THE SECOND MAYFLOWER

Other works by Kevin Swanson and Generations with Vision Publishing:

Upgrade: 10 Secrets to the Best Education for Your Child
ISBN 978-0-8054-4030-0

Psalms - A Family Bible Study Series
ISBN 978-0-9801910-3-5

Vision for Generations (Mp3)
ISBN 978-0-9801910-0-4

Vision for Generations (CD)
ISBN 978-0-9801910-1-1

Reforming the Church in the 21st Century (CD)
ISBN 978-0-9801910-4-2

THE SECOND MAYFLOWER

KEVIN SWANSON

GENERATIONS WITH VISION
www.generationswithvision.com

ISBN 978-0-9801910-2-8

Published by
Generations with Vision
10431 South Parker Road
Parker, Colorado, 80134
www.generationswithvision.com

For more information on this and other titles from Generations with Vision,
visit www.generationswithvision.com or call 888-839-6132.

ACKNOWLEDGEMENTS

With grateful acknowledgement to those who gave a
great deal of themselves for this project, including
Susan Malone, Michael Gobart, Ray Suzuki, Marie Suzuki,
Anna Storrie, Chad Roach, Laura Sechrist, and Larry Crawford
(who first planted the idea in my mind 20 years ago).

Kevin Swanson

CONTENTS

FOREWORD

Some of my fondest memories as a boy are of my father packing our family in an overcrowded station wagon, and trekking across the nation to locations renowned and obscure in search of the ancient landmarks to America's remarkable providential heritage.

Along the way we listened to tapes -- hundreds of them -- tapes of thoughtful preachers, teachers, and historians who boldly spoke of the inextricable link between the greatness of America, and the spiritual legacy of her true founders.

Through these epic family adventures, the home education we experienced by the side of my father, and the books he constantly provided to each of us, Dad's message to his children was unmistakable: "Blessed is the nation whose God is the Lord."

And the group which best exemplified this proverb, and whose legacy was the most blessed and far-reaching in terms of its impact on the American nation, was that rag tag band we have come to know as the Mayflower Pilgrims.

The pattern established by my father would years later become a principle within my own family. For five of the last ten years now, my bride and I have gathered our little ones for our own pilgrimage to the land of the Mayflower visionaries. We travel in the month of November to remember, to give thanks, and to gain perspective as a family committed to the Christ-honoring reformation of 21st century America.

And each time we return, we are reminded of the great themes of the Pilgrims who founded this nation: First, the Bible alone is the only infallible and sure rule of faith and practice. It is also the guidebook for men, families, and nations. The principles of moral law articulated within its pages are eternal, reflective of the unchanging character of God, and thus transcend time and civilizations. This means that true liberty can only survive under the law of Christ. Blessed is the nation whose God is the Lord.

Second, true greatness is borne out of sacrifice. Only persevering and principled individuals who look to Christ as their all sufficiency and who trust in his sovereignty can hope to shepherd a nation to God-blessed revival and reformation. This also means that parents must be willing to make great sacrifices to see their children prosper as covenant keepers.

Finally, Christians must think beyond the span and influence of their own lives. They must be multi-generationally minded. They must aggressively seek an abundant and godly progeny, and they must see their own lives as part of the unfolding plan of God through time and history.

It is a wonderful providence of God that this recent edition of Kevin Swanson's important manifesto, *The Second Mayflower*, comes on the heels of America's celebration of two remarkable events, both of which occurred four hundred years ago, and both of which point to the perseverance and faithfulness of those imperfect, but God-blessed men who founded this nation.

The first is the departure of the Pilgrims from England in 1607 in search of a land where they could cast a generational vision to their children, and have the freedom to obey the law of God without state interference. The second was the establishment of the first permanent English settlement at Jamestown expressly founded on a charter that declared the primary purpose of the colony to be the advancement of the Gospel of Jesus Christ.

Four hundred years later, Kevin Swanson is presenting the American people with a vision of victory that recognizes that charters and covenants before the Lord matter -- a vision which is rooted in the most noble and God-honoring ideals of the original Mayflower visionaries.

When I began the outline of the forward you are presently reading, I was actually standing on the shores of Plymouth Harbor. It was the conclusion of the 2007 Faith and Freedom Tour, sponsored by Vision Forum Ministries. My bride and I took our family to Cole's Hill overlooking Plymouth Harbor.

We took them there for a time of prayer. We desire the blessing of God on their hearts, their life mission, and the posterity that we hope the Lord will generously give them. So we prayed over them. We called upon the Lord to bless our children, Virginia, Faith, Providence, Honor, Jubilee, Liberty, Justice, and Joshua with a persevering spirit, and a multi-generational vision of victory.

We love to go to Cole's Hill. The view of Plymouth harbor is breathtaking. More importantly though, Cole's Hill is the spot were so many of our Pilgrim fathers and mothers were buried during that first winter under cover of darkness to hide the high mortality rates from the natives. It is a sacred place to all lovers of freedom.

But just days before this private time of family prayer, Cole's Hill was covered with protesters -- sign-bearing homosexuals, megaphone-carrying Gaia worshippers, and radical Indian activists. Their leader wore a shirt with a line drawn through the head of a Pilgrim, and displaying the words "No Illegal Immigrants." They had gathered on Thanksgiving Day, not only to demand their political rights, but to affirm their pagan gods and to denounce what they perceive to be the oppression of Christianity in general.

I let my sons observe the protest because I wanted them to witness the state-permitted desecration of America's holiest landmarks, and to see the duty incumbent upon their generation to boldly proclaim the providences of God to a Church that struggles dearly to persevere in our neo-pagan culture. I want them to understand the profound antithesis that exists between biblical Christianity and everything else. I wanted them to understand that if they do not honor their fathers and mothers (spiritual, physical, historical) that they will not "live long in the land" and it will not "be well with" them.

But I also wanted them to be encouraged to remain faithful to the legacy of pilgrim boys of past generations, whose faithful stand on the same few acres of land had resulted in the discipleship of a nation.

This is yet another reason why the message of *The Second Mayflower* is so timely. Kevin Swanson points us to the future by charting a course for the present, even as he reminds us of the greatest and most enduring truths of the past.

And this is precisely what is necessary if we hope to see our children prosper in a country whose leaders have broken our covenants with God, and forsaken the faith of our fathers.

But if there was hope for Nineveh, most assuredly there is hope for America. There is hope for this country, if the generation which will arise will honor their fathers, and remember that "Blessed is the nation whose God is the Lord."

I am persuaded that we should never underestimate the potential of our young sons and daughters to transform their culture for the glory of Jesus, through acts of honor, remembrance, and blessing. It is from the stock of faithful boys and girls that Jehovah raises up warriors to remind the people of God to never be weary in their well doing.

And this brings me back to Plymouth, because that is precisely what happened near the base of Cole's Hill some 352 years ago when an elderly William Bradford took a godly eight year-old boy, showed him an unusual rock, and exhorted the boy to keep its memory alive as an Ebenezer to the providences of God, and the duties of God's people to persevere.

In 1741, that eight year-old boy had become a 94 year-old man named Thomas Faunce. He was now the esteemed elder of the ancient church of the Pilgrims -- the congregation of those holy separatists who had more than a century earlier been commissioned by their pastor John Robinson to travel on the Mayflower and build a covenant community in the New World.

Faunce would live to 99 years of age. He was recognized to be one of the most honest men in Plymouth. But fearing his life would soon end, the hoary headed man asked the people of his town to lift him onto a chair, carry him down Leyden street -- the oldest in America -- and then place him by an unusual rock where the bay water meets the land.

Pointing at the rock before him, the now aged Thomas Faunce told the story of his boyhood encounter with Bradford, declared the rock to be the very spot where the Pilgrims first set foot in Plymouth, and exhorted the men of his generation to honor the faith of their fathers.

Thomas Faunce did more than simply fulfill the commission he received as an eight year-old -- he gave America her greatest "rock of remembrance."

Because an eight year old boy listened to his elders, Plymouth Rock has become America's "Gilgal stone." Visited by hundreds of millions, it is our most recognizable Ebenezer to the providence of God. Plymouth Rock reminds us that in the annals of history, since the early days of the great Apostolic commissions, perhaps no group has been more blessed, or had a greater impact for their size than the 102 people who - in the words of Governor William Bradford - dreamed of being "stepping stones to others" in furtherance of a multi-generational family vision of victory for the Church of Jesus Christ.

This last point is particularly significant: Of the men and women who would journey on the Mayflower, just over fifty would survive the first winter. But from that weathered, yet indefatigable band, more than thirty million would descend, and with them, a nation conceived in liberty - one of the most remarkable evidences of the blessing of God on a principled vision in the history of Christendom. It was that vision and that commitment to honoring God which served as the basis of freedom for the future United States of America.

And that is why America needs a second Mayflower experience. It is the Mayflower hope -- that multi-generational, covenant-keeping, Christ-honoring vision embodied in the ideals of our Pilgrim fathers -- that Kevin Swanson now rightly proclaims to 21st century America Christians.

Persevero,
Douglas W. Phillips

PREFACE

Two histories are found side by side in the annals of the world. Sometimes the histories of the city of God and the city of man weave in and out of each other, but they remain distinct. In short summary, the history of the city of man is only a sequence of empires that rise and fall. From Babel to Rome, and from Spain to America, empires collect their force and inevitably dissipate. Immigrations, imperialist insurgencies, civil wars, internal corruption, and natural disasters dismantle the towers that men build. It is quite an amazing thing to consider that the prophet Daniel retained his position through successive empires from Babylon to Persia. Here is a terrific picture of the city of God sustained from one generation to another. Empires come and go, but the church of Jesus Christ now spans the continents. What is done for the kingdom of God does not perish in time or eternity, even while man's empires rot in the ash heaps of history.

After an eight-hundred year respite from empire-building in Europe, the modern age of empire-building began with the Treaty of Meaux in 1229.[1] Here the north of France, with a little help from friends at the Vatican (an institutionally-centralized church), wrested control of southern lands from Raymond VII. The "Albigensian Crusade" was waged on the pretense of opposing the strange cult of Catharism, but political power was the major aim, and that is how the stage was set for

1 Madaule, Jacques, *The Albigensian Crusade*, Burns and Oats, London, England, 1967.

the modern nation-state. Similar struggles followed in the English isles (in the 14th century), Germany (in the 16th century), and the United States (in the 19th century).

The city of man is predicated on political power and will inevitably oppose individual liberty. Indeed, the last four centuries have marked the unprecedented growth of the political state. Of course, this centralization of power came under the guise of "democracy." Facilitating this brave new world was a combination of government-funded education, centralized control of monetary systems, the rise of mega corporations, the misuse of technology, and the systematic dismantling of the family as a viable social structure.

Ironically, when the Christian church cooperates or synthesizes with the power religion of humanism, it does so to its own demise. With the growth of the state, men began to put their faith in princes and horses, and in the great achievements of science and the economic inertia of the Western states, rather than in the living God and His revelation. They traded monarchies for "democracies" and centralized power in the process. Their attention turned from church and faith to the civil government, science, and secular education. Today even the most committed churchgoers listen far more intently to the humanist-existentialist, Jean Paul Sartre, than to Pope John Paul or to Pastor John of their local community church. That is why the lowest birth rate in Europe today is found in Italy.

In the race for empire status only America paused to consider whether she even wanted to be an empire. As Virginia considered ratification of the U.S. Constitution, at least one patriot, Patrick Henry argued persuasively against "converting this country into a powerful and mighty empire."[2] But the lure of centralized power was strong, and within a century the nation gave way to the proto project of the city of man - empire building. As the heart of this country turned towards

2 Campbell, Norrine Dickson, *Patrick Henry, Patriot and Statesman*, Devin-Adair Company, Old Greenwich, Connecticut, 1975, p. 343.

the idolatry of statism, secular education replaced a 250 year heritage of Christian education, the nuclear family came apart, and biblical morality became despicable in the public eye.

Nevertheless, the first 200 years of this country's heritage (from 1600-1800) represent a unique occurrence in the history of the last 800 years. Self-conscious Christians who wished to apply the Word of God to all areas of life, including the commonwealth, constructed a loose configuration of city-states that struggled to balance law and liberty, or anarchy and religious freedom according to the laws of God. It was a brief interruption in the conquest of humanism in the modern world that began with the Renaissance around the time of the Treaty of Meaux.

If God exists and He still blesses nations for their obedience to His laws, then America is another example of this great historical precedent. Here was a people that really believed those words of David, "Blessed is the nation whose God is the LORD." And the premise of this book is simply if God can bless us once, perhaps He will do it again. Could the first attempt at building a free nation upon God's law which took place in the middle of the humanist rush to build empires be repeated in a new era, as the empires fail? I suggest that there must be a connection between the First Mayflower and the Second that is to come.

In this book, I grapple with the future of a nation which at one time covenanted with the living God to walk in His ways and to be a city on a hill, a beacon of righteousness to the nations around. I wrestle with the future of a nation that has abandoned God's Word as the light to its path. I challenge the reader to identify what it means to be in the world but not of it, salt and light without losing the savor and becoming overwhelmed by the darkness.

I confess that I do not have all the answers. But I hope that I have here presented a vision such that we might be able to take the first few steps towards a godly life - a good life - which must be made up of godly families, godly education, godly communities, and godly politics.

This is the third edition of a book that has seen multiple and massive edits since the idea first germinated one Sunday afternoon in our living room in 1993. What is contained in this book is not a set of theoretical propositions. Rather, they are ideas that I have already incorporated into my life and into the life of my family. It is a life that represents a sharp contrast with the life proposed by the humanists and the socialists who have constructed the institutions of the modern world. It is community rather than communism, Moses instead of Plato, Jesus rather than Rousseau or Marx. It is the relational life of Enoch who walked with God, rather than vagabond life of Cain who built a city. It is a good life. It is the life that God wants us to live, and God's ways are better than those proposed by Plato, Rousseau, or Marx. It is the life of liberty rather than slavery. It avoids the tyranny of the one institution and the anarchy of the many individuals. It is the good life. A blessed life. I can tell you that because of the Divine promise.

> *"And it shall come to pass if thou shalt hearken diligently unto the voice of the Lord thy God, to observe and to do all His commandments which I command thee this day, that the Lord thy God will set thee on high above all nations of the earth. And all these blessings shall come on thee and overtake thee, if thou shalt hearken unto the voice of the Lord thy God. Blessed shalt thou be in the city, and blessed shalt thou be in the field."*
> *Deuteronomy 28:1-2*

1

THE FUTURE OF A CIVILIZATION

From all reports, Western Civilization is dying a wretched death. A civilization that was built on a synthesis of humanist thinking and Christian thinking is almost entirely corrupted. For the Christian faith is almost dead in the Western world and the raw humanist faith is unable to sustain that civilization alone. Church properties in Europe are turning over to the Muslims as Christian church attendance drops to single-digit percentages. With birth rates falling well below replacement levels in most of western Europe and in some parts of Asia, the modern world is quickly losing a vision for the future. Political commentator, Pat Buchanan recently explained the demise of Europe in his fittingly named tome, *The Death of the West:* "The Islamic world retains something the West has lost: a desire to have children and the will to carry on their civilization, cultures, families, and faith."[1]

What used to be the most powerful Christian church in Europe in previous centuries has now conceded a loss of the continent to the humanists and Muslims. A certain Catholic provost, Joseph Fessio, who was recently interviewed on an American radio talk show[2] reviewed the status of Western Civilization (apparently summarizing a high-level meeting with the pope and other Roman Catholic academicians). Basically, said Fessio, Western Civilization is dying in Europe and is soon to be replaced by the Islamic worldview, and religious freedom,

1 Pat Buchanan, *The Death of the West,* St. Martin's Press New York, NY, 2002), p. 118.
2 The Hugh Hewitt Program, January 5, 2006.

1

at least for Christians, will no doubt die out there as it does in most Islamic states. While admitting failure in Europe, Fessio told the listening audience that there was yet some hope for the future of Western Civilization in this country because of some who still have a "will to carry on their civilization and faith." Among those who have a vision for their families and the future are the home educators who have removed their children from the culture. He called America's homeschools "the monasteries of the New Dark Age," quickly adding, "You non-Catholic Christians have a lot more of them than we Catholics do ... and that is where families are having children."

The modern age of empires is about to end with the fall of each major power center from Spain to France to England and finally, America. But, as with the fall of Rome, Christians are not particularly pained by the fall of these empires. As the bricks began to tumble off of the city of man in 430 AD, that great Christian theologian, Augustine, penned the classic, *The City of God*, in which he contrasted the two cities and suggested that all that really mattered was the city of God. Throughout the succeeding eight centuries, the church rapidly expanded into Europe, converting pagans from Ireland to Germany, from Scotland to Gaul.

However, with the advent of the secular humanist university during the 12th century, knowledge was separated from faith and life. Education moved from the God-ordained spheres of family and church to the state, and man began building his empires once more. Almost immediately following the establishment of secular universities, the humanist renaissance formed and the reformation was barely able to slow the headlong rush towards man-centered thinking and living. But even as humanism emerged victorious from the last 300-year "war of worldviews," and built its cultures, societies, and institutions, it planted the seeds of its own destruction. Failure was inevitable.

By God's providence, in the midst of the raging floods of man-centered humanism that came to characterize Western thought, the sixteenth century reformation formed a small stream of God-centered thinking. It retained something of a distinctively biblical worldview, profoundly influencing nations like Scotland, England, Canada, and Holland. But by God's wisdom and mercy, one nation received more of that little stream than any other nation on earth and that was America. The first Christians settling this land were far more rooted in the perspectives of John Calvin and John Knox than in the thinking of Thomas Aquinas, Desiderius Erasmus, or even Martin Luther. By the time of the Great Awakening of the 1740's, the leading theologians and preachers of the day, such as Jonathan Edwards, George Whitfield, and Samuel Davies, were still more committed to John Calvin and John Knox than they were to Jacobus Arminius, Menno Simons, or Phillip Melancthon. Study the thinking of the men who founded this nation and you will understand their reformational commitment to a theocentric, biblical worldview. Ideas have consequences, and the ideas of the 16th century reformers culminated in the founding of the most God-blessed nation on the face of the earth.

Nevertheless, these reformation ideas were relatively short lived in their cultural impact. Now it is man-centered, humanist thinking that rules our world.[3] What we have today is a post-Christian Europe and America. Despite the efforts of Catholic and Protestant Christianity, the birth rate in Italy is the lowest in all of Europe and 37% of the children in America are born without fathers (up from 6% in 1960). The family is unraveling, the culture has become hopelessly nihilistic, and the state has grown tyrannical almost everywhere. For at least four generations, children have been educated in science and history without so much as a mention of the fear of God as the beginning of knowledge. Although some remnants of Christianity are still extant in the forms, these externals are quickly fading. Taking the obvious example of church attendance, we would find that it is still relatively high in America while

3 Humanism is the doctrine that man defines his own truth and ethics, and ultimately controls his own destiny. (I would also suggest that my reader refer to the Humanist Manifesto I and II for a more developed definition.)

it has virtually dissipated in Europe. But even while church attendance remains at 19th century levels in this country, God is hardly a factor in the thinking, the culture, and the reality of the average person. If you compared the art and literature of the modern world to that of the pre-reformation world, the contrast is stark. There is far less awareness of a transcendent God in the mind of the 21st century American and Italian than there was in mind of the 15th century Italian. Three hundred and fifty years of naturalism, materialism, existentialism, higher criticism, and evolution have taken their toll on the minds of men and their cultures. Humanism has won.

But, as Francis Schaeffer pointed out, man always builds his towers so high they fall down. He has been in the habit of doing that sort of thing since Babel. Humanist man insists upon defining himself even as Michelangelo forms his man cutting himself out of the rock. But there was something Michelangelo as the optimistic humanist didn't take the time to consider. How can his self-defining man even begin the work if he doesn't have any hands? How can he define a single truth if there is no starting point for truth? Thus, post modern man gave up his search for a unifying, absolute truth which has resulted in hopelessness, futility, and a loss of the will to continue building the empires. His thinking unravels and the towers come down.

However, the focus of this book is our country. Her future hangs in the balance. Tremendous forces tear at her, threatening to rip her to pieces. Among those forces is a heritage, that singularly unique heritage shared by no other country on earth. The specters of John Winthrop, William Bradford, Richard Mather, John Cotton, Thomas Hooker, and Jonathan Edwards still loom large over some part of this nation's consciousness. It is still carried forward in books like this one along with hundreds of other books and audio-visual presentations produced over the recent decades that depict the obvious contrast between America's godly heritage and the secular departure from the vision. The vision burns ever brighter in the hearts of hundreds of thousands of families who, unlike the dying cultures around them, are committed to passing on a vision to future generations. It is a heritage that must not be forgotten.

What is of concern to people like us is not so much the survival of our nation as it is the survival of the principles upon which this nation was founded - the principles of righteousness and liberty. Of course we are impressed that this nation became the most prosperous nation on earth, a bastion of freedom to which millions have come seeking refuge from tyrannies elsewhere. Yet, as we shall detail later in the book, this nation has, for the most part, abandoned this heritage in favor of building a centralized form of power in what has now become the most powerful government in the world.

When the empires of men fight for survival, two trends appear simultaneously: tyranny and anarchy. From historical patterns one can see that as man builds his towers high, the empires trend towards both centralization and decentralization at the same time, with the final breakdown resulting in decentralization. The immigration problem provides an excellent example of this. Centrists want to loosen border control and perhaps even move towards a North American Union, while the current immigration situation produces increasing disunity in the national culture in the name of trans-cultural equality. Some public schools now insist upon teaching in Spanish and Arabic, disrupting the nationally unified culture, and threatening to produce a situation not unlike Bosnia (with multiple religions and cultures) that eventually tends to either civil war or decentralization.

A commitment to humanism itself produces the same phenomenon. When man becomes his own god, he will endow the state (or the civil government) with god-like power and centralization is inevitable. But, at the same time, the individual retains a desire to be god. Anarchy develops as the family breaks down, and as men live more for themselves with less concern for the future. Thus, anarchy and tyranny grow side by side, feeding off each other for a time. The one builds upon the other. Eventually, the system cannot bear their weight, and the lack of character and will to survive takes the empire towards decentralization. This is the Babel principle which has persisted since man built his first tower.

Meanwhile, the Christian who retains a biblical world and life view is not interested in building empires. For he is busy building the kingdom of God made up of families, churches, and covenanted communities. In fact, the American experience was a brief experiment in biblical government between 1620 and 1800. But the sway of humanism succeeded in securing the modern "Babel" project during the following century. By the 1900s there was no looking back. America had become one more attempt at the centralization of power in the building of yet another tower that would "reach to the heavens" (Gen. 11:4).

For a while, America maintained a common cultural denominator which was basically Christian at root. This kept the country unified while allowing significant diversity in cultural backgrounds. However, having jettisoned the Christian faith almost entirely from its educational systems, political institutions, and cultural expressions, there is little basis for national unity remaining. Now with so little respect for any universal standard of morality by which freedom could survive, this nation's future hangs in the balance.

The Future of the Nation

So what is the future of this nation? Here is a question that rattles about in the mind of any person who has any stock in it, as I do and I trust my reader does as well. As a beneficiary of a tremendous heritage passed on by the fathers who founded the nation and as one who cares deeply for my own children and grandchildren, I seek God's blessings upon this land. What father in his right mind would be satisfied leaving his child in a country that is about to fail morally, economically, and politically?

Short of direct divine revelation, it is impossible for anybody to know the future of the nation with any certainty. But if one were to look at present trends and extrapolate them into the future, he would find a decline in personal morality, more homosexuality, higher incidences of molestations in public schools, more children born without fathers, more devastation to the family, more big government tyranny, more economic stress on the future (with the savings rates falling steadily and debt rates rising steadily), and lower birth rates. This has been the direction set by at least one hundred years of recent history and it has only accelerated over the last forty years. If our course is not diverted into massive reformation, there will be little hope that this nation's great heritage will be salvaged for our children and grandchildren. The Christian faith will languish and we may be subject to an Islamic invasion not unlike that seen in European nations. The era of Western Christianity may indeed be over.

But God is in the heavens and He does whatsoever He wills among the armies of heaven and the inhabitants of the earth. None can stay His hand, or say unto Him, "What are You doing?"[4] God is not done with this nation yet. I will make the point later in this book that there is a quiet movement of God that has been steadily spreading across this nation since the 1960s, and this movement I call "The Second Mayflower." History is a river that flows like a complex of a thousand currents and streams. From man's perspective, it is impossible to determine the direction it will head even twenty years hence. But one thing is certain: history's direction has always been changed by small minorities of men and women who are self-consciously and intensely committed to either what is right or what is wrong, and remain so committed for generations (Lev. 26:3, 8; Deut. 32:30).

Thus, this rising movement has the potential to impact history regardless of the direction this nation takes. Nevertheless, before I lay

---

4 Daniel 4:36

the groundwork for building this Second Mayflower, it is important that we consider the three possible scenarios.

Scenario #1: Repentance and Reformation on a Massive National Scale - A complete reversal of direction will only happen if the remnant begins that reformation. Such a reformation must include a renewed interest in the Bible and a conformance to God's demands on our lives, our churches, families, and communities. Although rare in the history of nations, there are several clear examples of this form of repentance recorded in biblical history (2 Kings 22; Jonah 3:10; Matt. 12:41).

Scenario #2: Tyranny - If we were to extrapolate the present situation into the future, we might realistically expect tyranny. That is not much of an extrapolation since the two predominant worldviews in control of modern civil governments (Humanist and Muslim) both produce tyranny. The limitations on government that come through Christian common law, from the Magna Carta (1215) to our own Constitution and Bill of Rights, are rejected by professed statists. For both the Muslims - trained in the Koran - and the Humanists - trained in the worldview of Rousseau, Marx, and Plato - the state must play a central role in their lives. That is, the world and life view of either Muslims or Humanists cannot be realized without a coercive state. For both Muslim and Humanist, salvation comes by the power of the sword or the gun. But for the Christian, salvation simply cannot come by means of state coercion - it can only come by the supernatural work of the Spirit of God through the sharing of the Word of God. The Christian state emerges as a derivative of that work.

Totalitarian states subjugate their citizens, maintaining control through fear while expecting fidelity from the masses. Of course a nation like ours does not produce the oppressive state overnight. It is far more common for a populace to accept tyranny, just as the proverbial frog in the pot passively takes the graduated temperatures until he is good and cooked. As the state tightens its tyrannical grip on a nation, the citizenry tolerate increased regulations on small businesses, increased taxes on families, more violations of privacy, and assorted onerous measures. It may not be long before certain biblical forms of child discipline are disallowed and pastors are imprisoned for preaching against the sin of sodomy. Should such a scenario unfold, there would be all the more reason for another Mayflower. Only men and women with such a vision as this could prepare a haven for such a time of oppression and persecution.

Scenario #3: Fragmentation and Decentralization - With the inevitable collapse of every modern empire, it is far more likely that we will see great decentralization occurring in the near future. Here again, I am only extrapolating trends which are presently seen everywhere. With the advent of the internet, communication and media have been radically decentralized. The major television networks are fast losing viewers. The webcast for my Generations radio program now reaches 60 nations and I broadcast from the basement in my home. How many thousands of other such programs now exist, something that was impossible ten years ago? While the major newspapers are losing subscriptions at a rate of 5 to 10% every 6 months, smaller centers of community and information-sharing are rising everywhere. For the first time in a hundred years, the cultural monopoly of a few wealthy investors in Hollywood is unraveling. Developments in technology have enabled small production companies (even local churches) to produce their own feature-length films that have sold millions of reproductions. The world is changing. Even nations that have drunk deeply of the well-packaged humanist, socialist, and materialist worldview coming out of Hollywood now prefer their own productions. For example, film companies in Lagos, Nigeria have produced 2,500 local features in the last year or two, and film producers in Bombay are pushing out 1,000 films a year.[5]

Already, economic trends towards decentralization can be seen in some forms of manufacturing. For example micro-coffee "beaneries"

5 Isaac Botkin, *Outside Hollywood*, Vision Forum Ministries, San Antonio, TX, 2007, p. 213.

provide variety in coffee that mass production could never provide. Smaller, local farms now produce organic food products with a far shorter shelf life. And those who would prefer unpasteurized milk must avail themselves of local provisions.

This trend towards decentralization is also apparent in education. While the American educrats worked hard to centralize the control and funding of education through the Federal Department of Education, millions of parents separated from the system entirely and established the ultimate in the decentralization of education - homeschooling![6]

But will technology continue to drive decentralization? Hardly any form of technology has supported the modern nation states as gas and oil. What will happen when technology enables the decentralization of energy? Whether it be hydrogen technology research developing a cost effective way to isolate the hydrogen atom from the water molecule, or advancements in solar or wind energy technology, such discoveries will radically free families and communities from centralized control of energy sources. Such developments will bring about significant changes in our geopolitical systems and will allow increased self-reliance and isolation for the state.

Historically, the major catalyst to decentralization comes by way of corruption within (philosophically and morally) and wars from without. Ironically, the centralizing power that formed the empires becomes the means of their own destruction. For example, weapons of mass destruction were first developed in a world where massive centers of power developed around cities and then empires. But these weapons in the hands of rogue nations, employed against the modern centers of power, will result in decentralization away from those centers.

Whenever great empires, like Rome, fall, men are overwhelmed with grief (Is. 21:9; Jer. 51:8; Rev. 14:8) as their faith in man shatters. Many assume that such tragedies must mark the end of the world and the years following a collapse are always considered "dark ages." But what

6 This trend towards federal control of education continues in full force. Incredibly, federal funding of education has almost tripled from 2000 to 2006, while funding for higher education quintupled.

can we say about towers that fall and the massive decentralization that follows? The tower of Babel was not the only tower to have met such a fate. For those of us who are not so interested in building empires, these tyrannies will not be missed. The Christian world is not built upon empires. This is not the supreme purpose for our lives. What we are really after is the kingdom of God which is built on relationships, peace between brothers, righteousness, and joy in the Holy Spirit (Rom. 14:17). It is built upon godly families, churches, and communities that maintain relationship by covenant. It is built upon the righteous laws of God, without which there can be no guarantee of maximum liberty for the people. Conversely, the city of man is always built on centralized, top-down power and tends to authoritarian rule.

America may very likely fragment into smaller nation-states defined by various socioeconomic, cultural, and moral lines. Some may embrace the Muslim religion, others may embrace socialism, and yet others may realize the vision of the first Mayflower: a country obedient to God and blessed by God. As the economy continues to languish, some states could choose to separate for economic reasons. Unfortunately, racial and cultural differences continue to inspire hate in some parts of the country. This hatred is partially encouraged by multicultural education and ethnic awareness programs that do little or nothing to unify the nation. It is also quickly becoming clear that religious pluralism without biblical constraints will always break down into ethnic, religious, and cultural division. The Muslim population in America is growing fast and is now pressuring the public schools to accommodate expressions of their faith as well. Without the choice of a biblical government, multicultural societies like those in France, Germany, Bosnia, and America face either tyranny or fragmentation (or both).

Nobody will be as prepared for such decentralization as those who have spent the last three generations building godly families and churches by cultivating relationships and applying God's law to their own lives!

Whatever the scenario will be - reformation, tyranny, or fragmentation- this great movement of God in the 21st century could not be better timed! For if God is really sovereign and if He blesses nations that bless him (as He has so singularly blessed this nation), then no social order will ever receive the blessing of God unless the people have covenanted together to obey His laws. The libertarians will never create political and economic freedom apart from a government that bases its judicial laws on the Law of God. It is only God's Law that can effectively restrain the tyrant's pursuit for power, while creating a social order in which community interacts peaceably and profitably. The law of the one who is both One and Many can resolve the difficulty of the one and the many in our social structures. As this nation's founding fathers pointed out on numerous occasions, freedom is impossible to sustain without a moral, self-governing people. Peaceful communities are impossible dreams without a virtuous, regenerate people. Certainly secular, multi-cultural programs in our universities will not cut it. We need covenanting Christians who have committed their entire lives to the Lordship of Jesus Christ and his revealed Word in the Scriptures.

It is the perfect time for another Mayflower. In many ways, present conditions and circumstances parallel the times surrounding the first Mayflower. Yet I wonder if there are enough of us to renew the Mayflower Compact of 1620. Have we the dedication and resolve to make a covenant based on the Word of God to form a community that will be blessed by God? Truly, we need hundreds of thousands of people who are willing to commit their lives under the Lordship of Jesus Christ. We need tens of thousands of fathers who have a clear vision for the future and are committed to leaving a legacy for their children and grandchildren. We need men and women who are willing to repent of complacency and lethargy, seeking God with their whole hearts, seeking His will revealed in Scripture by vigorous study, and who are willing to spend their lives applying His laws to their lives, their family, church, and community government.

Who are these people who make up America's foundations? To understand the nature and character of these people is to understand your history and your heritage. The Puritans and Pilgrims were a people dedicated to the Lord. In the midst of terrible social decay, they raised their children in the fear and teaching of the Lord. In spite of threatened persecution, they worked for doctrinal accuracy and personal obedience to the laws of God. They wrote some of the best treatises on biblical topics that the world had seen to that point. They were courageous, self-disciplined, educated, godly, and never afraid to address any subject from a distinctively biblical perspective. They kept the Sabbath day holy, held family devotions twice a day, insisted upon honesty and uprightness in business, and preached the Bible in the face of kings and princes, risking imprisonment and death. Half of them would die during the first year of their venture into the wilderness.

Do we have the commitment of the Puritans and Pilgrims in our churches today? Do we have what it takes? Are we ready for another Mayflower?

Second Mayflower

2

THE FIRST
MAYFLOWER

One great presupposition that undergirds this book is that God blesses nations that fear Him and covenant to walk in his ways (Deut. 28:1-14). In this chapter, I will establish the case that this nation was dedicated to precisely that principle, for at least the first 150 years of her existence. The founding of America was truly a remarkable occurrence in the history of nations, in the history of many a dark struggle for freedom and for an ever elusive blessed and prosperous state. Somehow this nation escaped the tyranny of dictatorships and monarchies, maintained small self-governed colonies of decentralized power, averted foreign entanglements and invasions, and enjoyed unprecedented wealth and freedom for several centuries. While this blessed state has languished over at least the last 150 years, I would argue that the first foundations of the nation were essential to the blessing she has enjoyed for succeeding centuries.

Indeed, we still enjoy much of the blessing of God on our nation to this day. An organization called Transparency International conducts a Corruptions Perceptions Index on an annual basis, in which they survey at least 100 nations around the world for the incidence of abuse of public office for private gain.[1] I cross-referenced the 16 least corrupt nations on the list with the predominant religion listed for the country in the *Information Please Almanac,* and found that of the 16 least corrupt nations, 13 were predominantly Protestant nations, one

1 ww1.transparency.org

was half Protestant and half Roman Catholic (Canada), and two were Buddhist nations with undoubted influence from the West. Of the 21 most corrupt nations, seven were Roman Catholic, five were Muslim, five were Animist, and four were communist or ex-communist (atheistic) nations. The two most corrupt nations in the world were predominantly Muslim nations.

If we were to make one more correlation with the gross national product per capita, we would immediately notice that the least corrupt nations were among the most prosperous, and the most corrupt were among the poorest nations in the world. Thus, do worldviews actually affect the way people live? Emphatically, yes! Without a doubt, the powerful ideas generated by reformers like Luther and Calvin really do affect the way people live 500 years later. Ideas are powerful things that will impact civilizations for many generations.

The heritage of a nation is defining of that nation. It defines the legal systems, thought patterns, social structures, the cultural forms, and a hundred other aspects of a nation. Despite the steady denial of our Christian heritage on the part of our educational institutions and programs, that heritage remains. Denying it cannot rid us of it, any more than denying that the sky is blue will turn it to violet. It is just as easy to throw off a national heritage as it is for a son to cast off the genetic code he inherits from his own mother or father. Though the genetic code may fade through successive generations, some remnant always remains.

Anyone who calls himself an "American" must acknowledge these Christian foundations, and thank God for the men who fathered the nation. We are the product of John Winthrop, William Bradford, Thomas Hooker, John Cotton, and Richard Mather - all great Puritan and Pilgrim leaders of the 1600s. Though these men may not have achieved sinless perfection in their application of faith and love in every regard, they were committed to the God of the Word and to the Word of God, both Old and New Testaments, as the standard for faith and practice. As a consequence, we live in the most God-blessed nation, the most free nation, and the most prosperous nation the world has known. It is a nation that produces $12 trillion of the Gross World Product of $44 trillion, and in consequence has shared the economic blessing with other nations the world over (including such countries as China, Japan, and Mexico).

Before I explore the possibilities of a Second Mayflower, I want to uncover the foundations of this nation laid with the First Mayflower. Then I want to leave my reader with a simple question. Could the powerful biblical ideas that set this nation on the right track four hundred years ago and impacted whole civilizations come alive in the hearts and lives of a new set of visionaries for future generations?

To understand the present and to plan for the future, we must understand the past and how we fit into the story. Although history does not repeat itself word for word, there are certain recurring patterns from which we can learn valuable lessons. From the past we can see God's blessing on those who obeyed Him and His curses on civilizations that embraced debauchery. We also see the impact of small groups on the course of human history. While we will be careful not to repeat their mistakes, we must imitate their faith, courage, and character.

History books are not as much about events as they are about people. History is changed according to the faith and character of the people involved. So if we would truly desire to understand the cause of the greatest movements in human history, we would do well to study the beliefs, practices, and commitments important to those people.

I don't want my readers to think that the modern age will exactly duplicate the circumstances of those who went before us. We will not find a deserted island where we can be isolated from the rest of God's creation, but then, neither did our forefathers. They entered a world sparsely populated by primitive humanity where property ownership and development was almost non-existent. It was a world that did not know God but was known by Him. It was a world of danger with constant threats of plague, fierce massacres, and starvation. Never again will history repeat precisely the same conditions, the same adventures, the same risks, or precisely the same movement that founded America. But we can be sure that the Second Mayflower will face challenges of similar magnitude. Such a dangerous voyage will call for the same faith, courage, and character of those Puritans and Pilgrims who founded a nation and forever changed the world.

Early Motivations

For Christians in Europe, it was the worst of times. To those Christians without a long term view of God's advancing kingdom, it must have seemed like the end of times! King Charles I had abolished the Puritan-dominated parliament on March 10, 1629 after parliament had condemned taxation without representation. Richelieu had taken La Rochelle, and the French Huguenots (Protestants) had nowhere to run. Attempts to impose state control over the church resulted in severe restrictions on the reform elements of the church in England. Indeed, it was not unusual for the king's men to impose fines, "assessments," or even to imprison unlicensed ministers there. During these years, Archbishop Laud's star chamber was well utilized for severing limbs, branding, and other forms of torture. Some Separatists, such as Robert Browne, had already done prison time and Puritan Thomas Hooker narrowly averted imprisonment by an escape to the Netherlands in 1631.

Moreover, the cultural decline in England at the time had become unbearable to those Christians, Separatists, and Puritans who were committed to the principles revealed in the Bible. John Winthrop complained that "all arts and trades are carried in that deceitful and unrighteous course." Drunkenness served as the preferred sin of the day, with taverns providing their services "around the clock."[2]

2 Peter Marshall and David Manuel, *The Light and the Glory*, Flemming H. Revell, Grand Rapids, MI, 1977.

18

The progressively worsening condition of the Christian church in England was a strong motive for the First Mayflower. Although the Separatists had already distanced themselves from the state church, many Puritans were also motivated to leave because of unbiblical practices and teachings propagated by the church. Especially distressing to faithful believers was the fact that the official head of the Church of England, King James I, had lived a homosexual lifestyle throughout the early part of the 17th century.[3] John Winthrop knew something of the corruption of the day as he watched his own son, Henry, taken by it. His assessment:

> "All other churches in Europe are brought to desolation ... and who knows but that God hath provided this place [America] to be a refuge for many whom He means to save out of the general calamity, and seeing the Church has no place left to flee into but the wilderness ... The fountains of learning and religion are so corrupted as most children are perverted, corrupted, and utterly overthrown by the multitude of evil examples and the licentious governments of those seminaries."[4]

These were the circumstances surrounding the First Mayflower, not altogether unlike those of the present day. Occasionally, a pastor or a father will register similar concern over the soaring single-parent birth rates, the omnipresence of pornography, the prevalence of drug abuse, public display of homosexual acts in public high schools, and the decline of the Christian faith in this nation. However, the breakdown is far more universal today than it was in the 17th century. When even ministers of mainstream evangelical churches confess to sins of homosexuality, one must conclude the church has sunk to a low standard indeed, not

---

3 Otto Scott, *The Great Christian Revolution*, Ross House, Vallecito, CA, 1991, p. 192.
4 Edmund S. Morgan, *The Puritan Dilema: The Story of John Winthrop*, Little, Brown, Boston, MA, 1958, p. 40.

unlike the lowest moral conditions found in the wider culture.[5] The church is hardly a holy standard anymore.

We may be amazed that a group of 40,000 Christians assumed the faith and resolution to attempt change under such conditions, but what were their options? There was little hope of change in England, for the churches and seminaries there were heavily regulated by a homosexual king, and the men who sought reformation were persecuted out of their pastorates. Men of vision will always seek something better for their children and grandchildren. They will act upon that vision, and that is how history is made.

Thy Kingdom Come ... on Earth as it is in Heaven.

> "We whose names are underwritten ... having undertaken, for the glory of God, and advancement of the Christian faith, and honour of our king and country, a voyage to plant the first colony in the Northern parts of Virginia ..."
> - The Mayflower Compact (Nov. 11, 1620)

I think it is safe to surmise that the greatest human movement in the next millennium will pattern in some regard after the greatest movement of this millennium. Thus it is crucially important to note that the greatest movement in the second millennium after Christ was the First Mayflower which was launched for the "advancement of the Christian faith." Although the terms "freedom," "liberty," "justice," and "peace" may be causes which we would hope could fuel the greatest of human movements, they are not enough of themselves to motivate change against overwhelming impediments. When human nature must overcome the tyrant's fury, the temptations of the flesh, and the discouraging pessimism of the short-sighted, it can only do so through

---

5 In 2006, two major evangelical pastors in Colorado (Ted Haggard and Paul Barnes) confessed to long-standing homosexual inclinations and activities. Both resigned from their pulpits.

firm reliance on a sovereign God and with a whole-hearted commitment to pursuing "the Kingdom of God and His righteousness" (Matt. 6:30).

This was the official motive written into the early compacts and charters, and I suggest that it was the chief motive and desire that beat in the hearts of the men who founded this nation. They wanted to see God's kingdom come. Exactly four hundred years ago, the first colony was planted on the shores of Virginia in a settlement called Jamestown. And it was the first Virginia Charter of 1607 that spelled out this same commitment with these powerful words:

"We, greatly commending and graciously accepting of their Desires for the Furtherance of so noble a Work, which may, by the Providence of Almighty God, hereafter tend to the Glory of His Divine Majesty, in propagating of Christian Religion to such People, as yet live in Darkness and miserable Ignorance of the true Knowledge and Worship of God ..."[6]

Such dedication to the Christian Gospel and worship of the true and living God may be well understood by missionaries today, but it would be hard to find wording like that on the walls of a public school, let alone in the hearts of the teachers who stand in front of children every day who happen to be "ignorant of the true knowledge and worship of the Christian God." Another father who laid the foundation of this country in that very first colony, Richard Hakluyt, specified the impetus that drove him to the new land,

6 Wording for the first Virginia charter is available at www.lonang.com/exlibris/organic/1606-fcv. htm. Upon landing at Cape Henry on April 27, 1607, the colonists' first act was to erect a large wooden cross and hold a prayer meeting. Later that year, at Revered Robert Hunt's death, the settlers left this tribute to him: "We all received from him the Holy Communion together, as a pledge of reconciliation, for we all loved him for his exceeding goodness. He planted the First Protestant Church in America and laid down his life in the foundation of America." - 1607. The inscription of the original 1607 testimony is engraved upon the bronze Robert Hunt Memorial, Jamestown Island, Virginia.
Reference Catherine Millard, *The Rewriting of America's History*, Horizon House Publishers, Camp Hill, PA, 1991, p. 308.
Catherine Millard, *A Children's Companion Guide to America's History*, Horizon House Publishers, Camp Hill, PA, 1993, p. 9.

"Wee shall by plantinge there inlarge the glory of the gospel, and from England plante sincere religion, and provide a safe and a sure place to receave people from all partes of the worlds that are forced to flee for the truthe of Gods worde."

Indeed, the founders of this nation had a deeply committed to seeing God's kingdom come on earth as it is in heaven! They would not be content with the mediocrity of the state church in England. Although England was more thoroughly affected by the Reformation than any other country, the Puritans and Pilgrims had become increasingly dissatisfied and disenfranchised with the State-controlled church which was given to compromise and corruption. They were similarly discomforted by a culture that was progressively sinking to lower levels of debauchery, so much so that many of them feared the judgment of God on that nation.

The Pilgrim pastor, John Robinson, saw the migration to America as an opportunity for the furthering of the kingdom of God.

"Now as the people of God in old time were called out of Babylon civil, the place of their bodily bondage, and were to come to Jerusalem, and there to build the Lord's temple ... so are the people of God now to go out of Babylon spiritual to Jerusalem ..."

John Winthrop had a vision of the new Plymouth colony becoming a "City upon a Hill." Winthrop's biographer, Edmund S. Morgan, expounds on the Puritan vision:

"The advantages of such a move [to the new world] to the Puritans who composed the majority of the membership were obvious. If the company moved to New England, it could become, in effect, a self-governing commonwealth, with the charter, a blank check justifying everything it did. It would thus be able to enforce the laws of God and win divine favor. It could create in New England the kind of society that God demanded of all His servants but that none had yet given Him. The colony would not be a mere commercial enterprise, nor would it be simply a hiding place from the wrath of God. It would be instead the citadel of God's chosen people, a spearhead of world Protestantism."[7]

These men of the 1620s and 1630s really considered themselves the spiritual grandchildren of John Knox, John Calvin, and Thomas Cranmer, the reformers of the previous century. Especially in England, the reformation had been continually hamstrung by state control of the church. King Henry VIII was only too happy to take the reins of the English church away from the pope, appointing an archbishop more to his liking. While Edward was more sympathetic to the Reformation cause, Bloody Mary opposed it, Elizabeth I was cool to it, while James I, Charles I, and Charles II were uncooperative at best and at times downright oppressive toward it. Hence, the reformation never quite achieved a foothold in England. Historian Perry Miller comments on this reformation zeal that burned in the hearts of the founders,

"Winthrop and his colleagues believed ... that their errand was not a mere scouting expedition: it was an essential maneuver in the drama of Christendom. These Puritans did not flee to America; they went in order to work out that complete reformation which was not yet accomplished in England and Europe."[8]

That complete reformation of which Miller speaks was undoubtedly a better separation of the state and the church, and a more thorough

7 Morgan, pp. 46, 47.
8 Perry Miller, *Errand Into the Wilderness*, Belknap Press, Cambridge, MA, p. 11.

application of the Bible to family, church, and state, a theme which shall be covered later.

While the kingdom of God was first and foremost in the minds of the Christians who settled New England, this vision was also attended by an optimism that such endeavors would meet success. The kingdom was on a roll, and their writings reflected their deep desire to be a part of it. Characterizing the Puritan theology of the day, Thomas Shepherd writes,

> "The utmost ends of the earth are designed and promised to be in time the possessions of Christ ... This little we see is something in hand, to earnest to us those things which are in hope; something in possession, to assure us of the rest in promise, when the ends of the earth shall see his glory, and the kingdoms of the world shall become the kingdoms of the Lord and His Christ, when he shall have dominion from sea to sea, and they that dwell in the wilderness shall bow before Him (Ps. 22:27; Rev. 11:15; Ps. 72:8-11)."[9]

One hundred years later, the Puritan vision had faded a little, but thanks to the Great Awakening of the 1750s, God was still central in their lives, and the kingdom of God still played an important part for the leaders of the emerging nation. The great father of our War for Independence, Samuel Adams, would clarify this covenant for delegates at the signing of the Declaration of Independence with these words:

> "We have this day restored the Sovereign, to Whom alone men ought to be obedient. He reigns in heaven and from rising to the setting sun, may His Kingdom come."[10]

---

9 Quoted by Iain H. Murray, *The Puritan Hope,* The Banner of Truth Trust, Edinburgh, U.K., 1971, pp. 94-95.
10 Marshall and Manuel, p. 309.

The Nature of the Kingdom

The Puritans did not consider the kingdom of Jesus Christ as a mere missionary endeavor, although that was certainly included. That kingdom extended into every area of human existence and experience. Thomas Shepherd's essay and the language of the early compacts and charters noted above would endorse the missionary expansion of the Gospel of Jesus Christ. But they also saw a kingdom where the kings of the earth would "kiss the Son." They envisioned a culture that would educate, trade, entertain, legislate, and interact according to the principles of the Bible. They understood the fact that Christ's kingdom includes all areas of human life and endeavor, and unless cultures are transformed, missionary movements, reformations, and revivals will wane. In the mind of the Puritans, the kingdom extended from the individual to the family, the church, the culture, and the state. The kingdom is the full-orbed application of God's order into the chaos of man's disorder and rebellion.

As for entertainment, contrary to popular opinion today, the Puritans were not a simplistic-minded cult of fuddy-duddies. As a matter of fact, they wrestled with proper forms of entertainment that would honor God and eschew excess or impurity. Some Puritans, such as Cromwell, Milton, and others smoked tobacco.[11] While most of the Puritans would not condemn the consumption of alcohol, ministers like Richard Baxter would preach and write in great detail on the evils of gluttony and drunkenness.

John Cotton would not even condemn mixed dancing, although he wrote that he would "bear witness against ... lascivious dancing." Cromwell had mixed dancing at the wedding of his daughter, and John Bunyan wrote favorably concerning mixed dancing in his *Pilgrim's Progress, Book 2*. In 1685, Increase Mather condemned "Promiscuous dancing" in a little tract entitled "An Arrow against Profane and Promiscuous Dancing." He registers his concern with a form of

11 Percy Scholes, *The Puritans and Music in England and New England,* Oxford University Press, Oxford, U.K., 1969, p. 158.

dancing that was sexually titillating and promoted a violation of God's Seventh Commandment. The Puritans were not so much concerned with tradition or traditional values. Rather, they sought to base social mores and rules for behavior on the Ten Commandments of God. Richard Baxter, a contemporary of Increase Mather, produced a 1,000 page Christian Directory in which he taught the application of God's Word to every conceivable aspect of human life. This masterpiece is still in print and is still used by many devout Christians four hundred years later. Again, here is a remarkable instance in human history of an entire culture attempting to apply the Word of God to every area of life. In previous centuries many cultures had heard a little about the laws of God, but few had made any real effort to apply them to life.

Despite some caricatures some have made of the Puritans, my reader should carefully note that the Puritans were self-consciously reformed in their teaching and in the application of the Bible to life. Although certainly we may find imperfections in these people who founded our great country, one thing is certain: this was a movement headed by Christians who were attempting to use the Bible to determine right and wrong, establish government laws, organize churches, and train their children "in the way they should go."

The Heart of the Men

The general sentiment of the people who founded this nation was a deep-seated fear of God and an acknowledgement of his absolute sovereignty. After hundreds of years of education systems that have carefully avoided teaching the fear of God as the beginning of wisdom, few people today live with a sense of God's presence, God's power, God's sovereignty, God's retributive justice, or God's holiness. Thus, God has become unreal to the modern whether he sits in the civil seat or in the church service.

It comes as no surprise, then, that secular humanists gasp with incredulity that the first civil law codes laid down by the Virginia colony would prosecute those who took the name of God in vain. These first settlers in 1610 sincerely believed that absent of the blessing of a sovereign God, their endeavors in this new world would be in vain. Even the most liberal of the deists such as Benjamin Franklin would not deny the absolute sovereignty of God over every aspect of man's existence. "If a sparrow cannot fall without the oversight of God in heaven, we must conclude that an empire may not rise without his permission." Such statements would be repudiated by the modern humanists and many professing Christians today who insist that the will of man will always trump the sovereignty of God. It was this shift towards man-centered thinking that produced a post-Christian age.

The Generational Component

There is one more important lesson we have learned from the First Mayflower, that first great experiment that established a free country which has brought the blessing of God to hundreds of millions. It takes more than one generation to lay a foundation. Any endeavor that would attempt to establish a nation with a legacy that will bless multiple generations requires a generational vision. Beyond any other era in the history of Christian civilization, the men and women who founded our nation had captured that vision.

Powerful orthodoxic doctrinal formulations from the Protestant reformation (such as Justification by Faith and the Authority of Scripture) produced cultural family formations. But equally powerful were the orthopraxic elements in family and church life, primary of which was the practice of family discipleship. Without the Deuteronomy 6:7-9 mandate worked into a the social fabric of a Christian culture, the faith will inevitably languish. Therefore, when the Bible was translated into the common tongue and made available to each cottage in each little Christian community throughout Europe, for the first time in centuries a vibrant familial piety revived in the hearts and homes of millions. It may have been the over-emphasis upon the piety of celibacy or the lack of access to the Word of God in common languages, but with the reformation came the practice of family worship.

The Puritan preachers especially were insistent upon this practice. Richard Baxter recommended excommunication for those fathers who refused to nurture their children in God's Word. Phillip Doddridge warned his congregation that God would "pour His fury upon the families that call not on His name." Doddridge passionately preached on the subject of family worship, "If after all you will not be persuaded, but will hearken to the voice of cowardice, and sloth, and irreligion, in defiance of so many awakening and affecting reasons … if your children raise profane and profligate families; if they prove the curse of their country, as well as the torment and ruin of those most intimately related to them; the guilt is in part yours and (I repeat it again) you must answer it to God at the great Day!"[12]

As the son of a Puritan, Matthew Henry wrote the most famous Christian commentary of the last four hundred years as a culmination of teaching derived from his father's daily sessions of family worship. Henry exhorts in a sermon to his own congregants with these words,

> "You are unjust to your God, unkind to your children, and unfaithful to your truth, if having, by baptism, entered your children in Christ's school, and lifted them under His banner, you do not make conscience of training them up in the learning of Christ's scholars, and under the discipline of His soldiers."[13]

In America, this commitment to family worship and continuity of faith across the generations continued in full force. Massachusetts' first governor, John Winthrop, was insistent that children be "brought up in the knowledge and fear of God." As early as 1648, even the Massachusetts' Laws required that parents teach their children "some

12 Philip Doddridge, *A Plain and Serious Address to the Master of the Family on the Important Subject of Family-Religion*, Eben. Watson, London, England, 1777, p. 27.
13 Matthew Henry, *Sermon Concerning Family-Religion*, Bible and Three Crowns, London, England, 1704, p. 19.

short catechism" and the law of God, including the Old Testament civil law codes on penalty of a fine.[14] Many Puritans and Pilgrims, including John Robinson, Cotton Mather, and Richard Baxter wrote extensively on child discipline and education, admonishing parents to these important duties. Parents were directed by law to teach children to read "at least to be able duely to read the Scriptures," to include "the Capital Laws ... and the Main Ground and Principles of the Christian Religion."[15]

Unlike the fragmented family vision that prevails in homes today, parents in early America were deeply integrated and involved in both the education of their children and their eventual courtship and betrothal. Speaking to the betrothal of his own daughter, Governor John Winthrop writes to his son,

> "As for your sister, her constant professions and resolutions have bene to doe nothing without our approbation, and so hath bene very well contented hitherto to submit to such condition as we should see providence directing us ..."[16]

Thus, family unity and cooperation was the norm in Puritan New England. In the words of Morgan,

> "It appears that parents and children had both to consent to a match [in a courtship] and that in practice either might take the first steps to bring it about."[17]

A generational vision was most sharply evident in the Mather dynasty, which reached a full century into the founding of America.[18]

14 Edmund S. Morgan, *The Puritan Family*, Harper & Row, New York NY, 1966, pp. 88, 98.
15 Brigham, *The Compact with the Charter and Laws of New Plymouth*, pp. 270, 271.
16 Morgan, *The Puritan Family*, p.84.
17 Ibid., p. 86
18 Michael G. Hall, *The Last American Puritan: The Life of Increase Mather*, Weslyan University Press, Hanover, NH, 1988.

Richard Mather became the archetypal patriarch of the great movement to the new world. But the source of the vision is found first in a home in Toxteth, England in 1611 where a 15-year-old Richard boards with a family that engaged in the practice of family worship. In this Puritan home, the family would meet twice a day for prayers and scripture reading, and the singing of psalms. As a part of this routine, the older children were given responsibility in reading, leading the prayers, and catechizing the younger ones. Needless to say, this experience yielded a profound change in Richard's life and provided the beginnings of what would become a great nation, three thousand miles to the west. Richard became a Puritan pastor and persecution in England led to his escape to the new world. There God gave him five sons, four of which would become important Puritan ministers in the colonies. In their early years the boys were homeschooled by their mother and as they approached their teenage years, their father assumed responsibility for their education.

There is no question that the discipleship of the children was foremost in the mind of this pastor and father. Richard would instruct his congregation regularly,

"You must not leave your children to themselves, neglecting to instruct them in the ways of God, but as you love yourselves and your own comfort, you must be careful of this duty."

Richard's son, Increase, married John Cotton's daughter and became the greatest, and some say the last, American exemplar of Puritanism. He was the last conservative hold-out at Harvard College which, upon his removal in 1699, was quickly captured by the liberal Latitudinarians. Probably the greatest preacher of that generation (1650-1720), Increase Mather's prayers and preaching were often directed towards his own nine children. He would frequently record his prayers for them in his diary:

"After I had prayed, as I was in my garden, and had this soliloquy 'God has heard my prayer for this child, God will answer me, and the child shall live to do service for the lord his God and God of his father ... My heart was melted before the Lord, and therefore I am not altogether with out hope that this child shall be blessed and made a blessing in his generation. Amen O God in Christ Jesus, Amen... Tears gushed from me before the Lord. I trust prayer and Faith shall not be in vain. Oh! I have prevailed and obtained mercy for my poor children.' Amen! Lord Jesus!"

The heart of a father's vision and a pastor's passion for the next generation betrays itself in the messages he preached:

"If you die and be not first new Creatures, better you had never been born; you will be left without excuse before the Lord, terrible witnesses shall rise up against you at the last day. Your Godly parents will testify against you before the Son of God in that day... All you disobedient children that are here before the Lord this day, hearken to the Word of the Lord. There is a Scripture which methinks should strike terror and trembling into your souls. Prov. 30:17 - 'The eye that mocketh his father and despiseth to obey his mother, let the ravens of the valley pluck it out, and the young eagles shall eat it...' I am not only willing to preach, and to write, but I am willing to die for the conversions of the next generation."

Without question, the biblical faith of Puritanism had staying power which came directly from such love of their own children, love for God and his kingdom, and a burning commitment to pass the faith on to the next generation and the next. But the story is not over, for Increase's son, Cotton, had fourteen children, and Cotton lived to eclipse his father's legacy by his own preaching and writing. But again, the same faith that founded this nation still retained a strong commitment to building generational faith in Cotton's life. The following is a short excerpt from Cotton Mather's "A Father's Resolutions."

RESOLVED --

1. At the birth of my children, I will resolve to do all I can that they may be the Lord's. I will now actually give them up by faith to God; entreating that each child may be a child of God the Father, a subject of God the Son, a temple of God the Spirit -- and be rescued from the condition of a child of wrath, and be possessed and employed by the Lord as an everlasting instrument of His glory.

2. As soon as my children are capable of minding my admonitions, I will often admonish them, saying, "Child, God has sent His son to die, to save sinners from death and hell. You must not sin against Him. You must every day cry to God that He would be your Father, and your Saviour, and your Leader. You must renounce the service of Satan, you must not follow the vanities of this world, you must lead a life of serious religion.

3. Let me daily pray for my children with constancy, with fervency, with agony. Yea, by name let me mention each one of them every day before the Lord. I will importunately beg for all suitable blessings to be bestowed upon them: that God would give them grace, and give them glory, and withhold no good thing from them; that God would smile on their education, and give His good angels the charge over them, and keep them from evil, that it may not grieve them; that when their father and mother shall forsake them, the Lord may take them up.

With importunity I will plead that promise on their behalf: "The Heavenly Father will give the Holy Spirit unto them that ask Him." Oh! happy children, if by asking I may obtain the Holy Spirit for them!

4. I will early entertain the children with delightful stories out of the Bible. In the talk of the table, I will go through the Bible, when the olive-plants about my table are capable of being so watered. But I will always conclude the stories with some lessons of piety to be inferred from them.

5. I will single out some Scriptural sentences of the greatest importance; and some also that have special antidotes in them against the common errors and vices of children. They shall quickly get those golden sayings by heart, and be rewarded with silver or gold, or some good thing, when they do it. Such as,

- Psalm 111:10 - *"The fear of the Lord is the beginning of wisdom."*

- Matthew 16:26 - *"What is a man profited, if he shall gain the whole world, and lose his own soul?"*

- 1 Timothy 1:15 - *"Christ Jesus came into the world to save sinners; of whom I am chief."*

- Matthew 6:6 - *"When thou prayest, enter into thy closet, and when thou hast shut thy door, pray to thy Father which is in secret."*

- Ephesians 4:25 - *"Putting away lying, speak every man truth with his neighbour."*

- Romans 12:17, 19 - "Recompense to no man evil for evil ... Dearly beloved, avenge not yourselves."

6. Jewish treatise tells us that among the Jews, when a child began to speak, the father was bound to teach him Deuteronomy 33:4 -- "Moses commanded us a law, even the inheritance of the congregation of Jacob." Oh! let me early make my children acquainted with the Law which our blessed Jesus has commanded us! 'Tis the best inheritance I can give them.

7. I will cause my children to learn the Catechism. In catechizing them, I will break the answers into many lesser and proper questions; and by their answer to them, observe and quicken their understandings. I will bring every truth into some duty and practice, and expect them to confess it, and consent unto it, and resolve upon it. As we go on in our catechizing, they shall, when they are able, turn to the proofs and read them, and say to me what they prove and how. Then, I will take my times, to put nicer and harder questions to them; and improve the times of conversation with my family (which every man ordinarily has or may have) for conferences on matters of religion.

8. Restless will I be till I may be able to say of my children, "Behold, they pray!" I will therefore teach them to pray. But after they have learnt a form of prayer, I will press them to proceed unto points that are not in their form. I will charge them with all possible cogency to pray in secret; and often call upon them, "Child, I hope, you don't forget my charge to you, about secret prayer: your crime is very great if you do!"

* * *

A handful of men changed history, but they were unique men. Rare are the men with this kind of vision for future generations, men who have a passionate heart for the kingdom of God and a generational vision for that kingdom. But this is precisely what it takes to establish a nation that will continue to receive the blessing of God for 400 years.

Men who live for themselves will have little or no vision for the future. But such was not the case for the men who founded our nation. They had a vision for the future, they had a deep love for children and were blessed with a full quiver. And they made sure to pass the vision on to their children. Without this component, it will be impossible to form another Mayflower. But think of what a powerful force a few fathers would produce, if God would give us a vision for children, for the kingdom, and for the future!

The Warfare Motif

The Puritans, unlike the Separatists, recognized the fact that the saved must remain in the world and reform the world with salt that had not lost its savor. They were therefore reluctant to separate themselves from the state church. According to Harvard Historian Edmund Morgan, the Puritan "must do what he could to prevent and punish evil, yet if he failed, he could not wash his hands of the world, and resign it to the forces of darkness... The men and women who hated evil as much as the Separatists did but refused to turn their backs on their brethren, were following the path that Puritanism (indeed, Christianity), in its deepest meaning commanded."[19]

For the Puritan, isolation, in and of itself, could be just as corrupting as being in the world. They saw the Christian life as a fight, a fight with the world, the flesh, and the devil. The 17th Century Puritan, Thomas Watson, wrote a treatise on "Taking the Kingdom by Storm." Simply isolating himself from all temptation was not enough for the Puritan. Thus, the Puritans would extend their spiritual exercise beyond the

19 Morgan, p. 32.

paltry levels achieved by the monks in the monastery. Mere asceticism would not do. "There is still new work to do," Watson would write, "new sins to mortify, new temptations to resist, new graces to quicken. A Christian must not only get faith, but go 'from faith to faith.' This will not be done without violence." He warns against moderation, "Moderation in the world's sense means not to be too zealous, not to be too fierce for heaven ... To keep on the warm side of the hedge is a main article in the politician's creed. Moderation in the world's sense is neutrality ... If any should ask us why we are so violent, tell them it is for a kingdom. If any shall ask us why we make such haste in the ways of religion, tell them we are running a heavenly race and a softly moderate pace will never win the prize." This violence, according to Watson, is engaged by the "Hearing of the Word," "Reading of the Word," "Obeying the Word," "Prayer," "Meditation," "Self-Examination," and "Sanctifying the Lord's Day."

The Puritans and the Law

The Puritans were much more influential both in England and New England than were the Separatists. This may have been due, in part, to their numbers and to their unwillingness to separate from the state system. However, it was also because of a strong emphasis on the importance of the law of God, found in the 1648 Westminster Confession of Faith or such works as Samuel Bolton's *The True Bounds of Christian Freedom*.

The antinomian sentiment that finds the law of God an offense would have been unusual in 17th century Protestantism. John Calvin, commenting on Matthew 5:17, maintained that Christ had "confirmed and ratified" God's law.[20] Martin Bucer was another important reformer who deeply impacted the English Reformation under Edward VI. He

20 *Calvin's Commentaries, Commentary on Matthew 5:17*, Associated Publishers and Authors, Grand Rapids, MI, 1978, p. 121

wrote these memorable words in his magnum opus, *De Regno Christi* (The Reign of Christ):

> "We, being free in Christ are not bound by the civil laws of Moses any more than by ceremonial laws, insofar as they pertain to external circumstances and elements of the world; nevertheless since there can be no laws more honorable, righteous, and wholesome than those which God himself who is eternal wisdom, and goodness, enacted, if only they are applied under God's judgment to our own affairs and activities ... I do not see why Christians ... should not follow the laws of God more than those of any men."[21]

> "So it is no longer necessary for us to observe the civil decrees of the law of Moses, namely, in terms of the way and the circumstances in which they are described, nevertheless, insofar as the substance and proper end of these commandments are concerned, and especially those which enjoin the discipline that is necessary for the whole commonwealth, whoever does not reckon that such commandments are to be conscientiously observed is certainly not attributing to God either supreme wisdom or a righteous care for our salvation."[22]

Such were the writings of the reformation, and their grandchildren did not differ much from these men in their perspective of the law. In speaking of the continuing validity of the law of God, the Puritan John Crandon wrote in 1634, "Christ hath expunged no part of it." Thomas Taylor wrote in 1631,

---

21 Martin Bucer, *De Regno Christi, Chapter 17.*
22 Bucer, *Chapter 60.*

"A man may breake the prince's Law, and not violate his Person; but not God's ... Every Beleever ... is answerable to the obedience of the whole Law."[23]

God's Law and Government

This healthy acceptance of God's law as the standard for human ethics gave the Puritans a concrete agenda for political action. It would serve not only to bind the tyrant's arms, but also to form the foundation of a biblically-based system of law in New England.

Connecticut's first minister, Thomas Hooker, preached a sermon on May 31, 1638, in which he admonished his parishioners not to elect magistrates according to their "humors" but according to the "blessed will and Law of God." Serving as one of the first and most important of the Puritan pastors of New England, John Cotton produced a work called *Moses His Judicials*, which influenced the laws of Massachusetts Bay, New Haven, and Southampton, Long Island.[24] The 1641 Abstract of the Laws of New England, published by John Cotton, was replete with biblical references, noting the proper biblical basis for each statute included in the compendium.

Such important historical context is nowhere to be found in the history textbooks used in contemporary schools. Nevertheless, we ought to accurately and honestly portray the people who formed our nation. These were men and women who truly acknowledged the Christian God, His revelation in the Bible, and the ethical authority of those words. What a far cry from the modern political situation where we debate special rights for homosexuals, government funding for killing babies, and whether we should pray to God or Allah in the public schools! Theologian and apologist Dr. Greg Bahnsen describes the Puritan commitment to the law of God as the source of ethics:

23 Greg Bahnsen, *Theonomy in Christian Ethics,* Presbyterian and Reformed Publishing, Phillipsburg, NJ, 1977, p. 550.
24 Ibid., 554

"The positive attitude of the Puritans toward every stroke of God's Law led them to oppose antinomianism in both theology and politics ... the New England Puritans sought a government which would enforce God's commandments, knowing that the sure word of the sovereign Lord required, endorsed, and undergirded this project."[25]

In England, the Puritans insisted that the king must be bound by the Law of God. King James I flew into a rage when Sir Edward Coke told the King that he was "under God and His law." James I claimed that "the King is above the law ... even by God Himself [we] are called gods." John Knox said it plainly, "Kings then have not an absolute power in their regiment to do what pleases them; but their power is limited by God's word."

Francis Schaeffer, a modern reformer himself, points out in his book, *A Christian Manifesto*, that the principle of "rex lex," that is, "the king is law," had governed nations for centuries. Then the Scottish Presbyterian, Samuel Rutherford, wrote his book *Lex Rex* in 1644, asserting just the opposite - the law is king. Schaeffer summarizes the powerful philosophical thrust of Rutherford's work,

"If the king and the government disobey the law they are to be disobeyed ... The state ... is to be administered according to the principles of God's Law."[26]

Thus the Puritans and Presbyterians, grandchildren of the reformation, would powerfully challenge the King to submit himself to the laws of God. This in itself became the true basis for our modern liberties and was key to the gradual collapse of the monarchy in England as a highly concentrated form of governmental power.

25 Ibid, pp. 551, 553
26 Francis Schaeffer, *A Christian Manifesto*, Crossway Books, Westchester, IL, 1981, pp. 99-100

The Puritans would therefore set out with a greater resolution to apply God's law to the construction of a new commonwealth. Still recognizing that man by nature rejects God and His law, the Puritans, undaunted, would attempt to reform the world around them. They were encouraged on by faith in the sovereign hand of God who blesses those who are faithful to Him. Many were stirred on by a confidence in the progressive victory of God's kingdom on earth. It had not been many years since the radical spiritual and sociopolitical changes of the Reformation had swept across Europe. Some had parents and grandparents who had experienced the effects of William Tyndale of England, John Knox of Scotland, John Calvin of Switzerland, and Martin Luther of Germany. They had seen what great things God could do with institutions, churches, and nations, even though all of these were made up of fallible, miserable men. Resting on the spiritual capital of their forefathers and carefully charting the course by the holy Word of God, could they take this reformation on to another continent and be successful in the venture? It was an enterprise with very good prospects and one that eventually paid off.

INTERLUDE

The Breakdown of the Vision

America is no longer the nation that she once was. This point will be made abundantly clear in the next chapter. Over the following century (from 1800 to 1900), the nation would abandon the God of the Bible in all of its institutions. Several influences broke the spirit of the nation and these seeds were planted in the 18th century. The best of men are but men. Even as we sow a legacy that we hope will produce a reformation that spans centuries, we will also plant the seeds of our own destruction. This inevitability was evident in the planting of this nation in several regards.

1. First, a rising antinomianism refused to use God's standard of law to determine ethics. As the 18th century progressed, Christians increasingly found God's law restrictive of freedom and sought for autonomy (or to be a law to themselves). They would speak of love, but would hesitate to define it as keeping God's commandments as love is framed in the Old and New Testaments. The only reason why education was so quickly co-opted by the social theories of Jean Jacques Rousseau, Horace Mann, and Karl Marx in the 19th century was because Deuteronomy 6:7 and Proverbs 1:7 were abandoned in the 18th century as having no real ethical force. As God's law was abandoned in American jurisprudence in the latter part of the 18th century, it was

not long before it was abandoned in the sphere of education and in the rest of life.

2. This antinomianism was attended by the right-wing enlightenment in which natural law increasingly replaced revealed law as the source of ethics in the minds of most of this country's leaders.

3. What may have influenced this repulsion to the law of God was the poor application of the law by some who wanted to make it more restrictive than it is. The badly handled witch trials in Salem coupled with an inappropriate state control of the church in some of the colonies produced more animus towards God's law.

4. Bad theological formulations increasingly separated faith and works, evangelism and discipleship, and grace and law in the minds of most Protestants. The Bible presents faith and works as distinct but not separate (James 2:26). When they were separated, an antipathy formed towards the latter. Faith was then reduced to a minimalized internal piety or a thin-coated personal experience that really didn't amount to anything. Most evangelicals today would repudiate the notion that hearing the law of God, being convicted by the law of God, and obeying the law of God is part of the Gospel of Jesus Christ. Jesus would disagree (Matt. 5:17-19, 7:23).

5. The seminaries or universities that were intended for the education of the clergy, quickly corrupted themselves beginning with Harvard; Yale, and Princeton followed. What the Christian faith is finally learning is that a system of education that seeks a marriage of classical humanist thought and Christian thought, and a form of education that separates itself from life is inherently corruptible. This humanist, secular form of education does not self-consciously root itself in the fear of God (Prov. 1:7), and certainly does not define itself as discipleship with faith and character as the primary content.

6. A man-centered view of truth, reality, and ethics eventually won out in the churches. The notion of "freedom" was gradually separated from the law of God. Over time, the definition of freedom changed from

freedom to walk in God's laws to the freedom for man to be sovereign, being the ultimate determinate of what will happen (what is real), what is true, and what is right. Either man or God will be sovereign. The denial of God as the source of law, truth, and reality was the point of departure from a Christian worldview. And it made way for a full-fledged humanism that now dominates all of our institutions.

Even many among the most conservative church groups, such as the Presbyterians who inherited the strongest reformation faith or the Mennonites who were self-consciously separatist from the beginning, eventually endorsed liberal theology, egalitarianism, socialism, and sexual perversion. The faith of the 19th and 20th centuries did not have a robust enough biblical epistemology and ethic to withstand the groundswell of Marxist, evolutionary, and humanist thinking. Even historically "biblical" or "conservative" strains of the Christian faith were quickly subdued by this distinctively humanist worldview.

Second Mayflower

3

THE RISING TYRANNY

Tyrant: "A monarch or other ruler or master, who uses power to oppress his subjects; a person who exercises unlawful authority, or lawful authority in an unlawful manner; one who by taxation, injustice or cruel punishment, or the demand of unreasonable services, imposes burdens and hardships on those under his control, which law and humanity do not authorize, or which the purposes of government do not require."

-Noah Webster's *1828 American Dictionary of the English Language*

A chapter bearing such a title as this might come as a shock to the average reader. For one thing, the word "tyranny" is hardly used anymore except perhaps to describe some third world dictator who has taken up the bad habit of knocking off his political opponents. So why should anybody be concerned about tyranny especially if he lives in the land of the free and the home of the brave? For the simple reason that the tyrannized seldom know they are tyrannized, and that is precisely the reason why they are tyrannized. It is the story of the frog in the Jacuzzi tub that is slowly approaching 212° Fahrenheit.

This book covers the past, the present, and the future of our nation, and this chapter will focus on the present. I cannot think that I should need to provide an extended polemic in defense of the case that this country is nothing like the nation that was forged two hundred years ago. When Laura Ingalls Wilder stepped into her first classroom in the frontier town of De Smet, South Dakota some 120 years ago, she did not see a single arrest in her school for the entire school year. There was no lesbian activity in the hallways. A police officer recently reported to me that he sees an arrest every day in a Colorado Springs high school where he patrols. Reports of public acts of homosexuality in local high schools are not unusual today. References to God have been purged from oaths in courtrooms of our state, and will soon disappear from all of the public institutions.

In this chapter I will summarize the present state of our nation by borrowing an axiom that became a truism for our forefathers. Two of America's most important founding fathers, William Penn and Benjamin Franklin, expressed the same point in two different ways.

"Those who will not be governed by God will be ruled by tyrants."
   -William Penn

"Either you'll be governed by God, or by God you'll be governed!"
   -Benjamin Franklin

These key founders of our nation certified from the beginning that tyranny was inevitable with an immoral people, and these somewhat prophetic statements are absolutely crucial for this nation's present direction. To the degree that men refuse to be personally governed by the morality of God's Ten Commandments, they would most certainly be ruled by tyrants. Therefore, in this chapter we will consider our current situation in light of this axiom. We will ask the simple question, what is the state of personal morality, and what is happening to the size of government in this nation? We will consider both the rise of tyranny and the decline of personal morality and the integrity of the family.

Let me warn my readers up front that I plan to establish the case that those who live in Western nations today live in what our founders would call "tyrannies." But our tyranny is unique in that it is really reasonably comfortable. No one is walking around in leg irons, no one is starving to death, there are no dead rats in the soup, and there is no large, fat fellow in a black mask whacking on the citizenry with his large black mace. So it is neither my intention to describe an unrealistic situation, nor to minimize the blessings of liberty that we still enjoy, or even to create paranoia and hysteria among my readers.

It is doubtful that the average citizen is going to sweat over the tyranny as long as his own economic condition is somewhere between comfortable and worry free, and as long as his social security check arrives on time. Moreover, if a man's economic security is his highest value (and if it seems to be in reasonably robust health) then he really can hardly be bothered by the loss of freedom to witness his faith, to own and control his own property, to home educate his children, or to own and carry a firearm.

The spirit that ruled in the hearts of our forefathers would have found such a life view utterly despicable, as should be obvious from this famous quote from the father of our War for Independence, Samuel Adams:

> "If ye love wealth better than liberty, the tranquility of servitude better than the animating contest of freedom, go home from us in peace. We ask not your counsels or your arms. Crouch down and lick the hands which feed you. May your chains set lightly upon you, and may posterity forget that you were our countrymen."

Even as one who would profess a love for liberty, I confess that I do not quite comprehend the meaning of those words and the passion behind them. But I know there is still some small part of this sentiment beating in the heart of a segment of our population today. So for those who still love the ideals of "liberty" and "freedom from big government," I offer the following assessment of a rising tyranny in our midst. Now we shall toss a thermometer in the water and take a reading for all the frogs soaking in the bath.

The Rise of Tyranny in the United States

"That government governs best that governs least."
    -Thomas Jefferson

Noah Webster's definition of tyranny included taxation that "imposes burdens and hardships" on the populace. Indeed, there is no easier metric by which one might assess the relative size and purview of government than the taxes and annual expenditures of that government as a percentage of the people's income.

Keith Hopkins from Cambridge University found that Roman taxation reached a maximum of about 13 HS (sestertius) per year for the average citizen, well under 5% of the GDP of the Roman Empire.[1] He also makes the point that the tax load on the Romans was greater than that imposed by England and France during the 1500s. But the tax load for the mighty Roman Empire was far less than that levied by the modern states of the 1700s, 1800s, and 1900s. Such tyrannies as found in the modern states are unprecedented in the history of mankind.

Historically and biblically, any government that would require more than a tenth of a people's income in taxation was considered a tyranny, as is clear from the prophetic statement made by Samuel:

1 Keith Hopkins, "On the Political Economy of the Roman Empire", Cambridge University
http://sshi.stanford.edu/Conferences/1999-2000/empires/hopkins.PDF

"And [the king] will take the tenth of your seed, and of your vineyards, and give to his officers, and to his servants ... And ye shall cry out in that day because of your king which ye shall have chosen you; and the LORD will not hear you in that day."
1 Samuel 8:15, 18

Even in preparation for the worst economic disaster in Egypt's early history, the Pharaoh never taxed the people more than 20% of their increase. It should also be pointed out that this special dispensation came by means of a direct prophetic word from God (Gen. 41:34). In our history, our founding fathers were especially concerned about taxes assessed on the colonies by the English parliament, and this served to motivate a war for independence. Dr. Walter Williams, Professor of Economics at George Mason University, recently commented that

"... in 1787, federal spending was about $3 million a year, or about $1 per citizen. By 1910, the Fed spent a little more than $600 million, about $6.75 per person. By 1929, the Fed spent $3 billion per year, $29 per person. Today, the Federal Government spends over $4 billion per day! That comes to more than $6,000 per year per person, or controlling for inflation, a 9,000 % increase in federal spending between 1929 and today. The Colonists, who were paying about 67 cents a year in taxes, went to war with Great Britain."[2]

The following graph provides one of the most succinct and important history lessons for every American, young and old. What incredible insight this trend chart provides into the heart of the American people as they made a radical shift in worldviews from a biblical perspective towards a Marxist perspective! By taking total government expenditures at the federal, state, and local levels as a percentage of the national

2 *Washington Times*, June 10, 1992, p. G1.

income, the chart illustrates growth in the size of government in the life of the average American.[3]

Growth in Government (percentage of National Income)

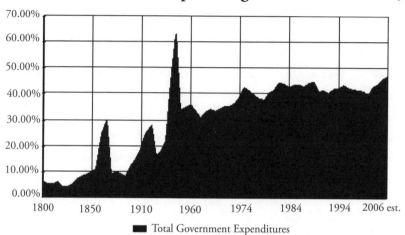

■ Total Government Expenditures

With only a few brief interludes in this Republic's 200-year history, the American people continually increased the size and purview of their civil government. As family and church became less important in their lives, Americans entrusted more power and importance to the state. Should it go without saying that government is far more significant in the life of the average person than it was in the 1850s? Never before in history has the state played so important of a part in the life of the citizens in huge nations on a worldwide scale!

Note also from the graph above that the size of government remained under 10% of the National Income for most of the 1800s. Most of the growth occurred after 1900. Each major war provided an opportunity for government to grow and to retain that growth in the years following the war. By 2007, government expenditures as a percentage of the nation's income achieved the highest level of our history. While there

3 Census Bureau (for federal, state, and local expenditures) www.census.gov,
Federal Reserve, St. Louis (for national income seasonally adjusted annual rates)
http://research.stlouisfed.org/fred2/data/NICUR.txtH.F.
Langenberg, Notes, 1994 ... 1995, Smith, Moore, and Co., St Louis, MO, 52, 53.

have been several slight declines in the relative size of government in the late 1970s and 1990s during the Carter and Clinton administrations, it is clear that there has been no serious attempt to decrease the size of government in America.

A trend such as you see in this chart can only be the product of a worldview that is taught to Americans and lived out by those who elect their representatives and those who "serve" in government. This is no accident. Ideas have consequences and those consequences are clearly displayed on charts like this, especially after 100 years of living out the ideas.

Presently, all governments in America have control of some 5.4 trillion dollars, of which the federal government spends 2.5 trillion dollars (almost one quarter of the National Income)! This amounts to more money than any government has ever had available to spend upon itself and to expand its purview over its people - more than Rome, more than cruel Babylon, more than the Soviet Union of the 20th century, and more than Hitler's Germany. Since money is power, we must conclude that the American government is the most powerful government on the face of the globe.

Once again, for most people who live under such government, this is hardly cause for concern. They would think men like George Washington a little odd for issuing his solemn warnings about the power of government.

> "Government is not reason. Government is not eloquence. It is force. And, like fire, it is a dangerous servant and a fearful master."[4]

Consider how men like Benjamin Franklin would look upon so cruel a master that should take as much as 46% of a people's income, as he would write:

4 Upton Sinclair et al. (eds.), *The Cry for Justice: An Anthology of the Literature of Social Protest* (1915).

"It would be thought a hard government that should tax its people one tenth part of their time, to be employed in its service!"[5]

More has changed than the percentage the government takes out of our income each year. It is amazing to think of how the worldview of a people can change so radically over just a century. Ideas have worked powerfully in the minds of the people. What we find in our current socio-political state is the fruit of 150 years of careful indoctrination on the part of powerful K-12 and university educational institutions.

Our government is now the most expensive tyranny the world has ever known! This money comes to the government in three forms - in direct taxation, inflation (which secretly deflates the value of the people's money), and debt, which places a severe tax on future generations. We are taxed on every level. At the beginning of the nation, the balance of powers separating the powers of local, state, and federal government was intended to decentralize power and limit tyranny. Unfortunately, the tyranny has tripled in size as all levels of government cooperate to oppress the people. We are taxed if we earn income. We are taxed if we invest what we can save after income tax. We are taxed if we sell our real property even if the only capital gains earned came by way of inflation (devalued money). We are taxed if we buy anything with the money that we earn after our income is taxed. We are taxed if we own anything of value such as property or business investments.

Then, after a lifetime of working to scrape together a tiny inheritance for your children, after paying 40% of your income in taxes, paying taxes on the 5% interest you made on your investments, and watching inflation consume 3-8% of your savings each year, you finally have a tiny bit of a heritage to pass on to your children. However, the base federal tax rate on your inheritance is 55%! Add to that an additional 10-15% imposed by state governments and there is little left to share

5 Benjamin Franklin, *The Way of Wealth*, Applewood Books, Beford, MA, 1986, p. 11.

with your children. Assuming there are no deductibles or other ways to protect their inheritance, a family could lose $700,000 of a lifetime's savings of $1,000,000 to the government! Imagine saving $1,000,000 for your five children over a lifetime, and then giving almost 75% of it away to the government in taxes!

The book of Proverbs reminds us that, "A good man leaveth an inheritance unto his children's children." But with the socialist worldview of the 19th century came the commitment to eliminate inheritance through taxation.[6] Again, worldviews clash on this issue and so do the sphere jurisdictions of family and state. If money is power, then government certainly could not afford to countenance any competition, and the family has the most potential of competing for that power, especially if a family legacy is allowed to grow economically from generation to generation.

The Toll of Taxation

A consequence of this onerous taxation is a huge surge in consumer and mortgage debt and a concomitant drop in the savings rates. The only years in our history in which the American savings rate dropped below 0.00% were 2005, 2006, 1933, and 1934.[7] Are we worse off today than we were during the Great Depression when 25% of the labor force was jobless? Today, people are desperately trying to maintain a fairly advanced standard of living with nothing but debt and the mere appearance of equity. Whereas in the 1930s families would rarely indebt themselves for longer than seven years, today the 30 year mortgage is far more common, and new equity loans, credit card loans, and reverse mortgages are just a way of life for many.

The toll of the steady growth of government on the American family has been devastating. As worldviews have shifted and the hearts of men turned towards the state, the family took has taken it on the chin and

6 Karl Marx, *Communist Manifesto*, Plank #3, "Abolition of All Rights to Inheritance"
7 MSN Money Online, "U.S. savings rate falls to zero,"
http://articles.moneycentral.msn.com/Investing/Extra/USSavingsRateFallsToZero.aspx

the future of this nation is now in the balance. For example, the birth rate for non-immigrant citizens is now well under the replacement level of 2.0 (down from 4.0 in 1900). Families have lost vision for the future, and make precious little investment into it. Back in 1880, nearly half of retired men lived with children or other relatives. Today, fewer than 5 percent of retired men live with relatives. They are busy spending their children's inheritance, to the point where they will spend their home equity by means of the "reverse mortgage." The number of elderly employing the reverse mortgage has increased 2,000% over the last 10 years! Incredibly, CNN Money.com reports that only 8% of the population will receive an inheritance and only about 1% will get anything significant.[8]

Even when the children are young, parents hardly invest the time required to nurture family relationships and raise their children with strong character. Increasingly, the health of the state and immediate economic concerns have become the only essential values, and hardly any investment of character is made for future generations. As governments at all levels have doubled and tripled in size, increased taxes, and debt-to-equity ratios have resulted in greater economic pressure on the family and the disintegration of family life. Struggling to retain a standard of living and "quality of life" that American families had come to expect, they began to trade relationships for economic status. Millions of mothers entered into the labor force. At the turn of the 20th century barely 10% of mothers in this nation had left the home for the labor market. By 1985, the percentage of mothers with children under six working outside of the home passed the 50% mark, and today it stands near 65%![9] *The strains on the solidarity of the family are increasing in intensity each day and are already taking a toll on the character of the nation.*

8 CNN Money, "What You Can Expect from Mom and Dad," http://money.cnn.com/2003/11/25/retirement/inheritance/
9 Mary Eberstadt, "Home Alone America," *Sentinel Trade*, 2005

Some say there are no limits to which governments are bound. Governments, they claim, are not subject to the law of God, and therefore there can be no limits to their purview. But the Bible indicates quite the opposite. In fact, the civil ruler is considered the minister of God to avenge the evildoer as defined by God's law standard (Rom. 13:4-6). There is little in the present system of government budgets and taxation that would reflect the biblical vision for government.

The Bible is careful to dictate what belongs to the government and what does not belong to the government. The government should not have free rein to take all of the people's property and money. The government engages in *theft* when it imposes a tax that exceeds the normative biblical limit of 10% of the people's income (1 Sam. 8:11-18). The government steals when it redistributes the wealth to certain privileged special interests (Ex. 23:3, 6; 30:15). It is nothing less than stealing when it spends money in any area not commissioned by the Bible. The government is stealing when it confiscates a family farm or a home as collateral for taxation (Prov. 22:28, 23:10). Our government today is entangled in a web of larceny and those righteous men who are left must demand repentance at the highest levels of political leadership, which must include a reversal of these trends. Tyrannical government must be bound by the chains of the laws of God or it will continue to expand as it has in the last 75 years of our history.

Since the Communist Manifesto of 1846 emphasized the importance of a graduated income tax as a means of redistributing the wealth, American governments have progressively moved in that direction. Those who work the hardest are taxed most severely. On the other hand, a biblical worldview calls for a level tax system: "The rich shall not pay more and the poor shall not pay less" (Ex. 30:15). As of 2001, the richest 10% of investors in this nation were forced to pay 65% of the United States' income taxes.[10] At the same time, the bottom 50% (most of whom do not invest in business) paid barely 4% of the taxes. This

10 http://www.rushlimbaugh.com/home/menu/top_50__of_wage_earners_pay_96_09__of_income_taxes.guest.html

envious trend of soaking the rich for the redistribution of wealth has escalated over the last several decades. "In 1980, the top five percent of income earners paid 36.4 percent of all federal taxes. In 1990, they paid 42.9 percent."[11]

What Government Does With All That Money

To make matters worse, we are taxed for services that we neither want nor endorse. We are taxed to fund educational, cultural, and philosophical programs that we despise. Few Christians would approve of the crucifix in a jar of urine, or pictures of Jesus molesting small children, but their tax monies have supported the pornographic and the blasphemous to the tune of millions of dollars through the ill-conceived National Endowment for the Arts. Thomas Jefferson warned that "to compel a man to furnish funds for the propagation of ideas he disbelieves and abhors is sinful and tyrannical." It is getting increasingly hard to find a dollar spent on educational and cultural programs that doesn't propagate ideas that I find abhorrent.

Replacing the Family

From the beginning, God ordained three governments for human society: the family, church, and state. When one sphere of government violates another sphere by encroaching on its jurisdiction, tyranny is the inevitable result. Unfortunately, civil government has set out many times over the last five hundred years to violate the other jurisdictions. In the 1600s, religious liberty was a concern of the Puritans and Pilgrims who founded this nation, largely because of the civil magistrate's iron-clad hold on the church in England. As the 17th century progressed, Separatist, Baptist, Quaker, Presbyterian, and Puritan alike fought hard at different times and in different ways against this unbiblical jurisdictional tyranny. These men of faith were committed to a separation of church and state governments, because they knew that if

11 *The Washington Times*, August 16, 1992, p. A3.

the civil government would interfere in an area not permitted by God's law, the state would only destroy it!

However, today the issue is not so much the state's attempt to control the church as it is the state's attempt to control the family. The first ideological movement came by way of the French philosopher, Jean Jacques Rousseau who abandoned his five children on the steps of an orphanage and proceeded to write a book on how to educate children. Historian Will Durrant summarizes Rousseau's work, *Emile*,

> "Rousseau wanted a system of public instruction by the state. He prescribed many years with an unmarried tutor, who would withdraw the child as much as possible from parents and relatives."[12]

Another important historian who has studied the modern age, Paul Johnson, comments on the influence of Rousseau:

> "What began as personal self-justification ... hardened into convictions, into the proposition that education was the key to social and moral improvement, and this being so, it was the concern of the state. By a curious chain of infamous moral logic, Rousseau's iniquity as a parent was linked to his ideological offspring, the future totalitarian state."[13]

How ironic that a man who threw away his own children became the philosophical father of the modern state and its educational institutions! Yet Rousseau was true to his own ideological commitments. If the state is of essence and family relationships and solidarity without value, why not consign the children to professionals on the day of their birth? Rousseau would later admit that he never bothered to check the gender

12 Will and Ariel Durrant, *Rousseau and Revolution*, Simon and Schuster, New York, NY, 1967, p. 179.
13 Paul Johnson, *Intellectuals*, Harper and Row, New York, NY, 1988, p. 23.

of his own children. He was too busy outlining a vision for K-12 education for the modern world.

The vision for the replacement of the family with the state came to fruition not long after Rousseau with the first state-mandated compulsory attendance laws. In 1806, a Prussian philosopher, Johann Fichte, gave a landmark speech called "An Address to the German Nation" in which he suggested that children ought to be turned over to the state and subjected to compulsory education. Fichte's point was that "through forced schooling, everyone would learn that 'work makes free,' and working for the State, even laying down one's life to its commands, was the greatest freedom of all."[14]

Later, Karl Marx honed Fichte's ideas, recommending the complete abolishment of both home education and the family in his *Communist Manifesto*. Yes. Those are his words. He certainly knew that family control over the education of their own children, or a family-based economy, would never allow for the centralizing of power in the state.

The humanist city of man has never seen much use for the family. In his introductory comments to *Emile*, Rousseau refers to Plato's *Republic* as "the best book ever written on education." No wonder! Plato configured the ideal state where temporary sexual liaisons produced the children and where "no parent should know his child, and no child should know his parent."[15]

These influential ideas of the 18th and 19th century philosophers profoundly affected modern institutions that eventually changed civilization everywhere from Europe to America and into Asia. One of the first steps taken towards implementing this new world and life view came in 1819 with the first public school-mandated, compulsory attendance law in Germany. America soon followed in 1852, when Massachusetts adopted its first compulsory attendance law. Such revolutionary encroachment of the state into the sphere of the family

14 John Taylor Gatto, *The Underground History of American Education*, Chapter 7, "The Prussian Connection," http://www.johntaylorgatto.com/chapters/7a.htm
15 Plato, *The Republic*, Book 5, Section 2: Part 6, Also, compare with Laws, 804d, where Plato says that children "belong to the state rather than to their parents."

was truly a watershed development! Never before had compulsory attendance been enforced in Europe, in America, in Africa, or anywhere. For thousands of years, families were free to raise their own children. There was no compulsory attendance law in 1700s France, or 1500s Netherlands, or 1300s England, or 800s Constantinople, or even in Rome in the 300s.

With government funding of education, both the responsibility and the freedom to educate the child are removed from the family and designated for the government. Every cent of the $536 billion spent on education loudly declares to every parent in America, "You are not responsible for your children's education. You are not responsible for the funding of it, the control of it, or the implementation of it." This is where the worldviews clash, for the Bible places the education of children at the foot of parents, not the state (Deut. 6:7; the Book of Proverbs; Eph. 6:4; 1 Thess. 2:11).

But the vision of Rousseau, Fichte, and Marx marches on. Over the last decade almost every state government has introduced legislation that would expand the compulsory attendance laws to include five and six-year-old children. Multiple attempts are launched across the country each year to fund kindergarten, pre-school, and day care. During one particular legislative battle waged in Colorado in 2005, a truancy judge testified in favor of a bill that would further expand the compulsory attendance law. In his closing words, he told the committee, "All of Colorado's children belong to us!" Rousseau, Fichte, Marx, and Plato all chimed in with a hearty "Amen."

In a ruling handed down on September 22, 2006, the European Union Court upheld the findings of the German Administrative Courts that would effectively outlaw homeschooling in that state. This decision stripped away parental rights, claiming that "the applicant children were unable to foresee the consequences of their parents' decision for home education because of their young age," and that this ruling would effectively maintain the "rights of the child." In the words of the high court,

"Schools represented society, and it was in the children's interest to become part of that society. The parents' right to education did not go as far as to deprive their children of that experience."[16]

The battle continues for parental rights, and such legal decisions are increasingly referred to as precedent for this country's courts as well.

Parental rights continue to disappear at an alarming rate in our country. For example, in the recent Ninth Circuit Court of Appeals decision *Fields v. Palmdale School District* (where parents objected to a psychological survey involving explicit sexual questions for 8-9 year old children), the court ruled that parental rights "do not extend beyond the threshold of the school door." This recent decision only confirmed rulings from other courts, such as the *Brown v. Hot, Sexy, and Safer Productions* (1st Cir. 1995) or *Mozert v. Hawkins County Public Schools* (6th Cir. 1987).[17]

The only exception to the trend towards obliterating parental rights has come by way of the homeschooling movement in this country. Since 1980, homeschool activists have worked hard to secure some small measure of freedom by way of laws that regulated home education at some level or another. As long as the freedoms are regulated by "positive" law, the freedom to homeschool will remain tenuous at best.

For now it is primarily the parental rights of those families who enroll their children in the public schools which are under siege. The freedom of parents to control what happens within the walls of the public schools continues to erode and the compulsory attendance laws

16 Michael Farris, "The Onslaught of International Law," *The Homeschool Court Report*, November/ December 2006,
http://www.hslda.org/courtreport/V22N6/V22N601.asp?PrinterFriendly=True
17 Michael Farris, "Has America Abandoned Parental Rights," *HSLDA Court Report*, July/August, 2006, http://www.hslda.org/courtreport/V22N4/V22N401.asp

continue to expand. If parents choose to remove their children from the public schools to homeschool them, homeschool laws will provide something of an island of freedom for parental decision making. But if parents have checked their children into the public schools, they have abdicated these liberties.

The irony of it all is that few parents even care to exercise these freedoms. During the socialist attempts to expand the compulsory attendance laws in Colorado, the only opposition from those favoring parental rights over the last two legislative seasons came from home educators. In order to quell this grass roots resistance, the legislature amended the bills to exempt homeschoolers before passing them into law. I'm sure the vast majority of parents saw these battles as petty or merely symbolic. Few really care, because few have any concern about salvaging freedom and family in the modern world.

As the 17th century was marked by efforts on the part of the state to control the church, the 20th and 21st centuries are marked by efforts on the part of the state to control the family. As the last fifty years have clearly demonstrated, in the process of usurping the family's jurisdiction, the state has made significant strides towards destroying the family. This should be no surprise, as it was the stated goals of the intellectuals, from Plato to Marx, who set out to build the city of man.

When we fight for the God-given responsibilities and concurrent freedom for parents to direct the education of their children, I believe that we are struggling for the very soul of the family. Without this freedom, we will see family solidarity, family responsibility, and family relationships disappear. As parents give up their freedoms, they give up their responsibilities too, and they give up the family. And that is why the family is fading away. Therefore, the battle for parental rights will constitute a gigantic struggle for the next generation. May God give us that courage to engage the struggle. Whereas the First Mayflower included a handful of men and women who were determined to salvage the church from the clutches of the state, the Second Mayflower will consist of those who have properly identified the battlefront for the 21st Century. We are struggling to salvage the family from the clutches of the state in a battle for the very soul of the family.

The Loss of Personal Freedoms

Fascism, as defined by Benito Mussolini, assumes government has an interest in every aspect of business and personal life, and therefore has a right to regulate it.

> "The fascist conception of life stresses the importance of the State and accepts the individual only in so far as his interests coincide with those of the State, which stands for the conscience and the universal will of man as a historic entity ... The fascist conception of the State is all-embracing; outside of it no human or spiritual values can exist, much less have value."[18]

Do a search for government agencies, state and federal, on the web and you will find pages and pages of government's all-embracing operations, thousands of programs that regulate every possible area of life. Such large and complex governmental systems existed only in the minds of a few philosophers and futuristic writers in the early part of the 1900s, 95% of which has appeared just since World War I. Discounting the huge expansion of the federal government, if one looks only at the growth of state and local bureaucracies in this country, there were *three times as many bureaucrats* per 100 citizens in 2006 as there were in 1946.[19]

Estimates of the cost of government regulations run between $8,388 and $17,134 per household. The total length of the Federal Register

18 Benito Mussolini, *Fascism: Doctrine and Institutions,* 'Ardita' Publishers, Rome Italy, 1935. http://en.wikipedia.org/wiki/Doctrine_of_Fascism
Complete text of the essay "Dottrina" (Doctrines). A translation of the Benito Mussolini "Doctrines" section of the "Fascism" entry in the 1932 edition of the Enciclopedia Italiana.
19 http://mwhodges.home.att.net/state_local.htm#Person

was 9,910 pages in 1954, 53,376 pages in 1988 and 78,851 in 2005.[20] Each year more regulations make life more difficult for the small entrepreneur and add layers of expenses on every product and service available in the marketplace. These regulations raise the prices paid by consumers, lower wages and increase unemployment, negatively impact the country's international competitiveness, increase uncertainty for businesses, discourage investments, and impair innovation.

Every real or perceived, local or national, disaster offers new opportunity for increased government involvement in our lives. For example, in 2006 the huge rise in the incidence of the sexually transmitted disease human papilloma virus, yielded a rash of bills in state legislatures across the country intending to mandate HPV inoculations for 11 and 12 year old schoolgirls.

Despite widespread disagreement on the causes of global warming, the extent of global warming, and the potential harm a few degrees of global warming would yield, governments all over the world (including our own) are now determined to use this as a pretense to regulate other aspects of our lives in unprecedented ways. The temptation to play God by pretending to both understand and control weather patterns is irresistible for scientists and politicians alike who haven't been rooted in the wisdom, knowledge, and fear of God for at least 150 years. Combine an overly optimistic view of the capabilities of science with the overly optimistic view of the abilities of politicians to predict the future and every possible ramification of each policy they legislate, and you will have a tyranny that just won't quit.

But will the increase in regulations produce a better world? Or would it be better to submit to the laws of God who knows something about the world He has made, the robustness of that world, and the limitations of the men that run it? The underlying assumption made by the modern regulative system is that men are better controlled by hundreds of thousands of regulations, millions of regulators, and billions of dollars

20 http://www.llsdc.org/sourcebook/docs/fed-reg-pages.pdf

in preemptive fines than they would be by a biblical system. Biblical law walks the delicate path between tyranny and anarchy, imposing personal responsibility and criminal penalties where there is gross negligence and somebody's person or property has been damaged.

Another faulty assumption held by the socialist mind-set is that government officials are less likely to make unwise decisions, engage in favoritism and fraud, and produce monopolies than business operators engaging in free market competition. Again, I would suggest that this places far too much confidence in politicians and bureaucrats than history and biblical record would ever warrant.

Property Rights

"They covet fields, and take them by violence; and houses, and take them away: so they oppress a man and his house, even a man and his heritage." Micah 2:2

The shameful history of property confiscation begins in the biblical record with King Ahab. Who can forget the sniveling Ahab coveting the fields of Naboth, and then offering a generous price for it in the first recorded act of eminent domain in human history? Naboth refuses, and after the trumped up charges, trial, and execution, Ahab takes possession of the vineyard, and gets a visit from Elijah the prophet with a message from God:

"And thou shalt speak unto Ahab saying, Thus saith the Lord, Hast thou killed and also taken possession? In the place where the dogs licked the blood of Naboth shall dogs lick your blood, even yours." 1 Kings 19:20, 21

Thus begins the sad story of power-driven, freedom-hating tyrants who cannot be content with other people having ownership and control over their own property, especially if it's a really nice piece of property.

A 59-year-old immigrant from Hungary, John Pozsgai, bought a lot in Morrisville, Pennsylvania. The usually-dry streambed bordering the lot was littered with tires. John cleared the tires and litter from the area and proceeded to place fill dirt on the property. Because he had no permit for fill dirt for his own property, he was fined $202,000 and imprisoned for 3 years.[21]

In another well-publicized story from California, federal agents confiscated farm equipment from a Vietnamese immigrant who was trying to cultivate his farm in the land of the free and the home of the brave. The spurious charges used to violate this man's rights was an environmentalist's claim that his land should be reserved as a game refuge for a species of rat.

In 1989, police stopped 49-year-old Ethel Hylton at Houston Airport. She was detained because police dogs had scratched at her bags. Upon searching her bag agents found no drugs, but they did find $39,110 in cash which was "money she had received from an insurance settlement and her life savings, accumulated through over 20 years of work as a hotel housekeeper and hospital janitor. Ethel completely documented where she got the money and was never charged with a crime."[22] The authorities released the woman, but not the cash. To this date, there is no record that the woman was compensated for this confiscation.

Property confiscations without benefit of trial, judge, or jury began in the 1980s and continue to expand at the federal, state, and local levels. Proceeds from civil forfeiture rapidly increased from $27 million in 1985 to $644 million in 1991, an increase of over 1,500 %.[23] According to one watchdog group, Forfeiture Endangers American Rights, more

21 "Net Loss of Freedom," *New American Magazine*, June 1, 1992.

22 Jared Wollstein, *How over 200 Civil Asset Forfeiture Laws Enable Police to Confiscate Your Home, Bank Accounts & Business Without Trial,* International Society for Individual Liberty, http://www.isil.org/resources/lit/looting-of-america.html

23 U.S. Department of Justice, Federal Forfeiture of the Instruments and Proceeds of Crime: The Program in a Nutshell 1, 1990.

than $1 billion in property is now seized each year from American citizens without the benefit of a trial.[24] These unlawful search and seizures are conducted by scores of state and federal agencies including the U.S. Marshalls Service, the DEA, the FBI, FDA, IRS, the Coast Guard, highway patrol, local police, the Bureau of Land Management, and the Department of Housing and Urban Development. Although, such forfeitures are undoubtedly conducted out of an interest for justice, such short-circuiting of the court trial is a blatant violation of both common law and biblical law (Deut. 19:15-21). Incredibly,

> "...there are now more than four hundred federal offenses and thousands of state and local offenses for which your cash, car, bank accounts and home can be seized – including shoplifting, hiring an illegal alien such as a maid (California), playing a car stereo too loud (New York), transporting illegal fireworks, gambling, having illegal drugs on your property, and merely discussing violating any law such as underpaying your taxes."[25]

If some government agency has any reason to believe that a visitor to some random house may have brought drugs onto the premises, the owner could lose his house, his bank account, and his car(s). In most states, he would have two weeks to register a complaint to the court if he had any money available for a lawyer. The widespread irresponsible and immoral use of drugs and alcohol have provided yet another convenient catalyst for more concentration of political power in the modern age.

Over the last fifteen years, private property owners have found their rights negatively impacted by increased government regulation on the federal and local level. Our founding fathers would be horrified if they

24 www.fear.org

25 Jared Wollstein, "Government Property Seizures out of Control," June 30, 2001, Newsmax.com, http://www.newsmax.com/archives/articles/2001/6/27/191414.shtml

could know of the power vested in our planning commissions and city governments. One local government in California recently sentenced a Francisco Linares to six months in jail for building a fence and a patio without a permit and approval from the local planning commission.[26] This kind of tyranny is new. Sometimes changes in local zoning regulations can make property effectively unusable and devaluate it to almost nothing. But what has become more common since the 1990s is the federal government's use of the Endangered Species Act (ESA) and the Clean Water Act (CWA) to keep owners from developing or farming their land.

Until the *Kelo vs. City of New London* Supreme Court decision of 2005, the exercise of eminent domain was reserved for an occasional government project. The landmark case began when fifteen families refused to sell their property to a developer who wanted to turn their little village on the Long Island Sound into a parking lot for Pfizer corporation. Interestingly, Pfizer was not a party in the case and agreed to build the parking lot elsewhere. But the City of New London was firm - the village must be turned into a parking lot, all for the purpose of increased tax revenues for the city. In the end, the nation's high court sided with the city.

The *Kelo* decision constitutes a substantial, resolute move towards tyranny in America. Now even Ahab's friends may confiscate Naboth's vineyard, as long as Ahab can expect a pretty good kickback in the form of increased tax revenue from his friends' use of the property. What made the *Kelo* decision yet another step down the road to tyranny was its inclusion of privately-funded projects in the list of properties where the state may wish to exercise eminent domain and pursue confiscation. The horror stories relating these confiscations have become more commonplace, evidenced by recent reports in mainstream news sources like *Reader's Digest*. The city of Lakewood, Ohio "recently proposed

---

26 "RHE man gets jail time for property fixes," *Daily Breeze*, August 27, 2007, http://www.dailybreeze.com/news/articles/9406861.html?showAll=y&c=y

bulldozing 18 private homes and businesses and handing the land to private developers to build condominiums."[27]

There was a time when "Thou shalt not steal," meant something because God said it and He didn't make an exception for government. But when government turned itself into a god, and when men stopped fearing God in university classrooms and the halls of the legislature, the government no longer considered itself constrained by the law of God. Thus, the government became the higher law, and the notions of absolute law and inalienable rights quickly disappeared from the consciousness of modern man. So Orwell's famed pig moseys up to the barn wall to make yet another slight modification. *"Thou shalt not steal, unless yur the government."*[28]

State and local governments also dispossess people of their homes every day for not paying property taxes. Of all the forms of taxation, property taxation is the worst and has no support whatsoever from Scripture. The right to own one's property is basic to the life of the free man. Harking back to the founding of this nation, men like Thomas Jefferson insisted that the essence of private property ownership was "the right to exclude everybody - even the government - from that property."[29] Jefferson would quote William Pitt the Elder,

"The poorest man may in his cottage bid defiance to all the forces of the crown. It may be frail, its roof may shake, the wind may blow through it, the storm may enter, the rain may enter, but the King of England cannot enter. All of his forces dare not cross the threshold of the ruined cottage."

Our forefathers cried out for their rights to "life, liberty, and property!" They would never tolerate the tyranny that we face today which is far worse than any threats made by the British tyranny. At

27 Tucker Carlson, "Home Wreckers," *Readers Digest*, August, 2003.

28 George Orwell, *Animal Farm*

29 Andrew P. Napolitano, Senior Judicial Analyst, FOX News Channel, "Property Rights After the *Kelo* Decision," *Imprimis*, January, 2007.

least the British army would only quarter in the homes of the colonists. They weren't confiscating their homes.

An elderly couple, having saved their money and finally paid off their house, should never be forced to pay additional rents on that house to the government or to some other fill-in "lord of the manor." It was property taxation that represented the end of private property ownership in America and which also constituted the very soul of Marx's vision for complete state ownership of private property. Without a doubt, property taxation was another substantial move away from a biblical model which provides clear protection for private property. Interestingly, Arkansas' state constitution still maintains to this day a prohibition on any government agency confiscating the property of a widow.[30] At the time that constitution was written in 1874, there were still remnants of a biblical law system and some inkling of the fear of God lodged in the consciences of the men who approved it.

"Remove not the old landmark and enter not into the fields of the fatherless." Proverbs 23:10

"Behold the princes of Israel ... in thee have they vexed the fatherless and the widow." Ezekiel 22:6, 7

Not everybody agrees that a man's property is sacrosanct. Occasionally, I will hear true blue "conservatives" question the right to private property. They ask, "how are we going to fund our public schools without property taxation? How can we build our empires without eminent domain? How could we ever build our modern world without confiscating a family's property now and then for important projects like military bases, highways, parks, schools, really nice malls, coffee shops, nail parlors, and adult entertainment stores?" The answer is simple. "You don't build empires. That empire-building project is the

30 Constitution of the State of Arkansas of 1874, Article 10, Section 6, Rights of widow and children.

outworking of the *other* worldview." As long as conservatives continue to buy into a centrist worldview, they will never form any effective opposition to big government socialism that gathers more power and influence through each successive generation.

Lethal government raids on eccentric and unconventional groups of citizens are also gaining some acceptance among the masses. While chronicling the growing tyranny in America, we should include mention of the raid on the 100 men, women, and children who made up the Branch Davidian cult in Waco, Texas, or the attack on Randy Weaver's family in Idaho. A good number of women and children were tragically burned alive or shot to death by government agents in these raids, the basis for which remain in question. Typically, the charges being investigated by the agents in such cases stem from alleged gun law violations. Resistance meets with resistance, and before you know shots ring in the air. After the dust settles and the bodies are buried, investigations are conducted and explanations for the mistakes are offered, but culpability is hard to pin down, and eventually justice is lost in the bureaucracy. As Washington warned, government is the dangerous servant and a cruel master. As powerful governments assume control of almost half of a national economy, they will eventually come to use that power badly. People will get hurt. In its attempt to be god, human government will turn itself into an inefficient, clumsy oaf with a tendency towards both gross incompetence and malevolence.

Plain Persecution

There are a variety of tyrannies. A tyranny like ours issues a long list of bothersome regulations and imposes heavy taxes that makes life difficult. While that may constitute a burden for the citizenry, no one is starving to death and nobody is getting beaten by the big man with the wicked-looking mace. But governments can cross the line into intolerable oppression when Christians are prosecuted and convicted for obeying the laws of God and living a righteous life before God and man. The prospects of such persecution are now visible on the horizon in this country.

With each passing year, thousands of parents are facing more regulations, investigations, and even prosecutions when they choose to homeschool or provide their children with biblical discipline. We have witnessed an increase in these investigations during the 1980s and 1990s. In one story, in which this author was very much involved, a mild-mannered Denver mother of three was dragged into court on charges of child abuse and harassment for spanking her son on his bottom. After months of trials and $12,000 in legal fees, she was finally acquitted by a hung jury. In early 1995, Colorado courts successfully prosecuted a case against a popular conservative talk show personality for spanking his children.

Families everywhere are subject to investigations based soley upon a single anonymous tip. Too often, fourth amendment protections against unlawful search and seizure are circumvented. In 1999, the Homeschool Legal Defense Association pursued a case to the 9th Circuit Court of Appeals (*Calabretta v. Floyd*, 189 F.3d 808), in which social services had invaded a San Bernardino, California home on the basis of an anonymous tip, insisting on entering without the benefit of a warrant The 9th Circuit decided for the appellant, holding that "the Fourth Amendment applies just as much to a child abuse investigation as it does to any criminal or other governmental investigation."[31] Unfortunately, the case is non-binding in other federal circuit courts. Last year, the social services departments in Colorado fought hard against a bill which would have restored fourth amendment protections for families subjected to social services investigations. The bill was killed abruptly in committee.

Public witness of the Gospel is also more of a risk today than it was twenty years ago. On October 10, 2004, eleven men and women were arrested by police, as they read from the Bible in the vicinity of a

31 Michael P. Farris, "The Fourth Amendment's Impact on Child Abuse Investigations," April 2, 2003, http://www.hslda.org/research/docs/200404020.asp

publicly-funded, homosexual event on the streets of Philadelphia. After their acquittal, attorneys from the Alliance Defense Fund pursued a suit for wrongful arrest. However, on January 19, 2007, a U.S. District Judge dismissed the case, concluding that a "permit granted by the city to the homosexuals allowed police to silence the Christian activists' message on public streets." One of the Christians in the case, Michael Marcavage, commented:

> "It is without question that Judge Stengel's decision has set a precedent to eliminate the First Amendment rights of others by citing that a 'permitting scheme' can be used by police and event organizers to 'exclude persons expressing contrary messages' in public areas and at public events."[32]

Legislation that targets disparaging speech of abortion and homosexuality is working its way through legislatures across the country. For example, the California 2004 hate crimes law expanded hate crimes to include speech interpreted as "threats, intimidation, coercion" and "anti-reproductive-rights crimes." If the victim can claim that the speech made him "feel intimidated," the violator could be liable for fines up to $25,000 and a year in jail.[33] How many parishioners might feel a little intimidated by hearing the law of God preached from some pulpit in California (assuming there might be a pastor who wishes to preach from the book of Leviticus or even Romans)?

Churches are also facing increased levels of opposition from city zoning boards. One large Midwestern city council passed an ordinance forbidding the opening of storefront churches.[34] A church in Evanston, Illinois, is unable to conduct worship services in their new facility. After the zoning commission unanimously approved the church's request for a special-use exemption, the city council nixed the decision, insisting

32 *World Net Daily,* February 16, 2007,
http://www.wnd.com/news/article.asp?ARTICLE_ID=54276
33 *Family Research Council,* http://www.frc.org/get.cfm?i=PW07B03
34 *World Magazine,* February 6, 1993.

that a tax-paying firm buy the property.[35] The Liberty Legal Institute, an organization that represents churches in religious freedom disputes, reports a 400% increase over the last two years in phone calls from churches fighting zoning battles.[36]

What does the future hold for freedom? It is hard to imagine that we will not see more government growth, more government regulation, more government control of the family, and more tyranny, at least in the near future. One hundred years from now, surely many will read these stories of the United States in the first part of the 21st century and wonder at the great tyranny that developed, and the minimal resistance generated against it. They will wonder why it happened.

Many of our citizens do not fully recognize the severity of the tyranny. Each incident that confronts us seems like a rare and random act of government coercion. In point of fact, the previous chart depicting the growth of government shows a steady increase that has progressed by ebb and flow. It creeps up on us. For a time, it seems that we will continue to live in a free country. But this is only because we have not lost our own property, and we are not the ones who have been arrested and thrown in jail ... yet. The reality of the situation only becomes strikingly apparent when the shrapnel hits close to home. But at that point, it is usually too late to protest. Nevertheless, the wise will take warning now and make proper arrangements beforehand so as to be sure that such tyranny does not strike unawares.

The Second Mayflower begins with a vision for something better than we have now, but we must know what we have today before we are ready to lay out a vision for something better for the future.

35 John R. Throop, "No Room for Churches," *Christianity Today,*
http://www.christianitytoday.com/yc/8y6/8y6020.html
36 Emily Bazar, "Cities opt for economics instead of religion to boost downtown areas," *USA Today,*
October 8, 2006,
http://www.usatoday.com/news/nation/2006-10-08-cities-churches_x.htm

Dependence on the State

By its socialist welfare and education programs, modern government lures people into a slave-like desire for security and dependence upon the state.

Government power expands every minute the legislature is in session, with every presidential election, and with every lecture in which government schools promote themselves s socialist institutions. Socialist government is inevitable for the modern state. What guarantees its permanent place in our socio-political systme are the breakdown of the integrity of the family and the promise of security from civil government. In short, government is able to perpetuate its power by promising 'free' welfare, health care, education, and sundry solutions to any other perceived problem. The promise is a lie and the fulfillment is always a mirage. And the cost to the citizen is his freedom and the prosperity of future generations.

Regardless of which party is in power, domestic spending for womb-to-tomb social welfare and education programs expand steadily from administration to administration. George H.W. Bush boosted entitlement and welfare spending by $175 billion per year adjusted for inflation, an expansion of 28% in just three years.[37] The following chart compares the first five years of two-term presidents who have served since the 1960s.[38]

	Party	Increase in Discretionary Outlays	Increase in Non-Defensive Outlays
George W. Bush	Republican	35.8%	27.9%
Bill Clinton	Democrat	-8.2%	1.9%
Ronald Reagan	Republican	11.9%	-11.1%
Richard Nixon	Republican	-16.5%	23.1%
L.B. Johnson	Democrat	25.2%	21.4%

37 Cato Institute, Policy Analysis, June 19, 1992

38 Nick Gillespie, Veronique de Rugy, "Bush the Budget Buster,"
http://www.aei.org/publications/filter.all,pubID.23352/pub_detail.asp

Discretionary outlays represent the portion of the budget (less entitlements) over which the present administration claims to have control in its budgeting. You will notice that party appears to have little influence on the direction of the nation. With the exception of the Reagan administration, we have seen a steady increase in domestic welfare spending since Lyndon B. Johnson's Great Society of the 1960s. Few politicians would commit "political suicide" by eliminating any of the welfare programs initiated in earlier administrations.

Increased taxes have contributed greatly to the disintegration of the American family unit. According to Senator Phil Gramm,

"In 1950, the average family with two children sent one out of every 50 dollars it earned to Washington, D.C. Today, that same family sends one out of every four dollars it earns to Washington, D.C."[39]

During the 1970s and 1980s, as the median individual income adjusted for taxation fell, millions of women went to work to compensate for the increased tax burden and to maintain a standard of living commensurate with lifestyle expectations. As children were increasingly relegated to bureaucratic programs and day care centers, parents had less time and energy to be involved in the education and training of their children.

Poverty rates remain fairly constant despite the increased government spending, tax increases, and government regulations. Meanwhile, the percent of children born out of wedlock has increased from 6% to 37% in just 40 years. Anti-poverty programs have absorbed 1.6 trillion dollars since 1960 without abating poverty.

After several generations of these government programs displacing the family by caring for our elderly, educating our children, and providing welfare for the indigent, the devastation to the family is immeasurable. Far fewer parents love their children enough to take

39 *New York Times*, August 16, 1994, p. A13.

responsibility for them. Far fewer children love their parents enough to care for them in their old age. Far fewer churches engage in their *diaconate* function of taking good care of the widow and orphan. And far more women have become the bedraggled, government-subsidized whores who strew the cities with millions of illegitimate children. The programs themselves are corrupting. They pervert justice by turning the widow and orphan into accomplices in the stealing schemes and redistribution of wealth.

There is an inherent lack of accountability and responsibility whenever centralized bureaucracies distribute charity. Suppose for a moment that I am an unwed welfare mom or, better yet, the live-in boyfriend of a welfare mom living in the inner city of Chicago. Would the funding of my family's sustenance by the local government welfare office have a negative impact on my character, on who I am, and who my family will become in a generation or two from now? What do these handouts do to the character of the families involved? If somebody else is going to feed my children, how does this impact my sense of responsibility, my own love and care for my children? Have the government programs done anything positive for the character of these families and the strength of a nation? Charity without personal accountability will only corrupt responsibility and make things worse.

Davy Crockett was a remnant of the First Mayflower as he fought the first vestiges of socialism in this country from 1827-1835. In the words of the old pioneer and Congressman,

> "We have the right, as individuals, to give away as much of our own money as we please in charity; but as members of Congress we have no right so to appropriate a dollar of the public money."[40]

---

40 Edward S. Ellis, *The Life of Colonel David Crockett*, University Press of the Pacific.

Liberals today have a hard time admitting that problems cannot be solved by stealing (welfare) and killing (abortion). The result of these modern day "solutions" lead directly to a breakdown of public morality, less commitment on the part of parents to their children, more poverty, increased human misery, and should I say it - the judgment of God?

Hypocrisy is a problem for every son of Adam and daughter of Eve. But the difference between conservatives and liberals is that liberals institutionalize hypocrisy. They build monuments to it. They make a great show of taking the "high" moral ground under a pretense of compassion as they "liberally" spend other people's money and kill other peoples' babies. All the while, they refuse to believe there are actual solutions to society's problems, solutions that will not aggravate the problems. What is the moral high ground but the law of God? Unless Christians will take a stand on the ethical principles of God's law and play by His rules, this nation is bound to fail, regardless of what party is playing engineer at the front of the train that takes us all over the cliff.

Legitimate Government

Whenever freedom-loving Americans register concerns over the encroachments of tyranny and the abridgements of freedom, some will assume that they are advocating a kind of libertarian anarchy. This is certainly not the case here. In fact, the founding fathers of this nation were insistent that proper government *defends* life, liberty, and property. Thus there is a legitimate function of government, and it is clear from Romans 13 that this is to bring God's justice upon the evildoer.

> *"For rulers are not a terror to good works, but to the evil. Wilt thou then not be afraid of the power? Do that which is good, and thou shalt have praise of the same: for he is the minister of God to thee for good. But if thou do that which is evil, be afraid; for*

*he beareth not the sword in vain: for he is the minister of God, a revenger to **execute** wrath upon him that doeth evil."*
Romans 13:3-5

If punishing the evildoer is the fundamental purpose of government, then a short review of the current status of the American system of jurisprudence is be in order. Based on the probabilities of arrest, prosecution, conviction, and punishment, the expected punishment for potential criminals in the United States today is listed below:[41]

Crime	Expected Prison Term
Murder	3.0 Years
Rape	125 Days
Robbery	59 Days
Burglary	9 Days

At present, America has more people in prison per capita than any other nation in the world. With the incarceration count now exceeding two million, the prisoner rate has quintupled in just the last 30 years. Although the United States retains only 5% of the world's population, it claims 25% of the world's incarcerated population. Generally considered "more oppressive" states, China ranks second with 1.5 million prisoners, followed by Russia with 870,000.[42] Most of those in American prisons have not murdered, raped, or robbed. They are serving time for possessing, buying, or selling a substance the government has chosen to call "contraband."

But what about *real* justice, biblical justice? If you refer to the ancient writings of the Jews and Christians, you will find that God revealed a single law to Noah after the flood, in order that society might re-establish itself. An omniscient God gave only one law:

41 National Council for Policy Analysis, Crime and Punishment in America, 1999, www.ncpa.org
42 James Vicini, "U.S. has most prisoners in world due to tough laws," *Reuters,* December 9, 2006.

capital punishment for the murderer. I suggest that this is the most basic definition of civil justice available to man, which is given to us by means of a transcendent law. But in our own country, of the 16,137 homicides committed in 2004, only 59 received the justice prescribed in Genesis 9:6. Do the math and you find that this judicial system fails to obey God 99.96% of the time.

To make matters worse, the rising costs of prisons (now at $37 billion) further tyrannize the victims of crimes and hardworking, productive taxpayers who are forced to pay for this fiasco.[43] Our justice system punishes the taxpayers while providing medical care, food, clothing, entertainment, and training programs for those who steal, plunder, rape, and kill. Such an unjust system that saddles the victims with the cost of room and board for those who commit crimes is quite a contrast with biblical law which wisely mandates that criminals restitute to their victims four to five times the value of what was stolen (Ex. 22:1).

A judicial system which abandons restitution for the thief and capital punishment for the murderer provides little justice for victims. And from all reports, the police in our cities are overwhelmed in their attempts to administer justice. Prosecutors settle almost all charges now by plea bargain in order to avoid the hassle and expense of court time. The courts are clogged such that "speedy trial" becomes nothing more than a mockery (Eccl. 8:11). The system as presently configured is simply unable to provide justice.

Whereas a biblical system brings hard justice to bear on gross crime and leaves the minor misdemeanors alone, the current system equalizes justice such that the rapist and the man exchanging contraband receive equal attention and sentencing. In the end, everyone gets the same free room and board to the tune of $25,000/year invoiced to the taxpayer and/or victim. The modern system attempts to reform criminals, while ignoring the standards of biblical justice proves itself to be yet another

---

43 Michael Myser, "Inside the $37 billion prison economy," CNN Money, December 6, 2006, http://money.cnn.com/magazines/business2/business2_archive/2006/12/01/8394995/index. htm?postversion=2006120608

example of man's arrogant foolishness. Indeed, the progressive reforms of the 19th and 20th centuries that ignored God's law for the betterment of mankind only produced worse conditions in the end.

"Thy princes are rebellious, and companions of thieves: every one loveth gifts, and followeth after rewards: they judge not the fatherless, neither doth the cause of the widow come unto them."
Isaiah 1:23

The Promotion of Immorality

For the Christian who holds a biblical worldview, it should be obvious that civil government should at least not promote that which is immoral, even if it is engaged in a good many useless or wasteful activities. But our governments today seem bent on using power and money to promote immorality. Then again, from the perspective of men like William Penn and Benjamin Franklin, this is the only way governments can expand their power. An immoral people will be enslaved.

Note, first of all, what the Bible says about those who reward wickedness:

"Woe to him that buildeth a town with blood, and stablisheth a city by iniquity! ... Woe unto him that giveth his neighbour drink, that puttest thy bottle to him, and makest him drunken also, that thou mayest look on their nakedness!" Habakkuk 2:12-15

"Wherefore thus saith the Holy One of Israel, Because ye despise this word, and trust in oppression and perverseness, and stay thereon: Therefore this iniquity shall be to you as a breach ready to fall, swelling out in a high wall, whose breaking cometh suddenly at an instant." Isaiah 2:12-13

"Woe unto them that are mighty to drink wine, and men of strength to mingle strong drink: Which justify the wicked for reward, and take away the righteousness of the righteous from him! Therefore as the fire devoureth the stubble, and the flame consumeth the chaff, so their root shall be as rottenness, and their blossom shall go up as dust: because they have cast away the law of the LORD of hosts, and despised the word of the Holy One of Israel."
Isaiah 5:22

The best way to anesthetize the frogs in the heating pot is to encourage the abandonment of responsibility, the breakdown of the family, and general moral dissoluteness. Unfortunately, that is precisely what is happening in practically every developed nation in the world today by the force of public policy.

From a cursory study of the Bible, one will quickly find two sins which especially meet God's displeasure: the shedding of innocent blood and sodomy. That is why these two issues are of the deepest concern to any Christian who looks to God as the source of ethics and the Bible as a real epistemological authority.[44]

Increasingly, homosexuals are insisting that children in government schools be taught how to perform homosexual acts as well as heterosexual acts, and the taxpayers pay the bill. The arguments in New York's school districts now concern whether or not fourth grade children should be trained in the use of condoms. In 1992, the Denver public school system used a Health and Science Education teachers' guide entitled "Gay and Lesbian Youth Tools for Educators" as a training tool for their teachers. The guide included a questionnaire designed to be answered by junior high and high school students. Here are several tax-funded questions from that questionnaire: "Is it possible your heterosexuality is just a phase you may outgrow? ... Is it possible that all you need is a

44 At the date of this writing, already the largest denominations in the West are poised to split on these ethical issues. We will expect ethics to begin to define the Christian faith in the next century or so, and a distinctively Christian worldview may once again be apparent in the Christian church in some places around the world.

good gay lover? If you have never slept with a person of the same sex, how do you know that you would not prefer to do so?"

Virginia government school districts tried another sex survey for 12-year-old children, suggesting that some children will have sex as early as nine years old with three or more people.[45] In the New York City school system, recommended books for first graders are *Daddy's Roommate* (about two homosexual men), and *Heather has Two Mommies.*

In 1999, then Governor of California, Grey Davis, signed AB 537 into law which added the topic of sexual orientation as required curriculum to the state's education code. Bills like SB 1441 passed in California last year, prohibiting discrimination on the basis of sexual orientation, a bill that has major implications for parochial schools and other faith-based educational institutions in that state. [46] A similar bill passed into law in 2003, disallowing discrimination towards cross-dressers. At least eight other states and ninety cities and municipalities have laws in place prohibiting discrimination against homosexuals even for private enterprise. Thus, homosexuality is now presented as something less than a sin, and in many schools a preferred lifestyle.

The movement towards a homosexual nation continues at a steady pace, not unlike the direction taken by Greece and Rome during the decadent years. Consider the fact that it was as recent as 1985 that the federal and state government programs began providing condoms to heterosexual high school students. By 1999, they were sanctioning homosexual clubs in the high schools. In 2003, the cutting edge schools included homosexual couples at proms. Then in 2005, newscasts reported regularly on homosexual teachers who would take sexual advantage of their students. In some cases, the judge recommended only house arrest. What developments can we expect in the next twenty years?

45 *Washington Times,* October 6, 1994, p. A1.
46 "Californian Governor Signs Pro-Homosexual Bill, Outrages Family Advocates," *Agape Press,* August 29, 2006, http://headlines.agapepress.org/archive/8/292006a.asp

On June 26, 2003, in a decision which was at least as important as the *Roe v. Wade* decision of 1973 (disallowing restrictions on abortion in America), the United States Supreme Court overruled a Texas sodomy law, effectively providing official state endorsement of homosexuality.

Social acceptance of homosexuality is now almost complete with the exception of a few pastors who might still dare to preach from Leviticus. It is hard to believe that it was just fifty years ago (1953) that President Eisenhower issued an executive order requiring the discharge of homosexual employees from federal employment, including military service. Forty years later, President Clinton initiated the "Don't Ask, Don't Tell," policy for the military, and on June 24, 2004, President George W. Bush signed legislation (named for one of the homosexual Safety Officers of September 11, 2001), allowing death benefits for "domestic partners."[47]

Now courts in almost half the states allow adoptions by both homosexual partners. According to a recent article from USA Today, at least 6 million children live with homosexual parents.[48] Laura McAlpine, executive director of the Women's Health Center in Chicago, reports that 70% of the women applying for artificial insemination are lesbians. The first seminar on lesbian parenting held in Chicago took place in the summer of 1992 and was filled to capacity.

Concerned Women for America reported on a most remarkable public event that would never have occurred in 15th century Italy even at the lowest, most depraved state of the Christian church prior to the Reformation. The historic occurrence was the "christening" of an infant reportedly belonging to two homosexual men.

"Cameron Frederick Fisher Davenport, 6 weeks old, son of Tim Fisher and Scott Davenport, was welcomed into the Christian community in the combined Episcopal-Presbyterian ceremony

47 Mychal Judge Police & Fire Chaplains Public Safety Officers' Benefit Act of 2002, Pub. L. No. 107-196, 116 Stat. 719.
48 *USA Today,* February 17, 2003,
http://www.usatoday.com/news/nation/2003-02-17-cover-samesex_x.htm

as about 80 other gay and lesbian parents and their children looked on... The christening of the infant, born to a surrogate mother artificially inseminated with sperm, was a vivid sign of the changing nature of gay and lesbian parenting ... Davenport has filed papers to legally adopt his newborn son, just as he adopted a 2-year-old daughter, Katherine Anne, jointly with Fisher in April."[49]

According to Dr. Paul Cameron, "children are increasingly being given to homosexuals and lesbians when their custody is disputed by a heterosexual parent."[50] This is frightening indeed when surveys of homosexuals show that nearly 25% of them say they would prefer sex with children.[51] "On September 28, an Orange County, California judge made [a] ruling in regard to an abandoned father. The judge told the father that 'your Achilles heel is your reluctance to accept the life-style your ex-wife has chosen for herself' and threatened his visitation rights with his child. The ex-wife is living openly with another lesbian. Both are employed by the Los Angeles Sheriff's Department."

Acts of public sodomy, once a crime meriting capital punishment in America, are becoming prevalent, particularly during the "gay pride" marches in the larger cities. The pedophiliac North American Man-Boy Love Association (NAMBLA) now marches proudly in "gay pride" parades, and meet freely in public buildings. Meanwhile, San Francisco, Chicago, and San Jose, California have informed local Scout troops that they can no longer use parks, schools and other municipal sites.[52]

All of which brings up that nagging question, "Does God really care anymore about things like this?" If you were to take into account

---

49 "New Trend: Homosexual Parenting," *Concerned Women for America: Issues at a Glance,* May 1993, Article sourced September 3, 1992 edition of the Chicago Tribune.

50 Paul Cameron, "Family Research Report," November 12, 1992.

51 "Effect of homosexuality upon public health and social order," *Nebraska Medical Journal,* 1985:70:292-99; ; Psychological Reports 1989: 64, 1167-79.

52 *New York Times,* August 29, 2000.

the biblical record, He seemed to care about what went on in Sodom, Egypt, Israel, Tyre and Sidon, Babylon, Assyria, Greece, and Rome. And these empires are gone now. But is God really all that interested in what is going on in our country today? Judging from what is said in New Testament passages (such as Heb. 10:29, 30; Matt. 10:15, 11:22), it seems that God is even more concerned with what is going on in America today than what went on in Sodom 2,500 years ago.

"And likewise also the men, leaving the natural use of the woman, burned in their lust one toward another; men with men working that which is unseemly, and receiving in themselves that recompense of their error which was meet ... Who knowing the judgment of God, that they which commit such things are worthy of death, not only do the same, but have pleasure in them that do them." Romans 1:27-32

The Shedding of Innocent Blood

Since 1973, America has produced her own "holocaust," resulting in the deaths of 48,589,993 babies. Forty-eight million babies is the equivalent to the population of 20 states. Who can hide behind ignorance with the millions of in utero pictures published, the ultrasounds, and fetal heartbeat monitors? Against all of the evidence that the child in uterus reacts to pain and his mother's moods, sucks his thumb, sleeps, kicks, thinks, lives, and dies, tens of millions of mothers have succumbed to these acts of murder (encouraged by varying levels of social and institutional coercion). Such wholesale slaughter is mind boggling, and again one wonders if God really cares, or if He still means what He says about fatherless children:

"If you shall afflict [fatherless children] in any wise, and they cry at all unto Me, I will surely heart their cry, and My wrath shall

wax hot, and I will kill you with the sword; and your wives shall be widows and your children fatherless." Exodus 23:22

Evidently God does care. But others don't. Since *Roe v. Wade* the Supreme Court of the United States had one opportunity to reverse the abortion holocaust. But on December 1, 1992, the Court refused to consider the case, effectively nullifying the Guam law that prohibited abortion in that territory. Justices Sandra Day O'Connor, Anthony Kennedy, David Souter and Clarence Thomas (all appointees of conservative presidents) joined the pro-death ranks to kill the law. Justice White, a Democrat appointee from the 1960s, dissented from the majority vote.[53]

To make matters worse, our tax money is directed to killing many of these children. Planned Parenthood received a record amount of money in federal funding in its 2004-2005 fiscal year, with a total of $272.7 million dollars in government grants and contracts. The total amount of blood money collected from taxpayers since 1987 now stands at $4.0 billion dollars.[54] Even "conservative" Republican presidents have continued to support federal funding of this national travesty. Title XIX funding continues to fund surgical abortions through Medicaid, in accordance with bills HR3061 signed by President Bush on January 10, 2002, and HR 2673 signed by the president on January 23, 2004. And the total increase for Title X Planned Parenthood funding between 2004 and Bill Clinton's last budget year (FY2001) is $26 million, an increase of about 10%.[55]

We have yet to describe what is newly on the rise, and still a little too edgy for government funding. On the bloody edge of the slippery slope sits the state of Oregon that legalized doctor-assisted suicide by popular referendum in 2001. The United States Supreme Court upheld

53 *Washington Post*, December 4, 1992, p. A1.
54 Gudrun Schultz, "Planned Parenthood Reports Record $882 Million Income, $63 Million Profit," *Lifesite News*, June 8, 2006,
http://www.lifesite.net/ldn/2006/jun/06060805.html
55 Covenant News, October 9, 2004, http://www.covenantnews.com/lefemine041011.htm.

the law in January, 2006. Furthermore, a general disregard for the value of human life is increasingly manifest in the growing popular support shown for candidates who ride the edge. A United States Senator and popular presidential candidate in the 2008 election cycle, Barack Obama, successfully defended *policies that legalized infanticide* while he was a member of the Illinois legislature.[56]

> *"Thus saith the LORD; Execute ye judgment and righteousness, and deliver the spoiled out of the hand of the oppressor: and do no wrong, do no violence to the stranger, the fatherless, nor the widow, neither shed innocent blood in this place ... but if ye will not hear these words, I swear by Myself, saith the LORD, that this house shall become a desolation." Jeremiah 22:3, 5*

But what does this have to do with you and me? It is doubtful my reader has participated in such criminal activity. Or have we? Imagine for a moment that you were riding in a bus down a mountain pass with 20 mph switchbacks and hairpin curves. The bus begins to accelerate to a breakneck speed as it approaches one dangerous curve. Suddenly, somebody in the bus discovers that the bus driver is drunk. As the bus careens over the guard rail and shoots into space over a deep ravine, somebody screams out, "This isn't my fault!" Another passenger cries, "I didn't vote for this driver!" Of course, none of this really matters. You are all in the bus together, and you are all inextricably connected in this horrific bus accident. In like manner, God holds all of us responsible for the conditions of our communities. This is called "covenantal culpability."

While some Christians would like to ignore the sins of their communities, God still considers them a part of it. And though Daniel and his friends were righteous men, they were still taken into captivity with the rest of the nation of Israel. As hundreds of millions of our

56 "Obama's constitutional crisis," *World Net Daily,* http://wnd.com/news/article.asp?ARTICLE_ID=53694.

fellow citizens passively accept abortion mills, elect politicians who will not oppose abortion, support candidates who allow the public funding of abortion, and silently stand by as their acquaintances kill their babies, it may be good to remind them that "the mills of God grind slowly but very fine." In 1998, I ran a political race against two candidates for United States Senate (a Republican and a Democrat), both of whom supported convenience abortion on demand. As the pro-life candidate in the race, I received 1% of the vote. Incredibly, 99% of the population in the state voted for candidates that were committed to the pro-abortion position!

Several years ago, I had a conversation with a pro-family lobbyist about the legislative agenda in the state in which he was lobbying. In the course of the conversation, I asked him about the life issue. His response: "Oh, that issue doesn't have any traction. We're going to put that on the back burner for now."

Of course, it is true that few people are troubled by the shedding of innocent blood in our nation. But what would happen if the God who created heaven and earth cared deeply about this issue? What would happen if God headed the conference table as conservative coalitions discussed public policy issues for the upcoming legislative session? What would God put on the top of the agenda in 48 point font? Does anybody care to know?

> *"If thou forbear to deliver them that are drawn unto death, and those that are ready to be slain; If thou sayest, Behold, we knew it not; doth not He that pondereth the heart consider it? and He that keepeth thy soul, doth not He know it? and shall not he render to every man according to his works?" Proverbs 24:11-12*

Conclusion

Our world has become a brave new world indeed, and it is fast changing. When Christians and Christian churches refuse to take a firm ethical stand at any point on the eternal principles of God's revealed law, this whirlwind of sin and moral decline will quickly sweep them and their children away. The courts, legislatures, schools, and media that enthusiastically promote these destructive sins will lead the churches into a tolerance and an acceptance of them. If the Grace Baptist Churches and Faith Presbyterian Churches in this country refuse to preach the clear law of God which defines sin and discriminates between good and evil, the other side will up the ante with each successive decade. From fornication and abortion to homosexuality, incest, and euthanasia, the church will ignore the conflict at each stage of the battle to its own demise.

It is hard to believe that it has been only 120 years since Laura Ingalls Wilder was complaining about the word "obey" in her marriage vows.[57] Sixty years later, prayer flew out the window of the government schools. And sixty years hence, we are debating the homosexual age-of-consent laws. There has been little break in this steady 120-year crushing of the Christian moral structure in our culture. Reagan's conservative revolution was a mirage and the moral majority turned out to be a pretty thin minority. We have yet to see a reduction in Planned Parenthood grants under any president. After all the photo-ops and prayer breakfasts that Christian leaders have shared with Republican Presidents in Washington, and after all the conservative talk radio programs, it is high time we admit the obvious: Christians have made no real progress in changing the civic and social direction of the nation.

However, at this point, I need to encourage my reader to not give up hope. Later, I will point out where we are making progress. I will argue that we are failing because we are incorrectly identifying the root problem. *Those who understand the root issues of our present decline will work on root solutions. And that is the charted course of the Second Mayflower.*

57 Laura Ingalls Wilder, *These Happy Golden Years,* Harper and Row, New York, NY, 1971, p. 270.

The Breakdown of Morality and
the Integrity of the Family

The fruit of this experiment in tyrannical and immoral government is precisely what we would expect. According to a Rutgers University study released in 2005, American families are *the weakest in the Western world*. The study found that "The USA has the lowest percentage among Western nations of children who grow up with both biological parents, 63%."[58]

Nothing depicts the devastating collapse of the American family in sharper clarity than the index of children born without fathers. The illegitimacy rate now stands at 37% and continues to increase at 1% per year over the last several years. With the rate standing just over 5% in 1960, this accounts for a 720% increase in the rate of single parent births in only 45 years! Sadly, minorities are hit particularly hard by the illegitimacy rates, with blacks now at 70% (up from 25% in 1965), and Hispanics as high as 48%.[59] All indices considered, the average minority child has only a 6% chance of living with their parents until the age of 18![60] What a sad irony that immigrants from Mexico come to America for a new life, and in the process they destroy their families! One would have a hard time finding any place at any period in world history where such devastation has eroded an entire civilization so quickly.

As of 2006, the American household where husband and wife live together fell under the 50% mark for the first time in recorded history. The number of families with husband, wife, and children fell from 40% in 1970 to 24% in the 2000s. The platonic vision of the individualized life and the dissolution of the family is finally becoming a reality.

Even more devastating than all of the above statistics is the disappearance of fatherhood in America. In 1970, 57.3 percent of

58 Sharon Jayson, "Divorce declining, but so is marriage," *USA Today,* July 8, 2005, http://www.usatoday.com/news/nation/2005-07-18-cohabit-divorce_x.htm
59 *Washington Times,* December 1, 2006, http://www.washtimes.com/op-ed/20061201-084845-1917r.htm
60 Suzanne Fields, *Conservative Chronicle,* January 11, 1995, 1.

men, ages 25-29, lived with their own children in the household. In 2000, that share had fallen to 28.8 percent.[61] The Rutgers University study just mentioned commented on the role of "adult entertainment," in undermining a vision for the nuclear family in the hearts of our people, "The adult entertainment industry, which includes gambling, pornography, and sex, is one of the fastest growing and most lucrative sectors of the consumer economy. Not only has this multibillion dollar industry gained respectability and power in the corridors of Washington, it has used its power to defeat every effort to restrict the access of underage children to its most misogynistic and hyper-violent products."[62]

The Connection

There is an intimate connection between a nation's social constructs and government policies, and the morality of the people. It is essential that my reader understand this connection, if he is to understand the thesis of this book. To illustrate this connection, consider the recent trend towards homosexual marriage that is fast taking hold in this nation.

Short of supernatural intervention, there are three overriding reasons why conservatives are set to lose the homosexual marriage battle, and why public high schools will move from homosexual clubs to homosexual classes and laboratories.

Historically, one finds examples of homosexual high schools and mentorships in decaying cultures from Greece to Rome. Unless something changes, America will likely meet a similar fate. There are now homosexuals who fill the highest positions of American government in the executive, judicial and legislative branches (of both Democrat and Republican stripes). Unless something changes dramatically in the

---

61 Barbara Whitehead and David Popenoe, "The State of our Unions, The Social Health of Marriage in America,"
http://marriage.rutgers.edu/Publications/SOOU/TEXTSOOU2006.htm
62 Ibid.

next ten years, there are three reasons why conservatives will lose the battle against homosexual marriage.

Reason #1 - Both the public schools and the media have already sold the vision to the country. It is true that the majority of America is still opposed to homosexual marriage. But recent polling reveals a significant trend in the other direction. While 52% of the populace still opposes homosexual marriage and civil unions, a full 67% of those who have post-graduate degrees support homosexual marriage, and 70% of those under 35 years of age support homosexual unions.[63] The bottom line is, education works. Those who were educated in the 1940s and 1950s are now in their fifties and sixties, and on average, oppose homosexual marriage, *because the schools had not endorsed homosexuality during the years that they were educated.* Today, however, homosexual indoctrination is pervasive. It is pervasive throughout the culture. One is marked as homophobic if he breathes a word against homosexuality in a high school classroom.

But more fundamentally, schools refuse to teach an education rooted in the fear of God. Rather, they teach a religion of tolerance, pluralism, and polytheism. The only opinion which is not tolerated is that which makes an unequivocal statement against sodomy or incest, or any sexual perversion whatsoever. The only god not tolerated is the God who says, "You shall have no other gods before Me." That is the religion of the public schools, and "Christian" children everywhere have learned it well.

Moreover, the official anti-monotheistic position of the schools establishes a cultural ethical relativism. Therefore it really doesn't matter how many Republicans you put in office, and it doesn't matter how much money you put into a referendum campaign endorsing traditional marriage, and it doesn't matter how many yard signs you put up in your yard. All the yard signs and bumper stickers in the

63 *Rocky Mountain News,* September 19, 2006

world will not make a difference. Conservatives will lose because they've already lost in the schools.

A valuable lesson may be drawn from another conservative in history, King Saul. In this story, God commanded a thorough annihilation of the enemy, but Saul held back from killing the king. Ultimately, he was never really committed to winning the war, because his heart was in the wrong place.

> *"And Saul smote the Amalekites from Havilah until thou comest to Shur, that is over against Egypt. And he took Agag the king of the Amalekites alive, and utterly destroyed all the people with the edge of the sword. But Saul and the people spared Agag, and the best of the sheep, and of the oxen, and of the fatlings, and the lambs, and all that was good, and would not utterly destroy them: but every thing that was vile and refuse, that they destroyed utterly."*
> *1 Samuel 15:7-9*

Lesson learned: if you kill what is vile and refuse, and leave the king alive, you will continue to lose the battle for generations to come. Our age exactly replicates the half-hearted obedience of Saul, who went after the gross and vile thing, but refused to kill the root and branch.

Now applying the lesson to the issue at hand, our education system will guarantee a liberal direction in the long haul. By definition, public schools will endorse statism and immorality. As long as the ACLU and the NEA refuse to allow public schools to teach the fear of God as the beginning of wisdom and knowledge, we will see conservatives continue to coalesce with the "progressive" agenda. Meanwhile, the Democrats will do their best to stay a year or two ahead on the road to Gomorrah. If conservatives and Christians really wanted to maintain a principled direction for the country, they would put every ounce of their resources behind dismantling the public school monopoly. But as long as Christians continue to support the godless agenda by supporting the government educational system, and as long as they send their children to these schools, they will lose every political battle in the long run.

Reason #2 - The second reason why conservatives are poised to lose the homosexual marriage battle is that this nation is producing a much higher number of homosexuals than ever before. What produces homosexuality is what produces all human behavior - a combination of nature and nurture. The nature of man is inherently sinful and therefore, latent homosexual inclinations are hardwired in the fallen, depraved hearts of men (Rom. 3:1-15). Nevertheless, homosexuals tend to come from fatherless homes. Clinical psychologist, Dr. Joseph Nicolosi makes this intuitively obvious point in his book *Preventing Homosexuality: A Parent's Guide.* Says Nicolosi, "In 15 years, I have spoken with hundreds of homosexual men. I have never met one who said he had a loving, respectful relationship with his father."[64] This is not to say that every homosexual is born fatherless, but a marked distance in the father-son relationship is a significant contributor to the homosexual phenomena.

Of all of the indices of the breakdown of the family in America, the clearest is the disappearance of fatherhood. And when I say fathers, I mean dads who invest themselves heart and life in their sons and daughters. Thus, a world where 37% of children are born without fathers *will produce huge increases in homosexuality.* The homosexuals raised in fatherless homes in the 1960s (when the illegitimacy rate was a mere 5-6%), are the 40-year-old "gay activists" today. But the fatherless problem is far worse today by a factor of 700%! What will this world look like 40 years from now?

Indeed, we have not even seen the beginning of the modern homosexual movement! I forecast at least double the current percentage of homosexuals in America by 2025, which means far more homosexual propaganda in the schools and a major increase in homosexual political

64 James Dobson, *Bringing Up Boys,* Tyndale House, Wheaton, IL, 2001, p. 121.

influence. We can expect to see even more homosexual perversions endorsed and promoted by civil fiat.

In the United States, 37% of children are born without fathers. But there is a much higher percentage of sons who have grown up without their fathers' hearts during most of their developmental years. The hearts of far too many fathers are consumed with work, sports, entertainment, and play. I wish a father would understand what he is doing when he prefers his golf game every Saturday to spending a little time with his son who is crying out to his father for attention, love, and discipleship. Do fathers understand that by their abdication they may be consigning their sons to a homosexual lifestyle? Or what about the father who abandons his little boy and his little girl in his heart when he grabs that Playboy magazine or surfs the porn sites? While I would not diminish personal responsibility, as each person must bear responsibility for his own decisions in life, neither do I want to the power of both nurture and nature in the life of a child. Without that nurture God requires of fathers and mothers, nothing will stop the unraveling of morality, family, and freedom in this nation.

All of the conservative activists and pro-traditional marriage yard signs in the world will not stop homosexual marriage or impede the rush towards wholesale social acceptance of aberrant lifestyles as long as the father-son relationship continues to decline year after year. Three years ago, 35% of children were born without fathers. Two years ago, 36% of children were born without fathers. Now it is 37%. Until this index shifts direction, I have little hope for the battle against homosexuality in the near future.

Reason #3 - The third and final reason that conservatives will lose the battle against homosexual marriage is that the church is unwilling to fight. In the most recent confrontation over marriage in Colorado, those working for the pro-family marriage referendums reported significant opposition to their efforts to disseminate pro-family information from "conservative" churches. Reportedly, these churches were afraid that the pro-family message would turn off the homosexuals they were trying to reach with "the Gospel!"

Now this brings up an interesting question. When you try to reach rapists with the Gospel of Jesus, should you state up front that rape is a sin? I would suggest that when you try to reach liars or homosexuals or anybody else with the Gospel of Jesus Christ, you need to put the law of God on the front of the brochure. It is interesting that Jesus brought up the problem of covetousness with a covetous man and really turned him off (Matt. 19:21, 22). For the apostles, repentance and faith were two sides of the same coin (Acts 20:21), but the modern church recoils from the law of God and the dreaded "R" word, because such a message is too confrontational with the culture and would "turn off" the crowd. Indeed the theological and practical separation of grace and law, orthodoxy and orthopraxy, or faith and repentance has done untold damage to the Christian faith across the West.

There is something fundamentally wrong with both the teaching and practice of the modern evangelical church. Recently, two of the most prominent evangelical pastors in Colorado resigned in shame, admitting to homosexual sins and patterns in their lives. Each had pastored area mega churches for 20+ years. For obvious reasons, one pastor had avoided "political agendas," and in one sermon, had suggested that homosexuality was a more acceptable sin than divorce.[65]

How To Win

The political battles of the 21st century have become symbolic reenactments of some old battle already lost. Our initiatives and referendums are nothing but carpet cleaning over a crumbling foundation.

If we are going to win, our reformations must be more fundamental. We must reform our theology, our parenting, and our education systems if we want to see *any appreciable change whatsoever* in the wider culture.

65 *The Denver Post*, December 11, 2006, http://www.denverpost.com/ci_4817067

And if Christians are unwilling to reform here, they might as well burn all their political yard signs and wait for the homosexuals to break down the door of the house. Our reformations must extend to both root and branch, flower and stem. Our repentance must extend to our own hearts and lives. But, are we ready to go that deep?

> *"See, I have this day set thee over the nations and over the kingdoms, to root out, and to pull down, and to destroy, and to throw down, to build, and to plant." Jeremiah 1:10*

*   *   *

For some reason we were born into the end of the second millennium, AD. We are a product of our generation and we strain to see beyond it. If we can see the standard of God's law and then contrast it with the situation and trends we face in our world today, we will be able to lay out a vision for the next voyage of the Mayflower.

In this chapter, we have seen the fleeting pictures of human misery from a civilization that has forgotten God. To some degree, all of us have a played a part in it. Pieces of flying shrapnel from this imploding culture have impacted each of us to one extent or another. Indeed, the Second Mayflower, not unlike the first, faces formidable difficulties. Those difficulties may be summarized as follows:

1. First, we face a rising tyranny of government. Let me be as clear as humanly possible on this point. A nation that takes 46% of your money in taxation is tyrannical. Any nation that forces every business owner to be a tax collector for the government and that maintains thousands of regulatory agencies to control every aspect of our lives is tyrannical. And a nation that employs a compulsory attendance law, forcing children into state institutions at early ages, is also tyrannical. Never, even in ancient times, did civil government interfere in so many spheres of the lives of citizens.

97

2. The vision-deadening influences of materialism, sexual addictions, and entertainment at the expense of duty have become almost overpowering. The sad fact remains that most people like tyranny and they do not like freedom. Generally, people are attracted to slavery as long as they can be slaves to big government and/or sinful impulses. As the man said, "Either you'll be governed by God, or by God you'll be governed."

3. The abandonment of the law of God as the standard of ethics. No institution or person is more to blame for the direction of the nation than the Christian churches of the 1800s and 1900s. When the church abandoned God's law as the source of ethics, it gave the nation up to the man-centered ethics of humanism. But more importantly, the people could no longer envision a godly direction for the future which would have come by the preaching of the law of God.

> *"Where there is no vision, the people perish: but he that keepeth the law, happy is he." Proverbs 29:18*

> *"My people are destroyed for lack of knowledge: because thou hast rejected knowledge, I will also reject thee ... seeing thou hast forgotten the law of thy God, I will also forget thy children."*
> *Hosea 4:6*

4. A growing pessimism has settled like a cold fog over much of the Christian church since the 1800s. When it came to building godly families, culture, and government, some Christian leaders went so far as to tell us not to "polish brass on a sinking ship."[66] Millennial fever towards the turn of the 20th century dogmatically held to an imminent return of Christ, and many Christians did not want to involve themselves in projects that would take more than a couple of years to accomplish. The world was going to hell in a hand basket, and the best anybody

---

66 A famous statement attributed to Dwight L. Moody of the 19th century.
Cf. Jane Lampman, "The End of the World," *Christian Science Monitor,* February 18, 2004.

could hope for was a few converts. So why try to salvage the education system, economics, or political institutions by taking them back to the standard of God's law? Such projects were deemed worthless. This theology played nicely into the hands of a humanist existentialism which taught the world to live for the immediate moment.

5. The disintegration of the nuclear family and the failure of fatherhood cut the legs off of any movement that would begin to build a moral and a free people.

6. Finally, the inherent weakness of the church in its theological formulations and practice have made it impossible for a few conservative activists to make any real difference in the sociopolitical world.

These are the challenges that we face at the end of the twentieth century. They are serious challenges but they are not insurmountable. For there are moments in human history when the hearts of good men and women are prepared to make the difficult choice when the choice presents itself. The status quo, the convenient course of action, the easy path all lead to an unthinkable, intolerable end for their families and must, therefore, be rejected. So boldly they advance towards the only reasonable alternative, the Second Mayflower.

*   *   *

"Mankind is in crisis ... a long crisis which began three hundred, and in some places, four hundred years ago, when people turned away from religion ... It is a crisis which led the East to Communism and the West to a pragmatic society. It is the crisis of materialism."
    -Aleksandr Solzhenitsyn

SECOND MAYFLOWER

4

CASTING A VISION FOR THE SECOND MAYFLOWER

The Second Mayflower starts today where the first Mayflower started - in the hearts of those who envision something better than this world. It starts with those who cannot live with the status quo, nor can they live without a dream for something better. It starts with those who can see where they are and have set a vision for that "something better" by the standards of God's transcendent law.

The Vision

"Without a vision the people perish, but he who keepeth the law, happy is he." Proverbs 29:18; cf. Hosea 4:6

The beginning of any movement is always found in the vision. Without a vision, the family perishes as do civilizations. And the lack of a biblical vision is precisely what maintains our present trajectory towards a continuing breakdown of family, law, and community. Vision provides a general direction for the ship, but it also dictates each tack in the journey, as well as the timing for the tack. Vision is the most difficult part of the project, and, in the end, it serves as the driving force behind the journey. Therefore, it would be worthwhile to lay out, at least in rough form, the vision for the Second Mayflower. That will be the focus of the remainder of this book.

A Generational Vision

As a vision begins to take shape, the sharp contrast between what should be and what is may yield some less than desirable effects upon the minds of those who would be part of the Second Mayflower. Some might be gripped with fear, pessimism, or even paranoia. Such responses are certainly not rooted in faith in God, and inevitably those consumed by such fear would also lose any sense of duty over time. For God has not given us a spirit of fear and timidity, but of power, of love, and a sound mind (2 Tim. 1:7).

There are also those visionaries who are overcome with impatience when they discover that what they envision today cannot be turned into a reality overnight. Such firebrands quickly burn out and produce little good in the long term. It should be obvious that perfection cannot be achieved on earth by mortal, sinful men. Rather, it is a vision, a direction, and steppping stones towards that vision that are needful.

Suppose that the National Aeronautic and Space Administration initiated a project to send a space ship to a planet beyond our solar system, and they selected a young man to navigate the space craft. Of course, it would take more than 200 years to complete such a voyage. If this be the case, the astronaut would need to be accompanied by his wife, and at least one other family. Because he would not complete the voyage himself, he would need to pass the vision for the mission on to his son, and then on to his grandson. Before passing on, he would carefully point out to his son the general direction of the planet to which they were headed. He would need to teach his son to navigate the craft, all the while reminding him to pass the vision of the mission on to his children.

Such an hypothetical example provides several points of analogy with the voyage of the Second Mayflower. First, the project we have set out to pursue will require a *multi-generational commitment*. In the history of man's dominion work, any project of real significance was accomplished with clear vision and hard work, over a long period of time.

The most important work came over a period of successive generations. For us, the sharing of the vision from father to son to grandson will be an essential component of the mission. If this transference of the vision is missed at any point, the mission will be forced to abort.

Capturing the Vision

If anybody is going to bring about change in the currents of world history and culture, it will not begin with those who are controlled by the major media sources. Television is the epitome of the status quo today, and those who have been well-immersed in the cultural environs of television will see no urgency or need for change. Never have societies been so manipulated or lulled into complacency by a mass media, as they have in the last fifty years. Many will accept a government that taxes up to 75% of their income, a society where 70% of its children are born without fathers and half of its marriages end in divorce, without so much as a shrug. Many will tolerate a culture where their children are deftly led astray into sodomy, fornication, drug addiction, and divorce. Many will accept a culture where entertainers regularly break all Ten Commandments with impunity. And far too many passively accept the life of a slave and shirk the responsibilities and challenges of freedom. They have no vision because they have television.

Those who play the part of the Pilgrims and Puritans will see the stark contrast between what is and what ought to be. If the First Mayflower gives birth to the second, some part of the vision will be discernable from the original founding of this nation. But not all of it. Indeed, the vision to which we chart our voyage cannot be a replay of the First Mayflower either geographically or ideologically. We do not face the identical problems nor do we share the same geo-political and social situation as the early founders of this nation. What we seek cannot be merely what existed in the 1950s or even the 1650s.

Times have changed, but the ultimate standard of truth and ethics has not changed. That standard is the law of God. According to Proverbs

29:18, our vision comes by the law of God. And that vision is clarified only as we come to understand God's truth and walk in it.

The Potential for Failure

But let us not over-simplify the task in laying out the vision. Eyes that are not trained to see the vision will have a hard time making out how the law of God has any relevance to this day. The potential for failure is very real. In our times we have seen many a good and promising vision fizzle and die. Indeed, short-sightedness and the lack of generational continuity will yield a movement producing little of long term consequence. But that is still not the *root cause* for the failure.

Visions fail when they are too superficial, that is, when they are not basic enough. Visions will fail when the epistemological and ethical base is neither basic enough nor self-conscious enough to produce very much in the long term. Indeed, the vision must contain both a strong foundational principle and a sufficient incarnation of that principle in life application. For example, freedom is a terrific principle, but if the application of the principle of freedom is only the liberty to grow marijuana plants in your back yard, that would be hardly a sufficient application of the principle to sustain the movement! Or illegalizing homosexuality may be a single application of a principle, but it would be hardly enough of an application to rid the world of that sin and the other sins that contribute to it.

First then, we will examine the fundamental principle that constitutes the vision for the Second Mayflower before introducing the various applications that incarnate the principle. Our vision must begin with a recognition of the Source of law, and a repentance for our failure to recognize Him as such.

The Rejection of the Lawgiver

"For as among the government of men, the great authority is obeyed in preference to the lesser, so God must be obeyed above all."

 - Augustine[1]

From the perspective of a Christian worldview, man's root problem is autonomy, a condition whereby a man seeks to be "a law to himself." It is a denial of God's right to determine what is right and what is wrong, and it is a lifting up of oneself above God to make that determination. How fundamental is the problem of autonomy? This is what characterized the first temptation of the devil and the first sin of Adam and Eve in the garden. When the devil challenged God's right to determine what would be good for man, he challenged God's right to be the supreme, sovereign Lawgiver. Then Eve made the determination herself, independent of God, whether eating the fruit would produce good for herself (Gen. 3:1-6). And this was precisely the point at which man first determined for himself the standard of good. As he abandoned God's ethical definitions of good, man became his own lawgiver.

"All we like sheep have gone astray. We have turned everyone to his own way." Isaiah 53:6

"And that ye seek not after your own heart and your own eyes, after which ye use to go a whoring: That ye may remember, and do all my commandments, and be holy unto your God." Numbers 15:39, 40

Natural man will have nothing to do with a God who will tell him what to do. What does he want with a God that will tell him how to

---

1 Augustine, *The Confessions of Saint Augustine*, Kensington House, New Kensington, PA, 1996, p. 64.

train his children, how to treat his wife, how to run his business, or how to set his public policies? What man does want is the right to make his own moral choices, independent of any authority above him. While he may be able to accept a God who loves him enough to save him, or a God that establishes some kind of a truth, or a God who created and controls his world, this God who gives order is utterly anathema to the mind of sinful man.

Humanist ethics are nothing more or less than a proud declaration and defense of the natural autonomy of the sinful heart. Unfortunately, the last two hundred years of human history have marked a radical departure from a God-centered ethic in every one of our public institutions. This humanist worldview now controls every outpost of our culture, all throughout the communities and institutions of the West, bringing with it the ethics of radical, blatant, rebellious autonomy. A modern humanist summarizes his system of thought in an introductory philosophy textbook in these simple words, "Any law that people are counseled to obey that is not of their own making enslaves them and robs them of their dignity."[2] Humanism comes into full bloom in its ethical outlook. The humanist faith begins by defending the dignity of mankind and ends with autonomy. But little does the humanist realize that in his autonomy he separates himself from the God who created him and in the process loses the only possible basis for any human dignity at all.

The problem, however, with humanist law is that it cannot provide a stable, effective system of law for men. It is unstable because it has no basis in tradition or transcendent truth, and it does not effectively provide for the rights of the one without in some way violating the rights of the many, or vice versa. Thus, humanism will often produce either anarchy or tyranny. Law is sometimes determined by the individual which brings about anarchy. At other times it is determined by the corporate body of the state which brings about tyranny. There

2 William H. Halverson, *Concise Introduction to Philosophy Second Edition,* Random House Publishers, New York, New York, 1972, p. 267.

is nothing more tyrannical than a perpetually changing civil law, changing by the whim of men who reject any transcendent law.

Even on the face of it, the humanist world holds the law of God revealed in the Ten Commandments in universal spite. Modern screenplays, academic institutions, and political laws increasingly encourage disobedience of all Ten Commandments. The first four commandments are rejected for their failure to accommodate polytheism and pluralism. The fifth commandment is culturally despised as evidenced by the generational rebellion from one generation to the next. The sixth commandment is ignored by the trend towards legalized infanticide, suicide, and euthanasia. It is rare to find any popular media source that in any way discourages fornication, adultery, or homosexuality. As mentioned in the previous chapter, government money in many Western nations now flows into programs that encourage the breaking of the seventh commandment. And the modern economy is built upon a systemic breaking of the eighth and tenth commandments, with hidden taxes, redistribution of the wealth at every level of government, and the perpetual encouragement of class envy.

The possibility of persecution for Christians is very real today, especially those Christians who take an uncompromising stand against evil, as defined by the holy law of God. A rejection of a biblical worldview will inevitably lead to intensified conflict between the kingdom of the devil and the kingdom of Christ. But a study of history will indicate that persecution of this sort is usually sporadic and limited. Inevitably, what follows in the wake of a self-conscious, rebellious rejection of Christian law in the West, is a disintegration of social structures, beginning with the family and education. And this must lead to a failure of economics and the larger structures of the state. Such a scenario is what characterizes the rather quick demise of the Western empires starting with the "Holy" Roman Empire, then the Spanish Empire, the English Empire, and one day, the American Empire as well.

However, the fundamental problem is not political, but theological. The breakdown did not occur in the legislatures, the schools, or Hollywood, but in the churches. To get to the root of the problem, we must examine the various ways in which Christianity in the West has abandoned a God-centered ethic, and undermined the authority of God as Lawgiver.

Ethical Confusion in the Church

Consider first the ethical confusion found in the church itself. Today, the Catholic and Protestant churches alike are filled with those in both clergy and laity who oppose the grossest of sins and others who support them. Take, for example, the sins of abortion and homosexuality which were once soundly condemned by the ancient Christian church. On June 7, 2003, the first openly homosexual bishop was elected by an Episcopal diocese in New Hampshire.[3] Another minister in a Presbyterian denomination retained his ordination after undergoing a transgender operation by a presbytery vote of 181-161.[4]

In the past several decades, American presidents have expressed public support for homosexuality and abortion while affiliating with the most conservative Baptist church denominations. Yet other presidents who have opposed these sins at least to some small extent, have been members of denominations of a much more liberal bent. Elders in the most conservative Presbyterian churches have served in state legislatures and carried pro-abortion voting records. It is not at all unusual to find the same evangelical churches attracting both legislators who endorse abortion and others who oppose it in their civil capacity. And the same can be said for the Catholics. If a candidate claims to be a Catholic, it would mean that he holds moral and political positions somewhere between Senator Ted Kennedy and Supreme Court Justice

3 http://en.wikipedia.org/wiki/Gene_Robinson
4 Lauren McCauley, "Transgendered Clergy Encouraged to Come Out," *Newsweek*, January 23, 2007.

Antonin Scalia, political polar opposites! For the most part, religious affiliation makes no appreciable difference today on the political and moral leanings of our leaders. The church has lost the authority to speak on ethical issues because it has abandoned the objective authority of the Word of God and the application of its ethical standards.

We have come to the point in Western Christianity where we must ask the question: on what single ethical issue can the church stand with unity and assume the authority to preach a clear standard? The church is simply unable to preach with a unified voice against evil promoted by the civil magistrate and practiced by the wider culture. It has no standard, no message, and therefore very little gospel to bring to the culture. But it does not end there. In its ethical paralysis, the church slowly amalgamates into the culture, conforming to its thought patterns and practices. The resultant anemic church slowly dies. Though it may remain a religious institution of sorts with a few superficial rituals, it becomes effectively irrelevant to direct modern culture and life.

In the mind of the average American Christian, the difference between the world's ethics, lifestyle, and thinking, and that of the Word of God is blurred or indiscernible. Even within the most conservative denominations, some pastors are approving homosexual civil marriages, while others within the same denomination register vehement opposition with the practice. Remember that there were no churches endorsing homosexuality and transgender operations in 1960. It may take about twenty years for a particular perversion to go "mainstream." The church trails behind the mainstream culture by about ten years, and conservative churches will take another twenty years to get there.

For the first time in history, the Christian church is poised to divide on the matter of the source of ethics. Previous debates dealt with the Trinity and the two natures of Christ. Now, a heavily synthesized church finds it almost impossible to define itself because it has abandoned God as the source of law. The world will continue its slide towards endorsing homosexuality, incest, infanticide, and other perversions. With each brave new advance towards perversion, the church will be pressed to make a decision. Some part of the church will endorse the biblical position on these issues (found in the books of Leviticus and Romans), while another part of the church will abandon it and join the slide into Gomorrah. Either the Bible speaks authoritatively towards ethics and the church must declare it, or it does not speak authoritatively and the church will be directed by the ever-shifting cultural norms of men.

Western Christianity has produced a weakened church in its abandonment of the centrality of God in ethics. There are several uses of the law, as categorized by the early reformers in the 16th century. The law convicts the sinner of his sin (Rom. 7:7), it gives believers a rule of obedience by means of which they show love to their Savior (John 14:15, 15:10), and it restrains evil men from the most destructive immorality (Deut. 18:19-21). When the church refuses to preach the law of God, there must be a loss of power in the ministry. To ignore the law of God is to shorten the sword, the weapon by which sin is conquered, men's souls are rescued, and principalities and powers are overcome. Without the law, few, if any, will really be convicted of their sins and come to Christ.

Without the law, Christians will cease to mortify their sinful flesh, forsake the world, and live godly lives. Without the law one will hardly be able to see his sin, and certainly will not love God enough to keep his commandments. When the Spirit of God comes to a man and regenerates him, the change of heart does not stop with the heart. It must work its way into the man's behavior and affect his relationships and his institutions. The means by which this is accomplished is through the Word of God, which in its entirety is "profitable for doctrine, for reproof, for correction, for instruction in righteousness, that the man of God may be perfect, thoroughly equipped for every good work" (2 Tim. 3:16-17). Christianity loses much strength and relevance to the world around it when it refuses to use God's law as a rule of obedience in the sanctification of the saint.

Without the law it is doubtful that evil will be restrained very much, whether that evil be the common criminal or the tyrant. This is very much what we are facing in the 21st century: the rise of tyranny and the rise of crime. The church is emptied of power and influence in the lives of unbelievers and believers alike. Justification is cheapened, sanctification is minimized, and the church is hardly what it rightly ought to be - the institution against which the gates of hell will not prevail. How much true religion is left among us when few will love God enough to keep His commandments let alone preach them? When the incidence of divorce is higher among Christians than among atheists and agnostics, one wonders if there is any husband loving his wife as Christ loved the church, and whether any wife is submitting to her husband in the Lord.[5] If those who have true religion are marked by avoiding fornication (Acts 15:20, 29, 21:25), bridling the tongue (James 1:26), and taking personal care of the fatherless and widow in the church and the family (James 1:27; 1 Tim. 5:1-15), one would hope to find these things in Christian churches.

The Decline in Christian Influence

Another indication that Christians have lost a God-centered ethic is evident in the sharp decline in Christian morality obvious in all of our major cultural institutions. There is a reason why America now faces the highest rate of divorce and the highest rate of children born without fathers in 400 years. For hundreds of years, the Bible and *Pilgrim's Progress* constituted the basic reading material for American families. Even the McGuffey readers contained rich portions of Scripture, treatises on keeping the Christian Sabbath, and the Christian vision of Christopher Columbus. Recently, a Christian teacher in an

5 George Barna Group, "Born Again Christians Just As Likely to Divorce As Are Non-Christians," September 8, 2004,
http://www.barna.org/FlexPage.aspx?Page=BarnaUpdate&BarnaUpdateID=170.

Oregon public school lost her job for keeping a copy of the Bible on her desk. Imagine what would have happened if she actually read it to the class! Even when the Bible is taught as literature, schools are required to teach it "objectively." If the beginning of wisdom and knowledge is the fear of God, one wonders what it would be like to teach the Bible without the fear of God.

A man-centered worldview has successfully infiltrated every level of our cultural institutions, replacing Christian culture with another law system. Clearly it is autonomous humanism that replaced Christian law in education, government, and church, producing a profound shift in the culture, evident in the divorce rate, the crime rate, the single parent rate, and the suicide rate. New ideas have produced new consequences. One must only look to the change of ideas of the previous 75 years to understand the consequences over the same time frame.

While Christ's kingdom has expanded in geographic area over the last 200 years, it has failed to make much of an impact in terms of *the way that people live*, especially in the West. This abdication of an objective ethical system has made way for the huge inroads of the foreign worldviews of Marxism and Islam, especially in Africa, North America, and Europe. As some have put it, everywhere it goes Christianity spreads a mile wide, but only an inch deep. Religions that do not bring an ethic to real life will soon lose their relevance and force. Hence, other religions with a more sharply defined world and life view will eventually fill the void; this is the case with Marxism and Islam in the West, as both of these religions retain well-defined world and life views, law systems, and objectives.

With this great abandonment of God as authority in the area of ethics, it should be no great surprise to find twentieth-century Holland lowering the age of consent to twelve to accommodate homosexuals, or that Denmark has legalized euthanasia, or that the socialism of Hitler, Lenin, Mao Tse Tung, and Pol Pot has murdered hundreds of millions of adult citizens, or that American tax monies are used to encourage the sins of abortion and homosexuality to the tune of billions of dollars each year. It should be of no great surprise that public schools in the country indoctrinate children every day in the practice of homosexuality, purging all references to the Bible from the curriculum, classroom discussions, and even the wall decorations. A Christianity void of a defined ethical worldview is powerless in the face of cultural depravity and tyranny and will itself be overcome by the ethics of another worldview.

Preferring Subjective Ethics

A rejection of God's authority as Lawgiver is evident in the rejection of objective law by much of the modern church. While many churches speak of love, they shy away from any objective law by which love might be defined. In the sardonic words of a 20th century poet,

> "On the first Feminian Sandstones we were promised the Fuller Life (Which started by loving our neighbor and ended by loving his wife) ..."[6]

The sovereign Lawgiver has always required love of His people (Ex. 20:6; Lev. 19:18, 34; Deut. 5:10, 6:5, 7:9, 10:12, 19, 11:1, 13, 22, 13:3, 19:9, 30:6, 16, 30; Matt. 5:43, 44, 19:19, 22:37-39). But God has also provided objective law whereby He defines that love, adding form and vibrancy to it. Love involves keeping all of His commandments (John 14:15). For example, we love our neighbor by respecting the chastity of his wife, his property, and his person. It is this "shape of love" to which modern man recoils. He cannot imagine submitting to a law so objective that it will determine how he will discipline and educate his children, how he will spend his time every seventh day, how he will worship in and rule Christ's church, or how he will engage in his business and politics. Therefore, this objective law is far too restrictive

6 Rudyard Kipling, "Gods of the Copybook Headings."

for the humanist man. He finds it much easier to love others in his own way, perhaps even "his neighbor's wife."

The Christian faith is a love that motivates to obey the laws of God. Without love that obeys, there is no faith. Those who have broken the commandments and sinned much are those who have been forgiven much and therefore they will love much, and keep His commandments much (Luke 7:37-50). To break the unity of this faith is to have no faith at all.

So, if autonomous man is going to be attracted to the Christian religion absent "the power thereof," the modern church finds that it must gut the faith of its objective ethical content.

This is precisely the position expressed by one influential 20th century Christian theologian.

> "Orthodox Christianity ... cannot come to the aid of modern man ... because its morality is expressed in dogmatic and authoritarian moral codes."[7]

The problem with objective law is that it cannot be easily re-interpreted. It is too clear. It is just the fact that God's law is objective that makes it too dogmatic and authoritarian for the modern "Christian." Such an autonomous approach did not characterize the spirit of the Apostle Paul who took *every* Scripture in Old and New Testament as objective enough to equip the man of God to every good work (2 Tim. 3:16, 17). Uncomfortable though it may be for the 21st century Christian, Paul has no problem applying the moral principle of Old Testament law as he argues for the just compensation of pastors (1 Tim. 5:18). And he is chillingly objective with biblical ethics when he roots his teaching on the woman's role in the church in Old Testament law (1 Tim. 2:9-15). This use of the Bible is far too objective for humanist man because he would rather live, work, and worship without any directives from

---

7 R. Niebuhr, *An Interpretation of Christian Ethics*, Seabury Press, New York, NY, 1956, p. 14.

a God who has the right to be God over man's ethics. Natural man doesn't want God hemming in his choices.

Who Will Preach the Law?

A rejection of God as Lawgiver is also evident in the absence of a recognition of the Lawgiver in the pulpit. Generally speaking, it is rare to hear mention of the fear of God and the law of God in the formal and informal liturgy of modern Christian worship. What Christians fail to understand is that they must first fear the God of the law before they can love the God who decreed the death of His beloved Son because they broke His law. Gone is a recognition of the One who gives His law in fire and smoke, and writes His law on stone. Gone is a sense of sin, a sense of grace, and a true sense of love that blossoms into obedience of the commandments of the Son of God. Because there is little preaching and little understanding of God's law, there is little understanding of grace. The eternal standard of God's law and the fear of God is a foreign concept. No longer is it part and parcel of the fabric of the land and the psyche of the people.

It is increasingly rare to find a man in the pulpit who is willing to preach with Elijah-like conviction against the relevant sins and heresies of the day. Among these, I would include fornication, abortion, institutionalized stealing (socialism's redistribution of the wealth), illegitimate divorce, dishonor of parents, immodesty, egalitarianism, existentialism, and feminism. As one church-goer told me recently, "I just don't like to be told what to do." Or in the words of another evangelical preacher in the little "chat" he had with his congregation, "I just want to make a few suggestions for you today. I don't ever want to tell you what to do."

During the worldview shift that occurred at the turn of the twentieth century, many Christians were caught up in side skirmishes that, in themselves, marked a departure from the standard of God's law. Such was the nature of the prohibition movement, which would have imprisoned the Son of God for manufacturing potent wine at Cana. Moreover, as this nation's institutions embraced socialism, it was not at all unusual to find Christians taking the lead in this shift towards humanist law. It was church-going Christians who worked hard to establish the government welfare and education systems now in place, which have come to undermine the biblical prerogatives, responsibilities, and integrity of family and church. First came the shifts in theology which rendered God's law impractical, inapplicable or irrelevant. Then came radical changes in the ministry of the pulpit. In the end, most Christians in America think and live like socialists, egalitarians, and humanists. The Nehemiah Institute has studied the worldview perspectives within Christian circles since 1988 by means of a worldview test, and has found a steady move towards secular humanist thinking among Christians. Executive Director of the Institute, Daniel Smithwick, reports that,

"From 1988 to 2000, average scores of Christian school students dropped by 30.3%. Results of evangelical students in public schools dropped 36.8% in the same period. Christian students attending public schools now regularly score in the lower half of Secular Humanism and students in typical Christian schools score just below the minimum score to be rated in the Moderate Christian worldview."[8]

The Slide into Gomorrah

Another clear illustration of the abandonment of God's authority over ethics is seen in the blindness of a nation given over to relativism. When the objective standard is lost, all standards fade into a blur. 19th century advocates of humanism and the natural law of the 18th century enlightenment would, no doubt, be horrified to discover the consequence of their ideas. But today there are no more objective definitions or laws that might place absolute limits on such things as body mutilation,

8 http://www.nehemiahinstitute.com/articles/index.php?action=show&id=18

cannibalism, incest, child abuse, bestiality, or obscenity. Neither the mainstream media, nor the universities, nor even the supreme court of the land would dare suggest any absolute law.[9] So without a recognition of the absolute definitions laid out clearly in God's law in passages like Exodus 21:23-26, Leviticus 20:11-16, and Isaiah 20:4, ethical lines begin to blur and after a while, all restraints and taboos disappear.

Nevertheless, God still holds His people responsible for maintaining a sharp antithesis between that which is good and that which is evil, and in the book of Isaiah He severely reprimands those who blur the difference.

> *"Woe unto them that call evil good, and good evil; that put darkness for light, and light for darkness; that put bitter for sweet, and sweet for bitter ... therefore as the fire devoureth the stubble, and the flame consumeth the chaff, so their root shall be as rottenness, and their blossom shall go up as dust: because they have cast away the law of the LORD of hosts, and despised the word of the Holy One of Israel." Isaiah 5:20-24*

The meaning of this text is plain. A society that casts away the law of God and thereby blurs the difference between good and evil will rot away into the dust. Does this not speak directly to our case today? Ethical ambiguity is the order of the day in the pulpits of church, school and media. Over time, evil is made to look good and people wander in a wasteland of ethical confusion. This ambiguity and relativism is communicated in language and the art forms of music, movies, news casts, dress, billboards, textbooks, novels, law, and documentaries.

Consider how the changes in language blur the antithesis. The murder of children is called "choice." The murder of the elderly is "humane." Miserable, unnatural perversions are "gay" activities. The

9 The mainstream newspaper Los Angeles Times recently referred to a Sun Dance Film Festival submission, which contained a positive portrayal of bestiality, as "strangely beautiful." (Kenneth Turan, January 27, 2007.)

abomination of witchcraft is sold to children as harmless fun and adventure. Drunkenness is a disease. Even the worst forms of evil such as cannibalism and murder are made voyeuristic fodder in the motion pictures and music.

One documentary aired on a major cable channel passed off cannibalism as "making a statement." And there are now university professors excusing and, in some cases, commending incest as "a fulfilling experience." Princeton University, once the great bastion of conservative Christianity, now keeps a bioethics professor, Dr. Peter Singer, in its Center for Human Values (whatever that is). To the delight of *avant garde* liberals, Singer speaks fondly of such matters as killing the disabled child with Down syndrome, or the beauty of bestiality and necrophilia. But he does take a firm stance against the consumption of animal meat.[10] One wonders what the other great Princetonians of the 19th century would think - men like Charles Hodge or Benjamin Warfield.

Is there nothing left to call evil? Actually, I think there is one evil thing left. It is *those Christians* that uphold the objective, eternal law of the Creator of heaven and earth! The Christians who condemn homosexuality are labeled "homophobes" and subjected to "hate crime" laws. Those are the evil ones! It is the Christians, who obey God's holy law in all of their spheres of activity and influence, that are the wicked. Indeed, it is only the Christians who use the law of God as a restraint to the potential wickedness of men who are almost universally labeled as "intolerant, narrow-minded, and unkind." In the minds of the self-conscious humanists, Christians are the evil ones because they have the audacity to hold to an authoritative, unchanging standard by which they would still call incest and cannibalism evil!

Where the law of God has been abandoned, the consciences of men over time can no longer make fine distinctions between good and evil. As time goes by, the grosser distinctions become equally fuzzy. While

10 Marvin Olasky, "Blue-State Philosopher," *World Magazine*, November 27, 2004.

the church itself stays about a generation behind the rest of the culture in drawing these ethical distinctions, the church bears less and less influence on the minds and the lives of its parishioners. This is because the media and the secular education system have far more access to the minds of Christians who patronize them, than does a church which hardly has the courage or the conviction to raise the antithesis of the Lawgiver against the worldview and ethics of the occupational force.

Selective Application of God's Law

Another indication of a rejection of God as Lawgiver appears when professing Christians ignore the Bible's authority in select areas of their lives. Though many would agree that God speaks with authority in the area of ethics, they still limit its potential application. They cannot see how God's Word will equip the man of God for every kind of good work.

Several years ago, I had the opportunity to engage a graduate from a conservative, reformed seminary on the application of biblical law. Amazingly, this man insisted that a Christian legislator must not love God with his heart, soul, mind, and strength while he sits on a state committee! Chief among those areas exempt from God's rule is the area of civil government. This reticence to recognize God's ethical authority in the state has largely to do with the predominance of statism in the average person's mind today. If the state will be god, it can hardly bear competition.

The men who built this country understood that government's purview was limited by God, especially as it attempts to control family, church, and private property. But this is a notion that is almost entirely foreign to the modern Christian. The Scriptures may speak to the spiritual areas of life, or even to the individual, but never to such material concerns as human government! I'm sure that reading from biblical law in the halls of American legislatures would seem inappropriate to even the most "conservative" mind!

Moreover, the average Christian today could hardly imagine that God would have anything to say about economics on the macro or micro level. So they feel they have the perfect ethical right to take on as much debt as they wish whenever they wish to do so. They cannot believe that the Bible has something objective to say about what one is to do if he comes upon his neighbor's wallet in the way (Deut. 22:1). They cannot believe that there would be any limitation to what the government could impose on one who has broken a speeding law, whether it be fine or the death penalty. They would never wish God to impose upon them any principles relating to their children's education (Deut. 6:7; Eph. 6:4).

But if the word of God is to equip the man of God for every good work (2 Tim. 3:17), why would anybody want to make an exception for economics, education, government, culture, business, and medical care, unless he had rejected God as the source of law? These are precisely the areas in which the man of God needs to be equipped! If he should lack any ethical principles by which he can make decisions, then he would be unable to determine what is right and what is wrong, and what is just and what is unjust. If there is no direction in God's Word by which we may make ethical decisions, then we are, with the rest of the post-modern society, lost and wandering in the same wilderness of ethical relativism and worthless utilitarian ethics.

If there are principles in the Bible relating to the real issues of life, then we will ignore them to our detriment. By ignoring them, we deny the Bible's relevance and moral authority over the family, the church, and the world. But Christians will eventually make their choices based on some ethical standard. And this is how the Christian faith melds into the humanist worldview - by denying the antithesis between the world and the Word, and by ignoring the Word in all of its richness of principle, Christians amalgamate into a foreign worldview. After a time, this syncretism becomes openly apparent in their attitudes, their behavior, their presentation, their education, their entertainment, their divorce rate, and their politics.

There are also those who respond to God's law in a selective manner, avoiding those directives that have direct application to themselves. Some are very careful to apply the Word of God to the political sphere with which they are little involved, but their churches are filled with gossip and unresolved conflicts (entirely ignoring biblical principles relating to conflict resolution), their families are torn apart by quarrels and bitterness, and their own lives are plagued with addictions to pornography, excess, and materialism. True Christianity must exhibit itself in real and significant ways, to include such things as loving the brethren, bridling the tongue, submitting to our God-appointed authorities, avoiding gross spotting from the world's sins, and taking personal care of widows and orphans (James 1:27-31).

Implying God is Unethical

Still another way in which Christians deny the authority of God in ethics is in subtle implications that God's laws are unjust or wicked. I do not intend to resolve all of the problem passages and difficult laws recorded in Scripture. Although I may not understand why such a law was written or how it will ever be applied in any way at all, it is quite another matter to act ashamed of those laws. In my experience, it is not unusual at all to hear pastors and teachers mock Old Testament laws. Sometimes they will use words and intonations which would imply that God's laws are somehow antiquated, unjust, or even wicked. And when some Christians *do* assert God as center in man's ethical life, they are labeled legalistic, irrelevant, or not "Christ centered" (as if Christ is not God).

Such attitudes are dangerous. To impugn God for a minute with injustice is flirting with blasphemy; because at its root is a blatant denial of His right to be the Sovereign Lawgiver. It would be far better to take a difficult Old or New Testament law application, identify a principle that one *can* both understand and apply, and then work for other applications. For example, if one were to come upon the law requiring a parapet around the rooftop of a house, he should not pass it off as an old-fashioned, irrelevant law unfit to equip the man of God for every good work. He should rather seek its principle. In this case, God requires reasonable safety measures employed where loss of life could occur. The specific *application* used in Old Testament Israel happened to apply the principle in a situation where roof top entertainment was common. It is doubtful that I would ever engage in roof top entertainment in my home, and so that *particular application* does not affect me. But the principle itself has thousands of modern day applications and should be taken seriously. For instance, one might own a swimming pool into which a small child might fall. To prevent loss of life here, a reasonable safety measure might very well include a fence.

In the words of Jesus himself, the best way to be considered least in the kingdom of God is to take the least of the Old Testament commandments, disobey it and teach others to do the same (Matt. 5:19). It would be much better to remain silent on some particular law about which one can imagine no possible modern day application, than to risk God's severe disfavor by encouraging others to violate it. Yet, it baffles me how quickly modern churchmen adopt a theological scheme that in one fell swoop teaches men to ignore whole sections of God's laws from the Old Testament or the New Testament. Today such theological systems flourish in almost every denomination. This failure to acknowledge God as sovereign Lawgiver is a far cry from the perspectives of the early Christians in former centuries.

"And I did not know that true inward righteousness which does not judge according to man's custom but out of the most rightful law of God Almighty to which the ways of people of certain places and times were adapted according to those times and places. The law itself, meantime, is the same always and everywhere." [11]

Kowtowing to the Humanists

Another strong evidence that the modern church has denied the sovereign right of God as Lawgiver is found in the ready enthusiasm with which it kowtows to the customs and the practices of the world, even when such customs conflict with God's Word. Forbidding women from holding positions of leadership in the church, to take an obvious example, is now a transgression of the highest sort according to the orthodoxy of modern humanism (and its doctrine of egalitarianism). Therefore, the last twenty years have witnessed a steady compromise to accommodate the cries of the gender egalitarians. Even the most conservative denominations have gradually incorporated women into leadership positions in the church, first into leadership committees, then into leading worship, and finally into the officer positions of the church.

This is the day in which the traditions of men have displaced the authority and application of the laws of God (Matt. 15:6). Indeed, the hearts of men are far from God (Matt. 15:8) as evidenced by the fact that there is far more interest in accommodating the traditions of men, than there is in attending to the laws of God. Christians simply are not asking the key ethical questions. Does the social security system in any way encourage families to ignore the biblical principle of children caring for their own parents? Is it just another system of Corban, relieving children of any responsibility of doing "aught" for their father and mother? Do our educational systems, church programs, entertainment, and lifestyles in any way undermine the prescribed biblical method of parental discipleship of their own children as they walk by the way, as they sit in their house, as they rise up and lie down (Deut. 6:7, 8)? Is there anything in an unaccountable, uncommitted

11 Augustine, p. 51.

system of dating that might encourage lust and fornication, rather than produce a proper marital relationship? As we shall see, reformation is in the air and there is a segment of the Christian population today that is beginning to turn towards reformation in the area of ethics. But the legacy of the last one hundred years of Christianity has been one of accommodation to the traditions of men attended by an unholy irreverence for the Lawgiver Himself.

This is not the first time that Christians have been reminded of their duty to subjugate all human customs in all times and places to the absolute standard of God's law. Augustine is firm in his commitment to the Lawgiver over all human standards and traditions. "But when God commands a thing to be done against the customs or compact of any people, though it was never to be done by them previously, it is to be done. If it was suspended, it is to be restored, and if it was never ordained, it is to be ordained."[12]

Mistrust of God's Word

Finally, the refusal to recognize the ultimacy of God in the area of ethics is manifest in a general, universal mistrust of the Word of God. For most of the 20th century, men and women were carefully trained not to believe that God's Word is sufficient to deal with psychological issues. For example, they cannot believe that proper child discipline and training as laid out in the Proverbs and elsewhere in Scripture will be effective, so they resort to "the experts" in psychology and child development for the answers.

I have two books in my library, both were written by Christian leaders on raising boys. One book is laced with hundreds of Bible verses (mostly from the Proverbs). The second book hardly mentioned a single Bible verse throughout but it was filled from cover to cover with empirical studies, expert advice from psychiatrists, and personal anecdotes. Of course the book that sold hundreds of thousands of copies was the

11 Augustine, p. 64.

latter. Unfortunately, a great many of our people are not particularly interested in what God has to say. The epistemological authority, or the truth that they trust, is not the Word of God. It is the proclamations of some scientist who claims to be very smart, and insists that he has identified what is good and what will produce it!

They simply can not believe that the principles of God's Word will work in human behavior, as well as in economics and politics. So they turn to the experts in utilitarian ethics, the scientists who seem to know what would produce the highest good in the long run. There is, of course, no substantial agreement as to what constitutes the highest good or even what would produce it. But many still hold tenaciously to the belief that the experts are well briefed on the millions of possible effects and interactions produced by any given action, in the long run! Of course, no scientific study could ever consider all of the effects of any one moral decision, especially those effects that result in ten years, 100 years, or even into eternity. But they are "the experts." Therefore, the fields of psychology, economics, education, and politics are controlled far more often by John Maynard Keynes, John Dewey, Karl Marx, Benjamin Spock, and Sigmund Freud than by the Word of the omniscient, sovereign God who created this universe and prints His law code deep in stone.

It is obvious that the law of God holds no place of authority in the minds of men who are only persuaded to a particular ethical course by the latest scientific study on self-esteem or sexually transmitted disease. Rarely does one ever hear anyone appeal to God as the highest ethical authority even to convince himself of a certain moral course of action. Instead, those who wish to convince themselves and others concerning the appropriateness of their position on abortion or promiscuity appeal to the utilitarian ethic They warn teens not to engage in fornication for fear of contracting sexually-transmitted-disease. What such arguments suggest to the mind of the average teen is that life's ethical decisions are nothing but risk assessments. "Why not take the risk of the STD and go ahead and engage in the act?" The individual still retains the ultimate right to make the choice. Moreover, with the advances of modern medical science everybody knows that man has virtual total control over his environment. Certainly, within a few years, science will have the cure for these diseases. If Christians are careful to stay clear of the fear of God, we certainly cannot expect the rest of the world to fear God enough to take note of His commandments.

Certainly not every Christian in the West is self-consciously opposed to God's essential right to hold the position as supreme Lawgiver. However, in a day where the occupational worldview has so thoroughly infiltrated the culture, it would be nothing short of arrogant for any Western Christian to think that he has avoided every piece of shrapnel in the enemy attack. I would hold that a careful look at our hermeneutics, our theology, our worldview, and our lives would find the marks of humanist autonomy throughout the Christian faith today.

A Profound Reverence for the Lawgiver

"As the Scripture says: 'The wicked have destroyed Your law, O Lord.' And God in His great kindness has just recently planted this law in Ireland, where it had been growing by His grace."[13]

As in all movements of good, brave and righteous men in history, ours must begin with a profound respect for the Lawgiver himself. The teachings of Jesus, Himself, reflect that respect (Matt. 5:17ff, 15:1-8). I do not intend to work out all of the detailed arguments as to what applications will be relevant to modern situations. It is only to underscore the sense in which God's law is permanent and authoritative, and "all of Thy righteous judgments endures forever" (Ps. 119:160). The principles of God's law stand as the standard of God's justice. This

13 Phillip Freeman, *St. Patrick of Ireland: A Biography,* "St. Patrick, Letter to the Soldiers of Coroticus," Simon & Schuster, New York, NY, 2004, p. 170.

unchanging standard must be the measure to which all men are judged. It is the standard that must be met by Christ's obedience and sacrifice for our disobedience, and it must be the standard that is obeyed by those who really love the Lord Jesus Christ. "If you love Me, keep My commandments" (John 14:15). "For this is the love of God, that we keep His commandments" (1 John 5:3).

If God established His law as a standard whereby all of man's behavior is judged, then I would think that only God could in any way modify an application of those principles, or produce any guarantee that an application will no longer be relevant. This is simply a call to reverence God as Lawgiver. There can be no playing fast and loose with the authoritative demands of the Lawgiver. "What thing soever I command you, observe to do it: thou shalt not add thereto, nor diminish from it" (Deut. 12:32).

Reverence for the Lawgiver in History

Four hundred years ago, the men who founded this nation had a much higher regard for God as Lawgiver than those who lead the nation today. The founding governor of the first of the early colonies wrote this in 1644:

> "Arbitrary government is where a people have men set over them, without their choice or allowance; who have power to govern them, and judge their causes without a rule. God only hath this prerogative, whose sovereignty is absolute and whose will is a perfect rule ... so as for man to usurp such authority is tyranny and impiety. The determination of law belongs properly to God: He is the only Lawgiver; but He hath given power and gifts to man to interpret His laws."[14]

14 John Winthrop, 1644, contained in *American Historical Documents*, P.F. Collier and Sons, New York, NY, 1910, p. 90, 105.

The dissolution of this respect for God as Lawgiver has come over a long period of time. On the side of the humanist offensive, the roots of modern autonomy lie in the new epistemologies of the 17th century which denied the ultimate authority of God in revelation. Natural law was, at first, seen as a complement to God's revelatory law. But one had to take precedence over the other, and by the end of the 18th century, natural law had taken precedence. No mention of the law of God is to be found in any of the major founding documents of the nation.

References to God as Lawgiver began to disappear in Christian writings and sermons as early as the 18th century. America's foremost theologian of the 18th century, Jonathan Edwards, wrote an entire volume on *The True Nature of Virtue* in 1755, and avoided all mention of biblical law. For Edwards, moral good was found more in sentiment, moral sense, and human reason. Autonomy may seem acceptable, reasonable, and even noble at the beginning. But eventually these seeds would produce fruits of total rebellion against God and His law.

Sounding the Cry for Reformation

Christianity today is faced with attacks on every side. The antithesis that marks this age include such wayward ideals as pluralism, ethical relativism, teenage rebellion, feminism, socialism, egalitarianism, evolutionary scientism, immodesty, fornication, irreverence of parents and generational discontinuity, nihilism, materialism, disrespect for human life, excess, slavery, and tyranny, to name a few. In this fundamental reformation, we can no longer separate the Christian heart from the Christian mind and the Christian life. God requires of us a renewing of the mind and a refusal to conform to the anti-Christian thought patterns and lifestyles (Rom. 8:1, 2). More than that, He requires us to cast down all imaginations that oppose the wisdom of Christ communicated to us in His Word (2 Cor. 10:5). Every human thought must be brought into captivity to the obedience of Christ, whether they be academic thoughts, scientific thoughts, marriage thoughts, sexual thoughts, economic thoughts, cultural thoughts, or political thoughts. We must love God with all of our heart, soul, mind, and strength, and if we love Him, we will keep His commandments - with all of our heart, soul, mind, and strength.

A Christian worldview without law simply cannot be considered a world and life view. Likewise, Christian thought without law makes God's grace of no account. Grace itself loses its relevance without a law standard and a Lawgiver. Of course, the law is ineffectual to justify the Christian, but without the law, there is no standard to which man is held accountable, and to which he may be justified and forgiven of his sins! The preaching of the law is essential, ultimately because it is in God's Word. Without the law, everything else unravels - the atonement of Christ is meaningless, sin is without definition, repentance is another wasted word, and love is without form.

Recognizing God as the Standard of All Good

The attributes of God are personalized to a Christian who knows God and knows God in relation to himself. In other words, God is not a standard of good floating in the ethereal. God is good *to us!* He is the standard of good to us in real and concrete ways. Therefore we will embrace Him as the standard of all that is good. If God is the ultimate determinant of all that is good and all that is right for man, then the Christian must recognize this, submit to it, and live in that realization. What is good is established by God, it is administered sovereignly everywhere in the life of the Christian, and it is made part of the believer's life by active obedience to what God has defined as right.

This has tremendous implications in the Christian's life. He recognizes that all that happens to him is meant for his good (Rom. 8:28). And this is so because God is both sovereign over all the facets of reality in his life, and He has the sovereign right to direct his ethics.

He is the sovereign determinant of what is good, and what is good for man to do.

The Christian bathes in the conscious recognition of the goodness of God. Indeed, the goodness of God is very real to the Christian, and it touches the Christian in every way. God defines what is good, so of course He knows what is good. Secondly, a man of faith will believe that God is good to him, and that God will sovereignly direct all things for his good. All the pain, distress, trials, and victories of his life will be channeled to produce what is good. But finally, if God is good, then unlike Eve in the garden, the Christian trusts in his heart that God's law is good (Rom. 7:1). And, unlike Eve, he will obey it because he believes that God is good.

The Real Need - A Change of Heart

> *"Thus saith the LORD God of Israel, As touching the words which thou hast heard, because thine heart was tender, and thou hast humbled thyself before the LORD, when thou heardest what I spake against this place, and against the inhabitants thereof, that they should become a desolation and a curse, and hast rent thy clothes, and wept before Me; I also have heard thee, saith the LORD."*
> *2 Kings 22:18, 19*

Josiah was commended for a heart that was tender to the law of God. This was the beginning of that great reformation 2,500 years ago, and it will be the heart of every great reformation to come. Upon every directive word of God, the autonomous, proud heart of man instinctively recoils away from it. But the loving servant heart of Samuel calls out to God, "Speak Lord, for Thy servant heareth" (1 Sam. 3:10).

From the outside it is difficult to tell whether a heart is tender to the Word of God. But there are distinctive signs of hearts that are hard to the laws of God. What kind of a heart would seek after every possible theological construct that would disallow relevant application of God's Word to life? Why would a Christian people follow after every human tradition concocted by men like Marx, Rousseau, Keynes, and Dewey, while circumventing the loving commands of a heavenly Father? The heart of Josiah uncovers the lost book of the law and instantly realizes the sinful conditions into which his nation has fallen. Immediately, he recognizes the voice of his God speaking through the law. As his eyes fall upon the pages, he scans and re-scans the word for something to believe and something to do. It is the heart that cries out to God, "Teach me, O LORD, the way of Thy statutes; and I shall keep it unto the end!" (Ps. 119:33).

What God wants is a man who will love his God with all his heart, soul, mind, and strength. It is the love of God that motivates him, that presses him to love His Word and follow Him. His heart attitude towards the law of God resonates with the psalmist as he says, "Oh how love I Thy law! It is my meditation all the day" (Ps. 119:97). He loves to hear those words that reprove him, convict him, and correct him. He recognizes the Shepherd's voice and follows Him. "My sheep hear My voice, and I know them, and they follow Me" (John 10:27). The sheep follow the Shepherd in objective ways. They move in the direction that the Shepherd leads in marriage life, in family life, in biblical peacemaking, in household economics, and in the voting booth. You know that you are one of His sheep when you hear His voice through this Word, and you follow Him. Such was the man Josiah of whom the Lord said,

> "There was never a king that turned to the Lord with all his heart, and with all his soul, and with all his might ... according to the law of Moses." 2 Kings 23:25

May that be said of us all!

Second Mayflower

5

THE BIRTH OF THE
SECOND MAYFLOWER

The Second Mayflower began in 1960.

As I pointed out in chapter three, since 1800 a worldview paradigm shift has swept across Western nations and any other nation connected to the West. This shift from a Christian worldview to a humanist worldview had solidified in Western institutions by the turn of the 20th century.

The humanist philosophies of the 18th century brought about a new faith in the next century - the faith of the empirical scientist who had rejected the fear of God as the beginning of wisdom in his pursuit of knowledge. It was not long before the Christian church capitulated to the new religion of science, and worked hard to re-interpret the Bible to accommodate the new and ever-changing pseudo-scientific theories produced by each new set of high priests in the temple of scientific empiricism.

This unwavering faith in man eventually yielded a world of scientists who were unable to distinguish between science and pseudo-science. Great Christian scientists like Newton, Boyle, Pascal, Kelvin, and others produced a tremendously useful science, based solidly in their professed fear of the Creator God and in a wise scientific method. However, a new "science" came into being with Charles Darwin. The science produced by Christian scientists was reproducible, observable, measurable, and useful! But the pitiful hypothesis that Darwin produced was neither testable, reproducible, or really useful. Nevertheless, this new evolutionary "science" brought about profound changes in education, psychology, jurisprudence, social ethics, and civil government. Such changes are graphically illustrated by important historical events as the Leopold-Loeb trial of 1924 where two young school boys confessed to killing a school mate because he was "an inferior specie." Towards the end of the 20th century, another pair of boys by the name of Harris and Klebold murdered 13 students and teachers at Columbine high school on the same pretense. One of the young murderers in the rampage reportedly wore a tee shirt bearing the message "Natural Selection." The pseudo-science that reduced man from the status of image of God to just another advanced form of cosmic dust has taken its toll.

But this was not the way it always was in this country. American education was Christian through and through for the first 200 years of her history. The first primer in New England, published in 1652, began with "A - In Adam's Fall, We sinned all!" The primer was fitly entitled *Spiritual Milk for American Babes*! In 1777, 125 years later, the primer was revised. Pictures were added. Other common textbooks included a Psalm book and a Hornbook containing the Lord's Prayer and Christian Doctrine. President Thomas Jefferson, not necessarily known for his orthodox Christian beliefs, saw to it that the first curriculum used in the District of Columbia schools included the Bible and Watt's Hymnal.

The bombs began to fall in the great worldview battle in the early part of the 19th century, and the succeeding 150 years brought changes to the American system of education with civilization transforming implications. Self-consciously consistent humanists such as Horace Mann and John Dewey worked hard to establish a new "secularized," government-funded education. By 1920, almost all remnants of Christianity were virtually expunged from the curriculum. It took another 50 years to complete the job and remove the mere accoutrements of Christianity (such as prayer and plaques bearing the Ten Commandments on the school walls), replacing them with instructions on aberrant sexual practices and the like. Curriculum professing either a polytheist religion (maintaining that "all gods in the classroom are equal"), or an atheist religion ("there is no god in this curriculum or classroom"), or a mix of both had won the day. Textbooks carefully avoided all mention of the Christian God or even a supreme, triune God. Bible stories and biblical doctrines are simply not a part of the *paideia*, or training, of a child today - for either those who call themselves Christians or non-Christians. The God-centered curriculum was gone. The pretense of a sacred-secular distinction opened the door for polytheism and atheism to reign in American public life.

Today, a quick survey of modern primary school curriculum will come up with a studied avoidance of the biblical God throughout. Instead, "the gods of the marketplace" are trotted out for review by a hundred million students. Recently, this author did a quick survey of textbooks used in a local public charter school, and within twenty minutes found himself well indoctrinated in evolution, egalitarianism, socialism, environmentalism, new age quackery, and ethical relativism. One fifth grade reader presented the Shinto ancestor worship of the Japanese, with a nice "non-judgemental" explanation. "This is how the Japanese boy expresses his values. How do you express your values?" This is called a polytheistic worldview, and most Americans see absolutely nothing wrong with it. All gods are permitted into the pantheon of public education, except for that "narrow-minded" God who insists that there will be "no other gods before Me."

The humanist worldview turns man into god. In the conception of the 19th century mind, man slowly evolved into a god-like form and, at the same time, the Christian God came to look increasingly like man. Put another way, the 19th century was the era that man stripped God of his "godness" and put it on himself. The characteristics once attributed only to God were increasingly attributed to man. Over 300 years of slow, transforming work, humanist man took on deity in his own imagination which in turn infected all of his institutions. The ultimate sovereignty once seen to belong to God alone was turned over to man. The salvation once attributed to God was increasingly attributed to man or the state (corporate man). The right to determine law was wrenched from God and turned over to man. When it came to who had the right to determine what is true, man moved himself onto the bench, shoving God into the dock.[1] A long time ago, the reformation catechism had taught all Christian children that man's chief purpose was centered on God - in glorifying Him and enjoying Him forever. With the humanistic corruption of the Western Christian worldview, man became the chief end of man in life, worship, and the ministry of the Gospel.

By 1960, the Christian worldview was effectively AWOL in the war of the worldviews. Throughout the previous century, the humanist worldview had infiltrated the Christian church. While Christians would still acknowledge God and the salvation of Christ, they would strip the faith of a God-centered worldview. They might still believe in God, but that God was hardly the source of reality in creation and providence any longer, he was neither the source of truth nor the source of ethics. Effectively, God had died the death of a thousand qualifications.

But all of that was to change in 1960. That was the year a small publishing house in Phillipsburg, New Jersey printed a book written by two Christian men, scientists by trade. Their names were Henry Morris and John C. Whitcomb and the book was *The Genesis Flood*. Although it was certainly an event of ignominious import in and of itself, the book signified an important shift for Christianity in the West. The book was the first serious argument leveled against the prevailing evolutionary model for origins.

But it was more basic than that. The book introduced an important epistemological question: "Shall we interpret the Word of God by rock layers, or shall we interpret rock layers by the Word of God?"

1 C.S. Lewis defines humanism this way in his essay, *God in the Dock*. C.S. Lewis, *God in the Dock: Essays on Theology and Ethics*, Eerdmans, Grand Rapids, MI, 1970, p. 220.

For at least 100 years, there was little fear of God and respect for His Word in the university science classroom. Few professors would acknowledge the Bible as the absolute source of truth or held the fear of God to be the beginning of knowledge in the field of science. Therefore, since the days of higher criticism, the veracity of the Word of God was tested by the higher minds of the enlightened scientists of the 19th century. Even the Creation account was interpreted by Christian theologians through the lens of this flawed science that refused to fear God. However, with the publication of *The Genesis Flood* in 1960, Christians in lab coats set out to *interpret science through the lens of God's Word*. Instead of using a pseudo-science (that was neither observable or reproducible) as a means of determining the truth and interpreting God's Word, these men used the truth of God's Word as a framework in which to interpret geologic data. This was a major epistemological shift, changing the way in which Christians would determine truth and establish certainty. With this hugely important move on the part of scientists, a revival of God's absolute authority in Christian thought entered the formative stage. Over the previous centuries, scientists applied their ultimate faith commitments and assumptions (such as atheism or radical deism, uniformitarianism, and the belief that God could never have created the world with the appearance of age) to the interpretation of the geologic evidence at hand. Now Christians were no longer bound to this single set of presuppositions. They could challenge the strength of the evolutionist worldview by the weaknesses and inconsistencies inherent in the model itself, because they were standing with confidence on the biblical record. These men had a renewed heart commitment to the absolute truth revealed by the God who cannot but speak with absolute authority.

This shift was the beginning of something significant. By 1960, the worldview war had basically ended in the West with the exception of an occasional skirmish. There was little left of the theocentric worldview in nations once dominated by Christianity. The major institutions were captured by this new worldview which glorified man as ultimate authority in truth, reality, and ethics. Christianity itself absorbed much of the humanist worldview and was thereby rendered irrelevant to the conflict. A distinctive Christian world and life view was all but gone from the institutions of education, seminary training, media, and politics. Christianity had lost the worldview war and no systematic, thorough going resistance to humanism was in sight. However, God was at work in the minds of a remnant. He was not done with His world. The battle waged over truth and error is not done. It has become a battle over the possibility of absolute truth and right. Now, another quarter of play has begun. Something significant happened in 1960, and what has begun has not abated. It continues to grow. From that point, there came an avalanche of Christian writing and thought. In field after field, Christians began to bring God's Word in objective and authoritative application to life. The intent of this book is not to analyze the particular merits of any single approach, but simply to point out the comeback of a self-conscious Christian resistance to the humanist worldview at all levels and in all areas of life.

Now huge ministries, research institutes, and schools are emerging as Christians self-consciously apply a biblical worldview to the field of science. One multi-million dollar ministry argues the creationist's perspective with the stated mission "to defend the authority of the Bible from the very first verse." One ministry, Answers in Genesis, opened a $30 million creation museum in the spring of 2007. Some of these ministries hold to the six 24-hour day creation week and others do not; and some commit more to the epistemological authority of God's Word than others. Unquestionably, we are witnessing multiple, serious efforts to test the validity of science by the truth claims of the Word of God.

Since the 1960s, men like Francis Schaeffer set out to define a distinctively Christian philosophy. Distinctively Christian forms of education began to develop through the writings of Christian educators and philosophers. The Christian school movement gained a major impetus in the 1960s, and the Christian homeschool movement formed by the 1980s. Meanwhile, various strands of Christian counseling developed during the 1960s and 1970s from men with disparate viewpoints - from Jay Adams to James Dobson. Then came literally thousands of books applying the Bible to various specific areas of life including conflict resolution, child rearing, education, marriage, dating and courtship, and to a host of other areas.

Around the same time, hundreds of books authored by educators and Christian historians sought not only to revive the rich Christian heritage of this country in the minds of young students, but also to bring a distinctively Christian perspective of history into the classroom. Attempts to bring a biblical worldview into news reporting came by way of *World Magazine*, American Vision's *Biblical Worldview Magazine*, and Focus on the Family's *Citizen Magazine*.

For the first time in generations, Christians are now bringing a biblical perspective to bear in both macro and micro economics. Moreover, Christian involvement in politics burgeoned in the 1980s and 1990s. Increasingly more vocal protests issue forth from Christian groups around the country against civil approval of abortion on demand, homosexuality, and other forms of moral degeneracy. By the time of this writing, there are worldview training centers and new colleges with distinctively Christian worldviews forming throughout America to counter the dominant secular humanist worldview.

Increasing numbers of Christians have a sharpened awareness of the antithesis between the ideas of the world and the ideas of the Word. Christians everywhere are asserting the sixth commandment as the normative ethical standard for a culture of death, abortion, legalized suicide, and euthanasia. Whereas one hundred years ago a desensitized Christianity gave way to powerful, centralized government, today Christians are coming to recognize what is at stake under the tyranny of unrestrained power. And while a hundred years ago Christians were fighting for laws without any basis in biblical law and without historical precedence (e.g. Prohibition), today many fight more appropriate battles rooted solidly in the revealed law of God (e.g. homosexual marriage and abortion).

This chapter could not possibly include the names of all of those faithful men and women who have already entered the worldview battle and are engaging in a reforming work to revive the centrality of God in ethics and life. The second half of the 20th century was a time of renewal for Christianity in the West. The times in which we live are thrilling indeed. The worldview battle has revived and the clashing of arms is heard everywhere.

The Twenty-First Century

Since 1960, the ultimacy of God in His rule, His law, and His truth has returned in Christian thought and writing. The ideas have taken shape. It is difficult to know for sure how much of this rising tide has correctly identified the fundamental principle and then effectively incarnated it in real life applications. Yet there is no question in my mind that the ideas of a modern day reformation are developing. The next one hundred years will provide opportunity to form the ideas into a unified force with strategies for application. Ideals and values are one thing, but implementation is quite another. How does one live a God centered, biblically based life anyway? How will we live out the applications sufficiently to incarnate the broad principle that forms the foundation of our reformation?

Understandably, there is much work to be done; but after all, that is the journey called the Second Mayflower, and I will proceed to chart out the journey throughout the remainder of this book. Suffice it to say that families must reform every aspect of household life in every possible area according to God's Word, incorporating such biblical principles as household unity, fatherly leadership, family worship, biblical economics, and biblical education. Each family must grapple with each of these areas and work out what it means for God to be central in their home. Somehow this vision must extend to the community of the church. In short, a Christian worldview must be taken into the broader culture by means of Christians who have self-consciously embraced a biblical, theocentric worldview. All of this must be done in the midst of great opposition, economic turmoil, political upheaval, wars, and cultural decline. Some view this as impossible. However, such has been the challenge for Christians since Christ issued His Great Commission! For example, Christians faced the same challenge in ancient Rome until the empire crumbled under its rotting cultural facade. Or consider a missionary like John Paton who met this challenge when he took the Gospel to the New Hebrides. In the face of cannibalism and the grossest forms of evil, and against the most severe dangers to himself, Paton preached the Gospel and stood in strong opposition to the evils of that culture. Thousands came to a saving knowledge of Christ, and today there are no cannibals left in the New Hebrides islands. Christianity has always faced the challenge of opposing worldviews and cultural declension, with a message of truth, renewal and hope. *That* is the faith that has conquered the world again and again in human history (1 John 5:4).

The Worldview that Corrupted America

The vision that formed the foundation of this nation has almost disappeared. As I painstakingly detailed in Chapter Three, the breakdown of the family and public morality along with the simultaneous growth of government remain the indisputable trends of the last century. In fact, there is not a nation in Europe, Asia, Africa, or the Americas untouched by the worldviews that drove these trends. But how do we best summarize these worldviews? I think the simplest way to summarize the world and life view of post-modern man is to call him lost and lonely. I am hardly saying anything controversial here, for the man himself would not deny it. He cuts himself off from truth and relationship resulting in the breakdown of morality and the family.

First Truth

Since the 14th century humanist renaissance, man has worked hard to define himself and his truth without God's Word as the foundation of wisdom and knowledge. The great renaissance sculptor, Michelangelo, produced the self-defining man who chips himself out of the rock. But it wasn't long before this humanist man realized that he could not very well chip himself out of the rock if he didn't start out with a pair of hands provided by a Creator. Thus he gave up any hope for determining absolutes on his own. Beginning with the skepticism of David Hume in the 18th century and concluding with the existentialism and pragmatism of Neitzsche, Dewey, and Sartre, man gave up his search for absolute truth and ultimate purpose in life. Modern man is hopelessly lost. Were he self-conscious of his relativism and nihilism, he would freely admit this plight.

Then Relationships

Relationships and community are also fast disappearing in modern cities. Some have blamed the Industrial Revolution for weakening these familial and communal bonds, but human economies and cultures are only a reflection of the hearts and minds of men. It was the ideas of men who disliked relationships that drove the transience and the superficiality of modern relationships and produced family-disintegrating education, entertainment, and economic systems. Since Rousseau abandoned his five children on the steps of an orphanage and set out to write the book on educating a child for the modern age, the world of professionals, psychiatrists, counselors, and instructors have replaced the old world of fathers, mothers, grandmothers, friends, and pastors. Mega churches and six month divorce recovery workshops have replaced long term relationships in community and closely integrated family life that had existed for thousands of years previous.

The modern city and churches are built for the anonymous life of the vagabond (Gen. 4:12, 17). Man is lonely.

As already mentioned, Francis Schaeffer was an important Christian thinker of the 1960s and 1970s. Most of his work was dedicated to describing the thinking and plight of modern man. In the end, Schaeffer reached the conclusion that man is lost and lonely and needs a personal relationship with the infinite, absolute, and personal God.[2] However, he was unable to incarnate the principle well. Many of his readers found themselves a little frustrated when he never quite answered the question posed in the title of his magnum opus, "How shall we then live?"

If man is lost and lonely, then how do we solve this problem? *How shall we then live?* Ironically, Schaeffer passed away in 1984, at the outset of the most important movement of the century which would capture his ideas better than any other. In the early 1980s, a small counter-cultural movement capitalized on these ideas, rallying around one verse which seemed to speak with particular force to the post-modern predicament. That verse was Deuteronomy 6:7.

> *"And thou shalt teach [My words] diligently unto thy children, and shalt talk of them when thou sittest in thine house, and when thou walkest by the way, and when thou liest down, and when thou risest up." Deuteronomy 6:7*

Truth and relationships were exactly what the modern world was missing. *So what about teaching truth in relationship? And why not teach absolute, transcendent truth in the womb of the parent-child relationship?* The homeschooling movement identified a near perfect application of an important biblical principle that spoke to the heart of a lost and lonely world. Here was a radical reintegration of family relationships through the reintroduction of teaching and discipleship in the home. With Christian homeschooling, the teaching of the Word was integrated into every aspect of our children's lives from rising up to

---

2 Reference Francis Schaeffer, *He is There and He is Not Silent,* Chapter 1, "The Metaphysical Necessity."

lying down at night (v. 7). That word was to be as a frontlet constantly hanging in front of their eyes (v. 8), and set before them on signs on the posts of the house (v. 9). No longer were God and His truth barred from the significant intellectual and academic portion of our children's lives. To a world that had come to despise close parent-child relationships and God's truth as the foundation of knowledge came a new paideia (system of training) for a child.

As the movement matured, it became clear that education was more about the discipleship of faith and character and the integration of knowledge into life, than it was focused on stuffing isolated facts into the heads of children. This form of discipleship resulted in better academics, stronger faith and character, and certainly, a better prepared student for life and eternity.[3]

And the effects of this movement are nothing short of phenomenal. According to research conducted by the National Home Education Research Institute, there are at least two million homeschoolers in America today. New colleges are forming to serve these homeschooling families. These students feed huge segments of the Creation movement, the worldview seminars, and conservative political organizations, to the extent that these other movements would hardly exist without the home education movement. One recent study conducted by Dr. Brian Ray (analyzing data collected from 7,200 homeschool graduates), indicated that these graduates, 18-25 years of age, were 14 times more likely to be involved in efforts to impact the civil government than their counterparts from public and private schools.[4] This is just the tip of the iceberg, considering that the movement is still young. We have yet to see the impact that 2 million homeschooled graduates nurtured with truth in relationship over 18 years will make on our world.

3 For an extensive development on the philosophy of Christian home education, refer to this author's book, *Upgrade: The Ten Secrets to the Best Education for Your Child,* Broadman and Homan, Nashville, TN, 2006.
4 Dr. Brian Ray, *Homeschooling Grows Up,*
http://www.hslda.org/research/ray2003/default.asp

A New Movement

In the early part of the 20th century this thing I call the Second Mayflower did not exist. Any call for a basic reformation of thought and life was drowned out by the demands coming from evangelicals for "conversions," and from those advocating a modernistic "social" gospel. Ironically, the social gospel had replaced the Bible with Marx and others as the source of ethics. Meanwhile, the evangelicals had so far separated grace and law, faith and works, that they could see no need for biblical law as the determinant of human ethics. Moreover, the social traditions and mores of the early part of the 20th century still enjoyed a remnant of Christian virtues. Sins like fornication, sodomy, Sabbath breaking, and convenience divorce were still stuffed in the closet, retaining little social stigma about them. It took at least one hundred years for the theological foundation of this nation to erode, and it wasn't until the 1960s that the building itself began to crumble. By 2007, 37% of children were born without fathers and homosexual marriages were practically institutionalized in many Western nations.

The Christian lifestyle of the first half of the 20th century was a moral lifestyle of sorts, though not necessarily a biblical one. Christians sent their children to government schools where they had minimal control over the curriculum. Meanwhile, the only significant activity in the political realm was a prohibition campaign for civil legislation - an autonomous initiative on the part of Christians who didn't care much for God's civil laws. They wanted their own laws. In 1913, Christian Protestants were busily working for laws against alcohol but offered little resistance against a system of unjust weights and measures and the illegalization of gold currency. They would have had our Lord arrested for making wine while wholeheartedly rejecting His endorsement of the civil law, "Whosoever curseth mother or father, let him die the death" (Matt. 15:4).

However, today the lines are more clearly drawn than ever. The homosexuals, the abortionists, the feminists, and the socialists are out of the closet and sitting in the living room. The result is that Christians are forced to reconsider their ethical positions and the meta-ethic by which they establish those positions. Either they will acknowledge man as the source of ethics, or they will embrace God's laws laid down by revelation. Either they will trust fallen man with the natural ability to discern law or they will rely on the written revelation of God Himself.

Common Ground with Our Early Founding Fathers

As we set out to define this second great movement of God to establish a city on a hill set upon biblical principles, we must find some connection with that first great movement of the 17th and 18th centuries. Indeed, this nation enjoys a unique heritage. No other nation still extant today was established on covenants appealing to the Christian God and His Word. No other nation was founded with a self-conscious commitment to the scriptures of the Old and New Testaments. Because of the deep roots of this rich heritage, if there shall be a Second Mayflower, it will draw from those roots and *the First Mayflower will give birth to the Second*. The seeds of this vision are found in the heritage of our nation.

Nevertheless, history does not exactly repeat itself. There will be some commonalities with the founding fathers of this nation, and there will be differences. First, we will expound on the commonalities.

The social condition of England in the 1600s was very much like that of modern America. Despite the growing movement of self-consciously consistent and reform-minded Christians, the society all around them had gradually sunk to deplorable levels of public immorality and civil tyranny.

It is true that there is little persecution of Christians compared with the persecution of the nonconformists in 17th century England and the bloody fields of Scotland under the reign of Charles II. Nevertheless, some small indications of persecution break the surface at points. In the 1980s, Pastors Everett Sileven and Ed Gilbert from Nebraska were jailed for their strong stance against state licensing of churches and church schools. Speaking against homosexuality in public forums is generally recognized as risky in those countries that pride themselves in "pluralism" and "tolerance." Also, parents who insist upon keeping their children out of state schools may continue to see persecution, not unlike that seen in Germany since the European High Court on Human Rights upheld a case against homeschoolers in September 2006. Fines, imprisonment, and the removal of children from the home continue in Germany.

Today we see great public immorality as evidenced by the rates of sexually transmitted diseases, adultery, illegitimate children, and crime. Through television, movies, public schools, and music, the culture is doing everything it can to bring all forms of immorality, instability, and destruction into our children's lives. The Puritans in the 1600s witnessed similar temptations and degradation, although on a different scale. Public drunkenness was rampant; and government tyranny and intolerance, particularly towards Christians, was the order of the day. Cotton Mather records this as one of the reasons why the Pilgrims were persuaded to leave Holland: "They beheld some of their children, by the temptations of the place, were especially given in the licentious ways ... many young people, drawn into dangerous extravagances."[5]

The tremendous moral decline which marks our society at large, equally affects those who call themselves "Christians." Indeed, both the orthodoxy and the orthopraxy of the Christian church have been severely compromised. Rates of divorce and fornication within the church equal or exceed that which prevails among the general population. One Christian news magazine reported that "Specific studies of sexual trends among Christian teens have been limited, but all indications are that, on average, there is little difference between their sexual behavior and that of non-Christian youths other than a tendency to delay their first sexual experience slightly longer."[6] Some mainline denominations

5 Cotton Mather, *Magnalia Christi Americana*, Vol. I, pp. 47, 48.
6 Jennifer M. Parker, "The Sex Lives of Christian Teens," *Today's Christian*, March, 2003 http://www.

allow homosexuals to be members, and others put them in leadership. Although such moral decline far exceeds anything seen in 17th century England, John Winthrop still commented on "licentious" seminaries and "corrupted" religion in England. This was high on the list of complaints from both Puritans and Separatists, further motivating the First Mayflower.[7]

Another commonality we find with our brothers who launched the First Mayflower is the bitter disappointment we have experienced in the political realm which has come by way of deception and political pragmatism. The Puritans had some access to political power by election to parliament and they enjoyed a measure of success for a time. In 1629 they demanded the elimination of taxation without representation and voted to quell the doctrines of pelagianism (humanism) in the state church. King Charles I responded by dissolving parliament. Taking this as the final straw, vast migrations of these people turned to America for a better opportunity at applying God's laws and enjoying the liberty that comes therewith. As far as they were concerned, they had tried everything they could in England to bring about righteousness and liberty. Professor Morgan captures the sentiment from the life of John Winthrop:

"Responsibility for England's wickedness lay heavy on Winthrop's shoulders. He had shared in the government of his county as justice of the peace, of his country as attorney in the Court of Wards. The utmost he and his Puritan friends could do in their various offices was not enough to stem the tide of evil. If God should descend in His wrath to punish England, as she so justly deserved, John Winthrop knew he would suffer with the rest. Not even if he resigned his offices and led the holiest

christianitytoday.com/tc/2003/002/7.28.html

7 Between the years of 1645 and 1686, 11% of the marriages in Plymouth Colony involved premarital sex (Deetz and Deetz, *The Times of Their Lives*, Anchor Books, New York, NY, 2001, p. 149.) Today, 95% of Americans engage in pre-marital intercourse. (Sharon Jayson, "Most Americans have had premarital sex, study finds," *USA Today*, December 19, 2006)

of lives as a private citizen could he escape responsibility, for where governors failed to uphold God's laws, God held the governed accountable."[8]

In a similar sense, twentieth century Christians have emerged out of the Reagan Revolution, the Moral Majority, the Christian Coalition, and other political movements only to find that abortion is still legal, homosexual marriage is an inevitability, taxation continues to rise, government continues to grow, and nothing resembling a biblical worldview is even close to implementation in the civil sphere today. In almost every case, the Christian agenda prostituted itself to the political pragmatism of the day, sacrificing the principle by endless compromise and a meaningless, unsubstantial form of incrementalism.

The commonality we share with that First Mayflower is a rise in true faith in the living God. These are men and women of God who take God's Word seriously. With the first reformation came several generations of men who would engage daily family worship, exhorting their families daily "so long as it was called today" (Heb. 3:13). Granted, this practice disappeared in the early 1800s in America, replaced by Sunday Schools, revival meetings, and small group Bible studies. But when the hearts of fathers turn back to their sons and sons to their fathers, a reformation of biblical proportion is in the offing (Mal. 4:6). Hundreds of thousands of fathers are rising to the occasion, many appearing out of the aforementioned homeschooling movement. These men are taking their responsibilities before God seriously and are no longer passing it off on to the church or the state. Such revival of fatherhood is the most important orthopraxic element of the present reformation. With the revival of a million men who are willing to rule their families well and disciple their children each day in faith and character, the church will finally again be blessed with men who will be

8 Edmund S. Morgan, *The Puritan Dilemma: The Story of John Winthrop*, Little, Brown, Boston, MA, 1958, p. 30.

able to rule the church well too (1 Tim. 3:4, 12). And these will be the nuts and bolts of the Second Mayflower.

True Christians are becoming increasingly aware of their responsibilities before God. We crack the Word and read, with interest and true commitment, the commands of God. We read the command to "remember the Sabbath day to keep it holy," and we begin to rest from our work one day in seven. We read the commands to give our children an education in knowledge rooted in the fear of God, and we remove them from the pagan schools that are forbidden by law to provide that sort of education (Prov. 1:7). We have family devotions with our children daily. We consistently discipline our children with the rod. We begin to tithe. We take care of our elderly parents instead of passing them off to the church or the state (Matt. 15:1-6; 1 Tim. 3:1-15). We find that the church is bound to take care of elderly widows without children and we stop passing them off to the state (1 Tim. 3:1-15). We read God's requirements for church discipline and we begin to faithfully engage our 1 Corinthians 5 responsibilities. We read the commands of God to appoint men to leadership positions who are "able men, such as fear God, men of truth, hating covetousness," and we support principled statesmen and principled political parties. In short, we begin to take our God seriously. We diligently search out the Bible for His commands so that we may obey them. We recognize His authority and lovingly and painstakingly endeavor to obey Him in all areas of life; for it was the Son of God who said it plainly, "If you love Me, keep My commandments."

The Second Mayflower Traverses New Waters

History does not repeat itself word for word, and as the Second Mayflower grows out of the First, there will be unique characteristics marking out this next great movement. The Second Mayflower must begin right away to rebuild the family and completely rework education. Indeed, the humanist juggernaut is found in their education systems, and the problem has lingered for 800 years. Since the first secular universities rooted their methodology and philosophy in Greek humanist thinking and removed education from family, church, and dominion work, our course towards humanism was set. This "secular" education necessarily separates knowledge from the fear of God, separates knowledge from life application, and builds up man's pride in himself. This is precisely what it takes to produce the modern humanist state. Our problem, therefore, dates back to the 12th century. When the university was removed from the context of family, church, and workplace, education was redefined in secular humanist terms. This is why Harvard adopted a humanist rationalism within 50 years of its inception, as did both Yale and Princeton. The university system is necessarily humanist in its conception because it will not define education as discipleship in faith and character, the substance of a biblical definition of *paideia* (Deut. 6:7; Eph. 6:4; Proverbs).

Think about the changes that have come about through the modern university institution as the minds of men were trained in a basically humanistic epistemology and metaphysic. Even during the latter half of the 15th century, during the darkest days of the pre-reformation period, there was still a deep sense of sin and a fear of God, though many would seek to resolve the sin problem by ineffectual means (such as the purchase of indulgences). But today, Catholics and Protestants alike hardly fear God at all. The notion of the fear of God as the beginning of wisdom and knowledge is utterly laughable in schools and universities. Reformation in the 16th century was concerned with the breakdown of the Catholic church. Today, reformation is concerned with the breakdown of everything and every denomination, with the all-but-thorough institutional abandonment of God-centered epistemology, metaphysics, and ethics.

Another difference between the two Mayflowers is the massive intrusion of the state into daily life. Tyranny is far more extensive though perhaps not quite as intensively engaged, in persecuting the church. The breakdown of the family, marriage, and morality is also far worse today than it was during the 17th century. Even with all of the complaints the Puritans and Separatists leveled against the state church in England, there were no pastors defending a homosexual lifestyle as there are now. I don't recall there being any transsexual pastors either.

Admittedly, the Puritans made mistakes. Though we may commend them for their faith, perseverance and courage, they were still humans and a product of their generation. They opposed religious pluralism and struggled with the intersection of church and state - a question still not entirely resolved in our day. With the Puritans in Massachusetts and several other colonies we find examples where state regulation and funding of the church was patterned more closely after that found in European nations than that warranted by Scripture. By the time of the War for Independence, a clearer separation of church and state had developed.[9]

Yet even as Americans so fiercely oppose state control of church today, they seem to welcome the state control of the family and education. Sometimes it takes a few centuries before good men will recognize the consequences of violating jurisdictions, as the state seeks to control the church or the family. Whereas the United States Constitution did forbid state control of the church by means of the "establishment clause," there was little mention made of state control of the family and education (although the tenth amendment may have sufficed for it).

Therefore, the next civil covenant must commit to a new direction for liberty. The issue that Karl Marx saw as core to his agenda was the destruction of the family, and this would come by means of public education. In his words, "we destroy the most hallowed of relations, when we replace home education by social."[10] Marx was aware of the radical nature of his agenda. No philosopher was more effective

9 Unfortunately, the nation quickly embraced religious pluralism in its eagerness to avoid the mistakes of confounding church and state. This relationship will be covered in more detail in Chapter 9.

10 Marx, *The Communist Manifesto,*
http://www.anu.edu.au/polsci/marx/classics/manifesto.html

at bringing about a vision in the modern world as modern nations proceeded to implement his immodest proposals. Economic systems changed only as education systems were socialized. Now it has come to the point that opposition to the statist agenda is futile as long as each successive generation receives an education at the hands of the state. In fact, opposition to government funded and controlled education and economic systems is tantamount to blasphemy of the darkest hue. But the journey of the Second Mayflower must begin with renewed empowerment of the family in the area of education. As far as the state has violated the jurisdiction of the family in the funding and control of education, we must reverse this trend. This is the only way we will salvage family and freedom in the next century. This will be the centerpiece in the incarnation of the reforming principle.

Christian columnist Cal Thomas correctly assessed the power of this system when he wrote, "Public education is not about education. In too many instances it is about propagandizing and controlling the minds and hearts (and bodies) of the next generation. Without public schools, liberalism would qualify as an endangered species. With them, liberals hope to train sufficient numbers of left-thinking drones to replace them when they are gone."[11] Columnist Joseph Sobran agrees, "Public schools ... should not even exist. The state has no business assuming power over its citizens' minds, and especially children's tender minds. The very thought of such power ought to chill us."[12]

As the First Mayflower took one positive step towards separating state and church, the Second Mayflower must take a meaningful step towards separating state and family. If the worldview of Marx and Platois sustained in the minds of those who head church and state, the family simply will not survive. If the responsibility of educating children has been assigned to the family, then the church or the state's usurpation of that responsibility constitutes a violation of rights. This is the very definition of tyranny. When civil government attempts to

11 Cal Thomas, *Conservative Chronicle*, January 13, 1993.
12 Joseph Sobran, *Conservative Chronicle*, November 30, 1994.

replace the family or the church by seizing their domain of authority, it progressively breaks down those institutions. Therefore, the challenge facing us is the demise of the family at the hands of the state. We are fighting to salvage the institution of the family in the 21st century.

All education is religious just as all ideas are based upon certain presuppositions concerning life, origins, purpose, and the order of the universe. All education assumes a certain theological and anthropological framework. To take God out of education as the humanists have done in America, is to assume and promote atheism. Therefore, just as the civil government has no business funding and controlling churches, so the civil government has no business funding and controlling education.

Separatists and Puritans

In our day, the Puritan-Separatist tension is obvious everywhere Christians engage the social and political institutions of our day. Some reformation minded Christians are active within the mainstream entertainment industry in Hollywood,[13] while others have all but abandoned it.[14] Some continue to work within the mainline denominations seeking some reform in the church, while many others leave those denominations. Some are constantly working to reform the more "conservative" political party, while others have given up and work to build another party. Some insist on reforming the public schools and send their children there hoping that they can make a difference. Meanwhile, the Separatists find little possibility of any meaningful reform in such institutions. Indeed, the balance of "being in the world but not of the world" produces a monumental challenge for any Christian.

Nevertheless, it must be admitted that when men and women climb aboard a ship and leave one nation to build another, they have embarked on a journey which is for all intents and purposes a Separatist venture.

13 Brian Godawa, *Hollywood Worldviews*, InterVarsity Press, Downers Grove, IL, 2002.
14 Botkin, *Outside Hollywood*.

Thus, the Second Mayflower constitutes something of a Separatist movement as well.

There are many reasons why the modern homeschool movement is a truly striking development in Western history. Chief among them are the political adjustments that have enabled the movement to flourish. While parental rights were eroded through abdication and through much legislative and court action during the 1980s and 1990s, hundreds of men and women fought for homeschool rights and carved out an island of freedom.[15] During the last two years of legislative battles in Colorado, the legislature sharply abridged parental rights with more restrictive compulsory attendance requirements, *while at the same time allowing exceptions for all homeschoolers in the language*!

Evidently, an island of freedom is forming for those who want it. Several other indications of this island include the child tax credit that came by way of the George W. Bush administration, and exceptions made available to those who wish to opt out of the expanding socialized health care systems and mandatory health insurance laws in this country.

If the survival of the family unit and obedience to Deuteronomy 6:7 and Ephesians 6:4 demands separation from the systems and institutions we have inherited from past generations, then the Puritans and Separatists of our own day had better be prepared to separate. May God continue to grant the remnant freedom in the years to come! Otherwise, our children and grandchildren will see family, faith, and freedom further diminished.

Problems for the Separatists

Removing children from the public schools is, without a doubt, a separatist action. Those who choose to homeschool their children are often criticized by those who see separatism as erring towards ungodly

15 Homeschool Legal Defense Association Attorney Chris Klicka records the remarkable providences of God throughout the recent struggles in his important book, Homeschool Heroes. Chris Klicka, *Homeschool Heroes*, Broadman and Holman, Nashville, TN, 2006

isolation and social inaction. While it is highly unlikely that Christian children will ever do much to purify the public schools, it is possible for Separatists to go too far, driven by strong human emotions of fear, disgust, and pessimism. Some Christian factions espouse the neglect of social duties, such as voting and other forms of political action, for a number of reasons. Some see engagement in any activity but a simple "gospel preaching" to be a waste of time. But such corrupted thinking originates from a misconception of the Gospel itself. It separates faith and life, and, in so doing, destroys the unity of faith and works (James 2:28). Moreover, the Great Commission was not proposing an evangelism reduced to some minimalist, three-point Gospel tract requiring some kind of a shallow assent. The content of the message was supposed to be *all* of Christ's commandments and the goal in mind was obedience, as specified in the Great Commission: "Teach them to observe whatsoever I have commanded you." That would include all 66 books (2 Tim. 3:16, 17; Matt. 28:18-20). If our faith incarnates in works and obedience to the commandments of God, then of course the gospel will impact every relationship and every institution with which we come into contact. A true Christian cannot help but bring a new law order and a new life to the marketplace, the corporation, the university, the science laboratory, the publishing industry, the economic system, and the spheres of politics and jurisprudence.

To make matters worse, the evangelical Christian population spent the last 150 years on an apocalyptic craze stirred up by cadres of false prophets. By the end of the 20th century, Christians still are not tired of the millennial frenzy, evidenced by a best-selling series of "Christian" novels bearing the apocalyptic theme, selling millions of copies.

As these believers scan the headlines looking for more hints that the world is getting worse, they will point to the abortion "holocaust," sundry wars, and the New World Order as certain proof that the world has "never been this bad" and is sure to end within a generation. Such notions form an insult to those severely persecuted in other eras as they were eaten by lions, burned alive, guillotined, or gassed to death. Nevertheless, as the 20th century millennial fever fades away, we must remember that our commission is still the same, "Occupy until the Lord returns. Go ye into all the world, teaching the nations to observe everything Christ commanded us" (Matt. 28:20; Luke 19:13).

Then there are those who are so afraid of being contaminated by the world that they are hesitant to influence the world in politics, arts, and education. To this notion, we would note that the only way that we will not be contaminated with the temptations of the world and the flesh is if we wage war. We must be as determined as the Puritans were, not to be neutral in interaction with the world's system. Either we will influence the world or we will be influenced by it. Either we will impress the order of God's law on society or we will succumb and adopt man's laws.

Still others have given up. They throw up their hands in utter disgust, refusing to pay taxes, vote, attend church, or maintain any influence in a public forum. While I can say that I understand the frustration and am quite intimately aware of the overwhelming strength of the opposition, this does not relieve the Separatists of the duty to be salt, yeast, and light (Matt. 5:10-16). Every city commissioner who wages the war, and every university instructor who goes down in flames teaching the fear of God in his classroom may not have accomplished much in his own time, however, the message he sends home to his children bears immeasurable value. By virtue of the standard he raises in those spheres of influence to which God has called him, he plants seeds that will bear much fruit in future generations. What would have happened if there had never been a message sent? No standard raised? No losing battle is a wasted battle if it was fought for God and His standard of righteousness! We know that we can be successful in our endeavors no matter how rough and corrupt the world becomes, providing the salt has not lost its savor and we are rooted in the Word of God.

There are others who are consumed with the fear of man because of their exposure to endless reminders of the progress made by the forces of evil and the great conspiracies that are active in world politics. Some write books claiming that our electoral system has been thoroughly compromised or "rigged," resulting in discouragement of any political involvement. What they fail to understand is that their message is paralyzing. Without a deep sense of duty which can only be rooted in a commitment to the law of a transcendent God coupled with a resolute trust in his absolute sovereignty over the most powerful evil forces, we would all eventually shrink from the battle. *We would be more driven and controlled by fear of man than the fear of God, insuring the failure of our mission.*

Unfortunately, the fear mongers are usually neither committed to God's law as the absolute source of ethics nor to the doctrine of God's absolute sovereignty over His created realm. They say education is the solution, yet their education contains no solutions. If there is no faith in God, no commitment to God's law, and no serious application to duty, being educated and aware of tyranny is a waste of time and resources.

To summarize, there are legitimate instances when we should separate ourselves from certain systems of the world. We do this to avoid needless temptations, to fulfill what we perceive as biblical duties (such as teaching our children), and when we are in imminent danger of physical harm. Meanwhile, we continue to apply all means at our disposal to influence our world according to the law-order of the King of kings and Lord of lords.

Striking the Balance

"I pray not that Thou shouldest take them out of the world, but that Thou shouldest keep them from the evil. They are not of the world, even as I am not of the world." John 17:15, 16

Jesus knew that the Puritans and Pilgrims of every age would be faced with the formidable challenge of living in this world. There is a tightrope to walk between irrelevance and involvement. How can we be culturally relevant in a time where the influence of true biblical Christianity has all but disappeared from our culture? Or how can we raise children who are culturally engaged in a culturally degraded age? To remain untouched by the influence of an ungodly culture while at the same time influencing a culture for God, is a balance that is almost impossible to maintain. Christians through the ages have resorted to various extremes in their attempt to live for God. But for some reason, Jesus wanted His disciples to be in the world, but not of it. Until Christ returns, we are commanded to "occupy" as salt, yeast, and light in a lost world.

There are three possible relationships we may have with the world. First, we may attempt to escape the world. The problem with escaping the world by withdrawing into convents, caves, or even our homes, is that it does not solve the problem of keeping us from the evil. Even within the modern homeschooling movement, the stories abound concerning children who were kept insulated from the world and its sexual deviance and they still fell into the trap of fornication. As one father told me, "We protected our children from everything ... except their own hearts!" Fundamentally, those who wish to escape the world are motivated by a desire to *escape the war*. The Christian life is battle - constant war against the world, the flesh, and the devil. Of course, when children are very young they are not equipped to fight the war. We must carefully *protect* them as we *prepare* them for battle.

But if we do not teach our children to engage in the battle and if we do not engage in the battle against the world ourselves, then we are disengaged from the war for the kingdom of God. If we do not fight the good fight we will passively accept the sin that remains in our own lives. The Christian life is such that we will either fight or die. Our battle with the world is part of our battle against our own sin.

"The kingdom of God suffereth violence, and the violent take it by force." Matthew 11:12

"For we wrestle not against flesh and blood, but against principalities, against powers, against the rulers of the darkness of this world, against spiritual wickedness in high places."
Ephesians 6:12

"For the weapons of our warfare are not carnal, but mighty through God to the pulling down of strongholds; casting down imaginations, and every high thing that exalteth itself against the knowledge of God, and bringing into captivity every thought to the obedience of Christ." 2 Corinthians 10:4

The Isaac Watts hymn, "Am I a Soldier of the Cross?" characterizes the necessity of this war in these words:

> "Must I be carried to the skies on flowery beds of ease,
> While others fought to win the prize and sailed through
> bloody seas?
> Sure I must fight if I would reign, Increase my courage Lord,
> I'll bear the toil, endure the flood, supported by Thy Word."

Furthermore it is impossible to escape the world, especially if we are to engage in trade with the world, and if we are to obey the Great Commission (1 Cor. 5:10).

The second relationship a Christian might have with the world is to amalgamate into the world by taking on the world's thoughts, attitudes, cultural expressions, and behavior, while neglecting the ethical standard of God's laws. This is the opposite extreme. These Christians will think nothing of giving their children a humanist, existentialist worldview in schools that will not teach that the foundation of wisdom and

160

knowledge is the fear of God. At the end of the day, they have the same economics, the same divorce rate, the same fornication rate, the same politics, and the same standards of immodesty as unbelievers. As one believer put it, commenting on her unbelieving days in an American day school, "Those Christian kids I knew in high school, they really didn't have anything to offer me. They talked the same way I did. They had the same attitudes I had. They listened to the same music. They just weren't quite as accomplished at it as the rest of us were." Such salt has lost its savor.

How to be Culturally Relevant without Being Contaminated

If the Christian cannot escape the world or amalgamate into the world, then I cannot think of any alternate approach but to take on the world to change it; to attack the world at every front; to impose God's agenda upon it; to impact it by salt, yeast, and light. There are really no alternatives. Either we will influence the world around us or we will be influenced by it.

Attempts to escape the world are usually motivated by an unhealthy fear which roots itself in a mistrust of our sovereign God. Often there is a sentiment that being in the world must necessarily include passive acceptance of the temptations, unbiblical philosophies, and sinful institutions of this world. This is why those who insist upon escaping the world are usually the first to be contaminated by it. They lack the faith to fight the war, and it is *faith* that overcomes the world! (1 John 5:4).

The Christian is left in a strange place. He is in the world but he is not of this world. In some ways, he will always be an alien, a stranger, and an outsider; but he still operates within the world. There is always a tension in his residence within the world. As he enters the world each day, he enters another battle in a gigantic war against the world's philosophies and temptations. We can never be at ease while in the world.

To aid in striking a clean balance between escape and amalgamation, consider the following points.

First, we need to recognize that we are engaged in war. It is primarily a war of ideas or imaginations that exalt themselves "against the knowledge of God" (2 Cor. 10:5). In this war, we must bring into captivity every thought, whether it be cultural, governmental, legal, or philosophical, "to the obedience of Christ." There is no neutrality at any point - in our music, politics, media, movies, or education. These things will either exalt Christ or they will set themselves against Christ.

Secondly, each of us should learn to recognize our own particular weaknesses and the peculiar temptations of the world that lure us, and avoid these temptations. Not everyone will be tempted by the same thing, and this is one reason why there is no need for a list of all of the activities and places in this world that Christians must avoid.

Thirdly, we strengthen ourselves by applying the means of grace daily in our lives. These include church convocations, church accountability, family worship, personal devotions, prayer and fasting. These things strengthen us in the important war against the world, the flesh, and the devil. In many years of pastoral counseling, I can't think of a single instance where someone had fallen deep into sin and had not shirked these spiritual exercises.

Fourthly, we must eschew ethical ambiguity and ground ourselves in the concrete morals laid out in God's revealed Word. We must begin to move from subjective, ethereal definitions of righteousness to the concrete, objective directives of God's laws.

As Christians begin to develop a strong sense of moral purpose and direction, they will begin to lead in society. Those with the strongest commitment to their religion in terms of its application to daily life are usually the ones who are most influential in society, whether it be Muslims or Marxists. If Christians will reclaim this culture for Christ, they must develop a strong sense of God's requirements on them in all areas of their lives. They will see that they cannot hide from God and His law in the voting booth, in the church, in universities, in movie theaters or in their homes.

Fifthly, we should develop a long term perspective on the kingdom of God, and see ourselves as fitting into the historical battle between good and evil. The kingdom of God advances gradually but steadily around the globe and into every area of life. We ought to see ourselves as a small part of this movement that is "filling the whole earth." Of course, we have much more freedom in our country today than in other times and places when Christians hid in the catacombs and were fed to lions in the arena. We can speak freely about the Bible on radio stations over this whole continent. But we must set ourselves to a lifetime commitment, a generational commitment.

Let us remind our children that there is a great expanse of work to be done for the kingdom of God. Without being overwhelmed by the magnitude of the project before us, let us challenge ourselves and our children to apply the laws of God to business, relationships, art, literature, government, the courts, science, economics and journalism. Many of these institutions have been almost thoroughly corrupted by unbiblical notions, sinful temptations, and evil philosophies. But as long as there are souls to save and Christians in need of sanctification, there will be corrupted institutions. So let us commit ourselves to be faithful to God in the specific calling to which He has called each of us. There isn't an area of life that does not have some contact with the world, and as we bring God's law to bear in each of those areas, they will taste the salt and see the light. Our lives are usually multi-focused and we are each called in different capacities to apply the law of God in the voting booth, in our children's education, in church government, in business, and in conversations with our neighbors. As we set ourselves on the firm foundation of God's Word, let us then commit ourselves to do it.

"I have inclined mine heart to perform Thy statutes alway, even unto the end." Psalm 119:112

This is the very heart of it; this is where the Second Mayflower begins.

*   *   *

The first church formed in Salem in 1629 covenanted together under this very succinct script, which thoroughly epitomized the early Puritan heart:

> "We covenant with our Lord, and one with another, and we do bind our selves in the presence of God, to walk together in all His ways, according as He is pleased to reveal Himself unto us in His blessed word of truth; and do explicitly in the name and fear of God, profess and protest to walk as followeth, through the power and grace of our Lord Jesus Christ.
> "We avouch the Lord to be our God, and our selves to be His people, in the truth and simplicity of our spirits.

> "We give our selves to the Lord Jesus Christ, and the word of His grace for the teaching, ruling and sanctifying us in matters of worship and conversation, resolving to cleave unto Him alone for life and glory, and to reject all contrary ways, canons, and constitutions of men in his worship ...

> "Promising also unto our best ability to teach our children and servants the knowledge of God, and of His Will, that they may serve Him also; and all this not be nay strength of our own, but by the Lord Christ: whose blood we desire may sprinkle this our Covenant made in His name."

6

MAKING PREPARATIONS
FOR THE VOYAGE

"Whoever will introduce into public affairs the principles of
Christianity will change the face of the world."
- Benjamin Franklin

Nobody will ever seek change anywhere in life unless they
have first got a vision for something better than what they
have. If you are quite content with what you have, why would you strive
for anything better? Those who are content to live in a world where 37%
of children are born without fathers, where 95% of the people confess
to pre-marital sex, half of marriages end in divorce, and where almost
half of the people's income is taxed, will have no particular interest in
change. Without a vision, the people perish (Prov. 29:18).

Clarity of Vision

But even where a vision is present, the movement it represents will
die unless the vision progressively sharpens in its clarity and purpose.
Many movements die because the vision was poorly communicated to
succeeding generations through teaching and example. Therefore, the
vision must either sharpen or it will die - there is no middle ground.
If the deep-seated and lasting cultural change that we are calling for is
going to come to fruition, it will only happen if the vision is sharp and
continues to become more defined with each successive generation.

Some will present vision enough to discern the problem but they produce little if any vision for the solution to the problem. Even if the windows of opportunity flew open and we had the opportunity to bring about change on a political level, most Christians would not know where to start and their efforts would turn out to be irrelevant or even counter productive. For example, take the Christian political activist who commits his resources and influence towards appropriating government lottery funds to an abstinence program. The rest of us are left wondering whether there is any biblical support for either government lotteries or government-funded abstinence programs.

Some Christians wander about in the wilderness of ethical relativism, not knowing what would constitute just punishments for child abuse or murder. They are unsure whether the civil government should fund art or homosexual erotic art, or education, condoms, welfare, needles for drug addicts, medical care, prisons, or random searches and seizures. Others have never taken the time to study what the Bible teaches us about these things. Sometimes Christians will take a determined stand on one isolated issue, but their worldview lacks coherence because it lacks a comprehensive and full-orbed view of history, politics, anthropology, epistemology, sociology, economics, ecclesiology, and medicine. Thus, this half-baked, piecemeal approach will produce very little, if any, long term, positive results.

For lack of vision, Christian activism is saddled with both lack of unity and direction. As the years pass and the fire burns, it becomes clear that all that energy and effort produced far more wood, hay, and stubble than gold, silver, and precious stones (1 Cor. 3:11-15). As long as the agenda is more framed by political pragmatism and utilitarianism than by a heart commitment to God's law, we will continue to fight losing battles.

Thus, in preparation for a voyage of similar scope and impact as the First Mayflower, we simply cannot be content with a small sliver of a vision. If our movement fails to progress, it will be from lack of purposeful vision. It takes years, even generations, to clarify that vision, and we often discover that our principles are too shallow and applications too narrow in scope. Once we have identified the vision, it must then be incarnated piece by piece into how we live. The Second Mayflower takes shape as we self-consciously live out the principles of God's law in our families, our businesses, and our churches.[1]

> *"Without a vision the people perish, but he who keeps the law, happy is he."* Proverbs 29:18

A Full-Orbed and Integrated Vision

If we are going to achieve critical mass in this movement, we must first adopt a full-orbed, cross-disciplined world and life view - and then fully integrate it into life. It must cross over from general epistemological, metaphysical, and ethical governing principles to social relationships, academics, and economics. Only after that will the movement bring any lasting effect to the political sphere. Those who ride the Second Mayflower must understand the inter connectivity of family relationships and church relationships with the economic, the academic, and the political spheres. It would, for example, be impossible to change the family in any meaningful way while at the same time leaving present economic and academic systems untouched, since sociology and economics are inextricably connected.

Educating the Basic Core of the Vision

Earlier in this book, I presented the core element of the Second Mayflower vision as an epistemological and ethical commitment to the revelatory Word of God. However, there is a more fundamental way of

1 Since the purpose of this book is not to present every constituent part of a biblical worldview, I would direct my reader to the excellent resources already available through ministries like Cornerstone Curriculum Project, Summit Ministries, Vision Forum, Chalcedon, American Vision, and Generations with Vision. These ministries have been particularly helpful in supporting the burgeoning homeschooling movement, but they have also reached into Christian schools and churches with some success. Typically these ministries focus on different emphases, but they play a vital role in the rise of the Second Mayflower.

expressing our worldview that wraps a God-centered understanding of reality (or metaphysics) into the ethical; it has to do with our perspective of God and His connection with us.

Those who will make up the first movements of the Second Mayflower will have a distinctively different perspective on reality than that which has come to dominate Western thinking over the last two centuries. With every television drama, with every science class, every hour in the classroom, every first grade reader, literature class and news cast, God is more distant to the modern mind. Modern man meticulously removed every remnant of God from the reality and the thinking of modern man by the introduction of purely natural mechanisms in origins via "scientific" theories. Then he denied God's providential guidance in all things and called into question His omnipresence, omniscience, and omnipotence. However, the most destructive death blow to a God-centered reality came when Christians left God in the Sunday School lesson on Sundays, while at the same time removing Him from day school classes on weekdays. God is much further from the mind of the 21st century fundamentalist Christian than from the 15th century European because the worldview of naturalistic materialism has utterly infiltrated every aspect of our world (particularly academics).

Nothing and nobody is more at fault for this tragic metaphysical revolution than the church and the academy. Three thousand years ago, the wisest man who ever lived wrote in his book about educating a young man on the foundation of all wisdom and knowledge.

"The beginning of wisdom is the fear of God."

The only way to teach anything about human reality and experience is to begin every lesson with the fear of God. If anybody will teach our children about the enormity of the universe, the complexity of the human body, and the magnificent beauty of nature, they had better begin and end the lesson with an insistence on worshiping the God

168

who made it all. The teacher may either roar it out or whisper it in awe, *"Fear God, people. Fear God!"* He had better say it. Anything less than that presents the wrong worldview, and will result in an impoverished education. No teacher should ever teach the great stories of history, such as the bubonic plague that destroyed one-third of Europe in the 15th century, without looking up from his notes for a moment to say to his class, *"Fear God! Fear the God who is behind it all!"* Such is the metaphysic of a Christian. But as my reader knows well, this form of education is hard to find in this country or in any other country for that matter. Most teaching colleges fail to even mention the fear of God, let alone emphasize it. Indeed there is little "fear of God before their eyes." But if a worldview or a movement were a house, this would have to be its foundation. Without a sure foundation, we would have nothing but a trailer sitting in a park in Kansas waiting for the next tornado. Jesus warned of the foolish man who refused to build his life, his family, his institutions on the Rock of His words. If a nation refuses to build its education system on Proverbs 1:7 and the rest of Jesus' words, that nation may not fall immediately. But when the storms come and the floods rise, you will see a nation fall, and "great will be the fall of it!"

Our children's education must begin with a heart attitude of fear towards God. This is more than a tacit understanding of a proposition: it is a heart attitude and metaphysical perspective of *fear*. Thus, the heart of the child, his attitude and perspective towards God, and his character represent the pre-eminent and essential substance of a Christian education. For the Christian, the process of education must be centered around fear of God, faith in God, love for God, and the character that flows out from these things. If God is a reality and He has created man for relationship with Himself, education will be far more focused on discipleship rooted in relationships than in learning the bare facts about geography, geology, and geometry. Where there is no fear of God, education will be perverted in its goal, its content, and its methodology.[2]

> *"Let us hear the conclusion of the whole matter: Fear God, and keep His commandments: for this is the whole duty of man."*
> *Ecclesiastes 12:13*

The Unified Family

As we carefully lay out the basic building blocks of the next Mayflower, we move from the cornerstone of the fear of God in education to the recovery of the integrity and unity of the nuclear family. I have already presented the alternate worldview of Rousseau, Plato, and Marx - each of whom were committed to the dismantling of the family by the reformulation of education, economics and revolutionary politics. Moreover, the rise of divorce, homosexuality and alternative lifestyles, abortion, fornication and illegitimacy rates all illustrate the "outstanding" success enjoyed by the worldview espousing this social construct. For some reason, humanist man rejects God's social relationships and replaces them with his own. However with the breakdown of the family, he will lose his civilization. Even the natural bonds of *phileo* love can be broken when powerful materialist and existentialist worldviews work on the minds and hearts of millions, as the parents abort their young and the children remaining move on to euthanize their parents. Without *phileo* love, man is left with either *eros* (sexual love) or pseudo-relationships held together by shallow economic interests - both of which are usually self-centered and short term.

The humanist agenda was segregation and fragmentation for the family in order to render that institution irrelevant. This came about by stripping away its traditional responsibilities such as education, welfare, and care for elderly parents. Throughout recorded history such obligations had always resided with the family. Even among pagan

2 For more on returning to a biblical perspective on education, reference this author's book, *Upgrade: The Ten Secrets to the Best Education for Your Child*.

tribes, if any would engage in euthanasia for the elderly or infanticide for the young, it would be family members. Then with the modern world came *state-funded and state-mandated* euthanasia and abortion. Thus, the family as a social unit became even more irrelevant in the modern world. At the same time as this humanist worldview minimized the family's obligations, rights, and responsibilities, it also fragmented the family in just about every imaginable way. Again, this was fundamental to Marx's agenda outlined in the *Communist Manifesto*. He repudiated the family: "Abolish the family!" he wrote. Allowing for women's societies in his *Manifesto*, he recommended placing all women in state-run or state-controlled businesses and corporations. He viewed the "bourgeoisie" family business as the great enemy of his plan because of the economic inequality it produced; and more basically, because of the threat that family inheritance and family property imposed against an all-powerful state.

So as women were "emancipated" to work in their state-run and controlled corporations, most did not anticipate two negative consequences - the family became economically fragmented and the freedom for families to operate their own businesses was curtailed. The change was simple and subtle. The feminist agenda "freed" the woman from her husband only to enslave her to a corporate manager. Thus society atomized as individuals saw themselves relating more to the corporation or to the state and far less to the family unit. It should come as no surprise that as of 2006, for the first time in history, the nuclear family makes up fewer than 50% of American households[3] The family is disappearing.

This, however, was not God's vision for the family. From the beginning God intended the woman to be a help-mate, fit, or appropriate, to aid her husband in his dominion task. God then took the two and made "one flesh" (Gen. 2). Thus unity is basic to the family. While a wife is expected to be an economic contributor to the family (Prov. 31:10-31),

3 *New York Times*, "To be Married is to Be Outnumbered."
http://www.nytimes.com/2006/10/15/us/15census.html?_r=1&pagewanted=1&oref=slogin

the radical economic individuation of the modern world was neither anticipated nor considered normative by Scripture. The Greek word from which we derive the word economics is *oikonomia*. Its roots are *"oikos"* and *"nomia,"* literally translated as the "vision of the family" or the "law of the family." From the very outset of human society, the basic economic unit was the family, not the individual person.

Biblically speaking, it is normative for the family to be unified around a single economic vision. Take Rebekah, for example, who tended her father's sheep in Genesis 24. Joseph and his brothers tended their father's flocks, as did David before he left his father's home to fight the Philistines. Even in the New Testament, Aquila and Priscilla were tent makers together (Acts 18:3). This unified economic vision within families slowly dissipated over the years. Increasingly, women came to see themselves as competitors in the marketplace instead of complementors in the household. This produced profound changes in social relationships in the modern world and led to the trends we've seen in birth rates, divorce rates, and illegitimacy rates.

I want to take care not to critique a woman's economic contribution to the home. Remember, it is the Proverbs 31 woman who considers a field and buys it. However, the modern family has lost sight of the biblical vision of unity, and increasingly lives out the vision of self-oriented, family-fragmenting individualism. Consider for a moment a few other examples. Since the turn of the 20th century, children are educated by the state in age-segregated, state funded classrooms for large portions of the week, further solidifying the statist/individualistic worldview. Entertainment has increasingly taken on noninteractive forms from television and computer games to the more recent ipods and portable DVD players. The cumulative effective of this is more fragmentation. During the latter half of the 19th century, significant numbers of fathers left the family farms for the corporations; by the end of the 20th century, 64% of children under 4 years old had made "latch key" status (up from 6% a generation earlier), as their mothers joined the corporate workforce. Again, the problem is not women as economic producers, but the loss of motherhood, the vision of household unity, the value of family relationships, the blessing of children, and freedom from big government and corporations. These are the values surrendered to this "brave new world." To the extent that day care, corporations, public schooling, colleges, and the suffrage movement have removed from the hearts of women any desire to serve as complementarian helpers and home managers according to God's normative mandate, one must conclude that these changes have served to destroy the unity of the nuclear family in the developed world.

Families do not recognize their own covenantal unity nor do they function as a unit much anymore. This abandonment of the creation mandate in the modern world would appear unnatural and abhorrent even to the pagan tribes untouched by a Judeo-Christian influence. It was entirely natural for Gentile families to fear God as a unit (Acts 10:2). They were baptized together (Acts 16:15, 33), and they were saved together (Gen. 6:18; Acts 16:31). They worked together (Acts 18:3), and ministered in the church of God together (1 Cor. 16:15). As individualism and statism worked so thoroughly into the consciousness, the lives, and the institutions of modern men, many Christians also began to find these verses strange. Such practices are almost entirely foreign even to the Christian family today. I would suggest that this atomism has effected evangelism and church ministries as well. The church responded to this individuation by shifting its focus to women's ministries and child evangelism. Instead of the biblical focus on evangelizing fathers and equipping them to minister to their own households, the church has followed the vision of radical individuation. Could this be one of the basic reasons why 80% of children raised in Christians homes leave the faith? Families simply do not consider themselves as a unit anymore. If families will not see themselves as a covenant unit in a radically individuated society, they certainly will not fear God together, believe together, and serve in the church of God together.

For various reasons, modern corporations did not retain a family-integrated vision as family farms and businesses had done for centuries previous. But the root cause for the dissolution of the family unit was a heart rejection of the value of family unity in modern life. These large business power centers simply would not accommodate whole families or hire households as units. Individuals served in narrow, specialized positions. Generally, contractual arrangements were rare and the benefit/retirement package offered a security that few could resist. Mother went to work for one corporation and father went to another. Some would auto-deposit the pay checks into separate bank accounts. All of which added to the fragmenting vision. Again, the problem here is not with a wife's economic contribution to the household. The humanist agenda will prevail when her role is reduced to a bare economic value and when economic independence disrupts household unity.

This emphasis on economic independence is especially obvious in the *raising of daughters*. Assuming that God's normative goal for daughters is to be a help mate (Gen. 2:18), and home manager (Titus 2:5; 1 Tim. 5:14), few schools, churches, or colleges even consider these over-arching norms in the *paideia* (education) of women for modern life. The independent life and career is always of essence in the mind of the modern young woman. (Of course, the same could be said for the young man.) What is forgotten is the biblical standard of the unified household and the normative gender-specific goals which should drive the *paideia* of the young person. The Bible makes it clear that the normative *telos* (goal) for the young woman, by creation ordinance, is that she may be a helper for her husband in his dominion task, with "home manager" being a subsidiary of this wider vision (Gen. 2:18; Titus 2:5; 1 Tim. 5:14). However this is not the *telos* in the mind of modern day universities. Is the goal of our daughters' academic preparation to serve the corporation and maintain her independent career track or is it preparation to be an effective help mate and help manager?

Two Traps

Now there are two traps awaiting the incautious step, on either side of this issue. The first trap obliterates the principle of family unity and the biblical vision of help-meet and home manager. I would also hold that "*oikos despoteo*" or home manager is central to the calling of help mate. But the second trap would fail to see home manager as only a *part* of the wider calling of help mate, and ignore the economic contribution of the wife to the *oikonomia* of the home. Those who would take this rendering would give their young daughters the course in "How to Wear an Apron 101" for 18 years and call that a *paideia*. Let me elucidate by example. If my daughter is gifted in medical science, she certainly should study medical science. But for what purpose? Is the objective in mind a purely economic relationship with a corporation controlled by the state? Certainly that would be a fine Marxist or Socialist goal. Assuming she is not called to the unmarried state, I would expect that she should marry some day and she would see her socio-economic relationship far more defined by the family unit than the corporation. I would hope that her talents and abilities serve a household economic vision as she fulfills her God-given, created role of help mate to her husband's dominion task. For example, her husband's economic vision may be to serve as a missionary in the heart of Africa and a wife trained in medical science may serve well in that household vision.

The old concept of the two becoming one in order to complement one another in a dominion task is gone; now the individual relates far more to the corporation and to the government than he does to the family. This independent economic vision, combined with the abdication of parental responsibilities in taking care of their children's education and inheritance, has served to do immeasurable harm to the integrity of the family as a relevant social sphere.

The Second Mayflower calls for a radical shift in the way we perceive the family. If we are going to reform the modern social construct, efforts must be taken to reunify the family in economics, beginning with the way we educate young men and women. When the family is united around an economic vision, it will yield far more loyalty, security, vision, investment for the future, and economic strength than could any other economic structure.

A Conflict of Values

All of the above forces have weakened the family unit and strengthened the power of the state. Yet there was another economic force that played hard against the family - and that was debt. In the 1950's the average mortgage was less than seven years. But with the combined forces of a materialist worldview emphasizing material wealth as the ultimate value, and the short-sightedness and self-oriented philosophy of existentialism, a new form of economics developed: fractional reserve banking, inflation, thirty-year mortgages, and massive consumer debt. Long-term savings and family inheritance were replaced with exponential debt, the wrong-headed utopian notion of "retirement," and an unhealthy reliance for security upon corporations and government.

Fewer than one in a hundred persons will speak of any real desire for freedom today. Instead, many will speak longingly of a life of leisure, retirement, higher mortgages, social security and a job with a "great benefit package." This is because they do not define their values by the ethical statements of God's Word; their ethics are driven by the worldviews of existentialism, socialism, and materialism. If we were to search Scripture and live by its values, here is what we would find:

"A good man leaves an inheritance unto his children's children."
Inheritance is a value (Prov. 13:22).

"Six days shall you labor and do all your work."
  Work is a value (Ex. 20:9).

"If you may be free, use it rather."
  Freedom is a value (1 Cor. 7:21).

"The debtor is servant to the lender."
  The debt-free life is a value (Prov. 22:7).

"The fruit of the womb is his reward ... Happy is the man who has his quiver full of them."
  Children are a value (Ps. 127:3).

Either the Bible will set our values and define what is good or our values will be determined by worldviews that favor debt, few children, a work-free life, and tyranny. A nation that rejects the Bible's ethical definitions of the good life will inevitably prefer more dry wall to more children, security over freedom, and debt over leaving an inheritance for our children's children.

The Value of Freedom

I doubt that there are many who would reject freedom as a positive value. But there are widely varying definitions for "freedom." Some see it as freedom *from work* or freedom *from responsibilities*. Others interpret freedom as the right to get high and commit fornication on the weekends. But if we will submit to God's laws as the source of ethics to define what is good and right for us, then we will define freedom God's way. Following the biblical definition, true freedom at its most basic level is freedom from sin, freedom from debt, and freedom from the unnecessary servitude of men. Freedom is clearly an important biblical value. "If the Son will make you free, you will be free indeed"

(John 8:36). There are, of course, various levels of servitude, including bond slaves, indentured servants, hired servants and debt.

The idea of freedom is foreign to most who live the modern lifestyle. With the possible exception of a motorcycle enthusiast or an occasional libertarian cultivating a pot crop in his back yard, the word itself is rarely used anymore. For a populace who has, during the preceding one hundred years, traded freedom for security and embraced multiple layers of servitude, such words as "liberty" and "freedom" are strange and unwieldy indeed. When I use such terms in speeches, or employ an impassioned plea for liberty found in a quote from an American patriot like Samuel Adams, I seldom meet opposition. The response is more of a nonchalant disinterest.

So how then can anyone grasp a vision for a concept which has disappeared from his world? Freedom will grow gradually in the hearts of free men through the generations. First, the fathers will taste a little of it and then must intentionally pass the vision on to their children. We may never experience it, but if we can pass on a vision for freedom to our children, they will pursue it and enjoy some small part of the blessing of freedom.

We can also gain an understanding of freedom from the history books and the biographies and testimonies of men who pledged their lives, their fortunes, and their sacred honor for that freedom. Indeed, political freedom is largely dependent upon the existence of free men, not the complacent slaves who, as Samuel Adams stated, "lovingly embrace their chains." If we are to build freedom, we must build free men. Based on what I understand about the men who founded this nation, what follows is a description of that "free man."

First and foremost in the thinking of our founding fathers, that free man must be a self-governing man. Simply put, he submits himself to Jesus Christ and obeys the commands of the Bible. If we are to advocate for limited government that eschews tyranny, the individual must learn to govern himself. Tyranny will prevail when men are self-centered, quick-tempered, envious of the wealthy, and always eager to take their neighbors to court instead of working out their differences privately. Moreover, a free man embraces his responsibilities with vigor and enthusiasm. Filled with deep conviction of those duties imposed on him by 1 Timothy 5:8, Ephesians 6:4, and Deuteronomy 6:7, he assumes responsibility for his family, his children's education and discipleship, and his elderly parents' care and refuses to turn these obligations over to the state. Translating his vision into concrete goals and values, he leads his family with love, wisdom, courage and faith.

The Clearest Indication of a Rising Movement

The clearest and brightest indication of a rising movement of free men to launch another Mayflower will be the return of fatherhood - visionary fathers fully engaged in the discipleship of their children, saving an inheritance for their children's children, and preparing their sons to be men of God themselves and to rule their households well so they can rule in the local church (1 Tim. 3:5). Such men are hard to find. Much more prevalent are men who are irresponsible, spineless, dishonorable, passive, heartless, and treacherous. These are men who will not keep their covenants. There are conservative men who will not, under any circumstance, risk their own lives for that which they believe; and liberal men who will only risk the lives of others for that which they believe. We have men who have learned to insulate themselves from relationships that demand reservoirs of wisdom, courage, and love. There are the men who spend their days smoking peyote, engaging in tribal (gang) warfare, and impregnating half the village. We have men who lack the courage to be sacrificial lovers and leaders for their wives. We have angry patriarchs and macho men who couldn't lead a poodle on a potty walk. But mighty men of faith are much harder to find.

Those few men who have eyes of vision, heads of wisdom, backbones of courage, arms of strength, and hearts of love are despised by the majority and admired by only a rare few. Occasionally a man of faith will stand to speak, but he is despised in the valley of the deaf. He must be remanded to institutions where his eyes, head, backbone, arms, and heart are surgically removed. Call them schools, churches, television, or corporations - call them what you will. The surgical process is hard to watch, if you still have your eyes.

Considering that 37% of children are born without fathers, this is only the tip of the iceberg. The rest of the iceberg is under the water. Without the recovery of fatherhood, the recovery of a biblical social order of any kind will be impossible. Either fathers will begin to regain an economic and spiritual vision for their homes by teaching their children God's Word as they sit in their houses (Deut. 6:7), or they will default to a monolithic, freedom-stilting vision of the state. There is no middle ground. Top-down, big-government structures, in either the state or the church, will always form when fathers share little vision that is biblically based with their families. This is the legacy of many nations today.

Economic Freedom

According to a biblical ethical understanding of debt, "the debtor is a servant the lender" (Prov. 22:7), debt is undesirable. Debt is slavery. Though debt is an undesirable condition, it is not necessarily sinful. What is evil is not necessarily sinful. For example, it would be inappropriate to refer to the contracting of the measles as sinful, though it is an evil. Yet, if one were to consider measles as an ethical good, we would have just cause to be concerned. Unfortunately, this country has adopted a positive perspective of debt as a "good" - in clear opposition to divine revelation - and this has contributed to the breakdown of the family, not to mention the national economy.[4]

It is interesting that even as bond slavery was rightly rejected as an "evil," other forms of slavery became more attractive in the modern day. Slavery to government at federal, state, and local levels has expanded

4 America is now the greatest debtor nation on earth, a clear indication that its days as a world power are numbered (Deut. 28:12,24).

dramatically since the 19th century. Slavery to debt in this country is beyond anything we have ever seen before, and the percentage of individuals working as hired servants has increased substantially. In the days of the ancient Roman empire, about 40% of the populace were bond slaves, 5% served as hired servants, and 55% were free men.[5] Comparing this to most modern nations with 90% hired servants and 10% free men, one would wonder if the world has changed that much (in aggregate). Rejecting one form of slavery in the 19th century, the modern world wholeheartedly embraced other forms of slavery. We could refer to it as "slavery lite." Not wishing to acknowledge the true nature of the conditions we have embraced, we put it all under a cloak of respectability. In the end, we must conclude that the Son did not make us free because we would not bow the knee to His law (John 8:36). We would not submit ourselves to his yoke, which would have been lighter than the yoke of humanist man (Matt. 11:30).

> *"Art thou called being a servant? care not for it: but if thou mayest be free, use it rather ... ye are bought with a price; be not yet the servants of men." 1 Corinthians 7:21*

Paul is dealing with bond slavery in this passage, but by implication we can extend to all levels of unnecessary servitude to men. The principle is clear: if one has an opportunity to be free, he is under obligation to take it. Be careful to note that this is not a universal and absolute requirement. If it were taken this way, we would all be pressed to throw off all government tyranny, debt, and corporate structures instantly. Of course that is a practical impossibility and to pretend otherwise would bind burdens too heavy to carry (Matt. 23:4). Some must borrow money or borrow a home by renting because they cannot otherwise afford to purchase a home. Many live under government tyranny because they can neither leave it or change it. If nothing can be

5 http://legvi.tripod.com/id27.html

done to alter our circumstances, we are called to receive our lot in life with contentment and joy, and submit to our masters (Phil. 4:11; Eph. 6:5-8). However, if we have embraced tyranny and debt-consumed lives because our hearts sought after idolatrous security and materialism; if we are serving the idol of materialism and trusting in government social security and corporate retirement packages in lieu of trusting in God, we are not living out the 1 Corinthians 7:21 principle.

Consider the reason for the above admonition to pursue freedom from the unnecessary servitude of men: "For ye are bought with price" (1 Cor. 7:23). Such a statement appears strange to those not trained to see the full-orbed implications of Christ's redemption. Yet men of faith must embrace this freedom because the redemption price that our Lord paid at the cross extends to political and economic freedom (Lev. 25:40; Is. 61:1; Luke 4:18-21). Sadly, men too often refuse this freedom in Christ. It is their idolatry and sin that results in the institutionalizing of some forms of slavery and a voluntary submission to tyrants whose yoke is far heavier than that yoke we would have under the law of Christ (Matt. 11:30).

Therefore, the free man values the debt-free life. Typically, debt will drive a man to seek security in the steady paycheck and the faux security of the corporation or the government; it will also undermine his independence and flexibility. If he becomes dependent upon a corporation, he will be beholden to a corporate agenda that may not reflect his values, and he may be forced to play political games he finds repugnant. But this is often the cost of forfeiting freedom.

Unfortunately, our institutions favor debt and put the debt-free man at a disadvantage. Generally, investors expect nice leveraged profits in an inflating economy, as long as the fractional banking system keeps inflation on an even keel (and recession is averted). Also, provisions such as Attachment A, interest write-offs on income tax, and the capitol gains tax on real estate sales encourage the debt lifestyle. Against all of this the Word of God stands and declares simply, "The debtor is servant to the lender ... and ... "owe no man anything."

Between 1970 and 2000, the decline in the American character betrayed itself through the concurrent exponential rise in government, corporate, and personal debt. As the debt to Gross National Product ratio increased exponentially in the 1980s, one 23-year-old man encountered an overpowering vision for freedom from debt. It took six years to realize that vision. During the early years that this author engaged his initial struggle for freedom, few, if any, financial counselors and investment advisors supported this mortgage-free, debt-free vision. The economic gurus that play the current system will call such an approach imprudent, impractical and even immoral, but they forget the intangibles because they have never experienced the debt-free life themselves. How does debt damage the character, confidence, and inner strength of the human soul? These losses are seldom compared with the gains on the balance sheet of life.

While God does not promise a particular material blessing to each individual that adopts His law as a standard for what is good and right, He does bless nations that submit to Him (Deut. 28:1-13). Therefore, our obedience to Him must come out of a true love for Him, and the blessings are never merited but they are varied and concomitant.

Political freedom may be difficult, if not impossible, to regain when the masses have embraced the security of their chains over the "animating contest of freedom." However economic freedom is more within the reach of the Christian family that desires it than other forms of freedom. Even so, the path towards freedom is long and tedious. The rewards of freedom are great, but freedom is not achieved without sacrifice. Debt free living is not easily achieved. Typically, it is instant material gratification that will trump any other value on the road to freedom. Not many middle-income families would be satisfied to live debt-free in an 800 square foot house at a value of $100,000, when they could live in a house three times that size carrying a $150,000 mortgage.

Yet throughout the 19th century families raised as many as 6-8 children in 800 square foot homes. But over the last century, Americans have come to love material comforts more than the blessings of freedom.

Once the freeman has tasted freedom, he will desire more of it. The debt-free life can birth even more freedom, especially in the pursuit of entrepreneurship. The single most significant drawback facing those who desire the freedom of self-employment is the absence of the steady paycheck. Typically, the man with debts is responsible to pay those debts on a timed schedule. Without a regular and dependable income source, that man would be unable to make the payments and could face potential bankruptcy. On the other hand, the debt free man with savings has the margin to absorb losses and survive the famine years when the crops fail to yield.

When the debt free man is paid on contract, commission, or in direct exchange for his own products, services, or capital, he has more flexibility to prioritize his work days, integrate his family into his life and regulate his own business philosophy and practice. Ideally, it will be the kingdom of God that benefits, because every hour of his work is dedicated to the advancement of God's kingdom. There tends to be less overall kingdom influence when a Christian works deep within a system or institution which is utterly opposed to God's law in its philosophy and policies.

Yet there are still traps on every side of the economic picture. On the one hand, debt undermines a man's confidence and abilities, weakens his leadership potential, and stresses the value of materials over the more essential values of life. However, even the man who is debt free and earns a million dollars a year in some successful entrepreneurial venture can easily fall into the same trap of trusting in himself and his money instead of trusting in God (1 Tim. 6:9, 10, 17, 18). When covetousness and greed replace a passion for Christ and His kingdom, the passion for freedom wanes, and the ship founders. That became the legacy of this country as the First Mayflower ran aground.

All of this presumes that the free man is industrious, frugal, and innovative. He must love his work as God's calling on his life. Those qualities marked the character of the early Americans, well exemplified in many an issue of Benjamin Franklin's hugely popular *Poor Richard's Almanac* which contained such sage advice as: "Industry pays debts, while despair increaseth them ... Be ashamed to catch yourself idle." These character traits come directly from the book of Proverbs in the Bible, and parents especially are responsible before God to work them into the fiber of our children's lives.

Economies cannot survive where the preponderance of hearts are consumed with leisure and where men work for the primary purpose of enjoying leisure and retirement. Because their hearts are in the wrong place, they will live for the present and debt will drive the nation into the ground. The free man achieves great satisfaction, fulfillment, and financial reward from his work, but not without the expense of great pain. Only when hundreds of thousands of men work a lifetime to save an inheritance for their children's children while passing on a vision for God's kingdom first, will we begin to see a brighter future for generations to come.

Saving an inheritance is yet another essential element in the construction of this new Mayflower (Prov. 13:22). As we pass a vision for freedom on to our children, we can help them realize a financial freedom that we never had - a freedom to live free from debt, enjoying the blessing of large families, and making an impact on the kingdom of God with their finances. Yet both federal and state governments will tax as much as 75% of the total inheritance. Imagine spending a lifetime saving an inheritance for your children; and after having paid tax on your income, tax on the interest income, and tax from inflation on the savings over a lifetime of work, the government could take as much as $750,000 of the $1,000,000 savings (depending on where you live and the exemptions for which you may qualify). If there is any doubt that the state has displaced the family and is committed to demolishing family legacy, this should eliminate it altogether! Those who have, by God's grace, received a modicum of vision for their family's future should carefully plan the inheritance; one of the best ways to accomplish this is to take advantage of the gift tax exemption. By combining a $1,000,000 life-time exemption with a $10,000 annual, per child gift allowance, one may still be able to avoid all inheritance taxes on several million dollars.[6] This assumes that the inheritance is passed along prior to the death of the progenitor. But if our children are raised on the principle that they are responsible before God to care for their parents in their old age (Matt. 15:4-6), then this approach to inheritance should work well. Of course, this also presumes that there are strong relationships of trust, love, and care built up within the family over many years. Assuming we have raised our children with strong character and in wisdom and the fear of God, we can strengthen their position greatly if we are able to pass on an inheritance to them as they establish their own households. This may help them into debt free living so as to perpetuate a legacy of freedom for successive generations!

Granted, those who have adopted the present worldview will see no need of taking responsibility for their children's education, providing an inheritance, or even taking care of destitute elderly parents. This is because the only significant relationship left in the socialist state is the relationship of the individual to that state. However, those who can recapture the vision for freedom will renounce government control and funding of the education of our children, save an inheritance for those children, and rely on those children to care for them in their old age. Therefore, the renewal of both family and freedom is simultaneous.

Finally, a free man will be a man of integrity engaging his dominion work in the market place according to God's rules. As almost every one of our founding fathers said in a hundred different ways, freedom is impossible without moral constraints and self-government. Even free

6 One should contact a tax attorney or professional tax accountant before solidifying plans for the inheritance as tax laws change every year. There is significant biblical and historical precedence for passing on an inheritance before the death, in order to strengthen the economic conditions of the generations to come (Gen. 31:14, Luke 15:12, 13).

enterprise can be corrupted when greed begins to dominate the hearts of men and they begin to cheat, lie, and steal. Unfortunately, the last century produced a corrupted capitalism. Labor-management relations broke down through oppression, mistrust, lying, sexual intimidation and economic inequities. The principles of the Bible are basic to the maintenance of free enterprise. "Masters, give unto your servants that which is just and equal, knowing that ye also have a Master in heaven" (Col. 4:1).

If there is anything we can glean from history's battle for freedom, it is this: freedom will never be won without generations of struggle and sacrifice. But it is not an impossible battle if it is waged every day in every home in this country. Our very economic systems are constructed such that they guarantee servitude and lead the populace to seek security over freedom. Entire economic, educational, and political institutions are arranged to guarantee the dismantling of the nuclear family. If the family is going to survive the 21st century, individual families must commit to building back economic systems that will strengthen the bonds of the family unit. Of course each family will develop their own financial vision as they recover the values of family and freedom, but I would suggest the following general strategies for building freedom back into the souls of men, weaning the family from financial dependence upon the state, and bringing the family back as a meaningful socioeconomic institution in the new dark age of humanism:

* Pay for your own children's food and education.
* Work towards a debt free life.
* Incorporate your family into your economic vision.
* Raise your sons and daughters with the idea that they will never have their independent career. They will work as a team with a household economic vision.

* Opt out of social security if at all possible. At the very least do not
  count on a government social security system. Consider your
  contributions to be money thrown away.
* Save an inheritance for your children.
* Do not plan on retiring.

Each one of these strategies is aimed at strengthening the bonds of
the family economically in every place where the modern world has
weakened it.

My intention here is to encourage a biblical view of finances. The
Bible warns us not to trust in riches, to cast our bread on many waters,
to avoid debt, and to give generously to the poor among us. As we
teach our children a good work ethic and use our money to train them
in the calling God has on their lives, we will have invested wisely in the
future.

The Bible also warns us not to run with a crowd to do evil (Prov. 1:10,
11). Before leaving this important subject of economics, I would fail my
reader if I did not warn him of an economic system based on greed and
debt, that has increasingly ignored the future. Such a system is bound
to fail. I would conclude that the best investments are those that are
closer to home and are debt free investments. They are investments over
which you have direct control. When you combine your investment
with those whose hearts are filled with greed and who do not share your
worldview perspective on debt, you will assume the same risks that they
take and you will suffer the same consequences that they will suffer.
Therefore, the ethical perspectives of the corporations and the mutual
funds in which you invest are important. Moreover, monetary systems
operating in most modern states have incorporated some measure of
inequitable "divers weights and measures," something God declares an
abomination (Proverbs 20:10). While these fractional reserve banking
systems may prosper for a short time, failure is inevitable as history has

eloquently illustrated time and again. Take this into consideration as you prepare financially for the Second Mayflower.

A Compassionate Man

Finally, a free man will be a compassionate man. After a one-hundred-year experiment in socialist solutions for the problem of poverty, it is clear that government funding has only exasperated the conditions. When considering the significant rise in inner-city welfare dependence and illegitimacy rates, not to mention the disappearance of fatherhood and the highest incarceration rates in the world, we can't help but conclude that the modern system of redistribution of the wealth has utterly failed. Until we recover the biblical approach to charity which demands love from the hearts of individuals, our communities will be cursed with the counter productive, humanist methodologies. Effective charity cannot be dispensed by impersonal government agents who are only redistributing wealth. Such immoral scams have only served to involve the poor as accomplices in the Marxist thievery. It has perverted their character and destroyed their dignity, all the while discouraging families and churches from fulfilling their responsibility to the poor. Taking the current state of social decline in the light of a biblical view of charity, *one wonders if a single government welfare dollar was well-spent.*

The only solution to this hopeless morass of misplaced intentions is to recover a true compassion as Jesus would have it, in accordance with His laws. This must begin in the family. Instead of leaving our aging parents to the government social security and Medicare programs, we will take responsibility for the care of our aging aunts, mothers, and grandmothers. This is the clear mandate of 1 Timothy 5:4, 8, 16. According to verse 8, failure to take responsibility in this area is a sin worthy of excommunication. It is assumed that only unbelievers would fail to fulfill such a basic obligation. Jesus also confirms this in Mark 7:10-13.

In the case that a daughter is widowed or divorced, it seems that the normative biblical approach in such a situation is that she return to her father's house as in the days of her youth (Lev. 22:13). The family is the first line of offense in economic crisis and should provide a godly form of security. But this will only be the case if those family relationships really exist and if family unity has been cultivated over the years.

Another biblical form of charity is the principle of gleaning on the edges of the fields (Deut. 24:19-21). Since the relative benefit of this form of charity is minor, the reception of the gift may or may not be anonymous. Certainly, it is voluntary charity and cannot be enforced by the state. Nevertheless, this field gleaning did involve a measure of work on the part of the poor that received the benefit. How do private businesses apply this gleaning principle today? Certainly, manufacturing plants could provide partially assembled or defective products (that might consume unwarranted resources to rework) to the poor free of charge. Retail outlets and restaurants may also provide defective or similarly unmarketable resources to the poor without cost.

Also, Jesus' story of the Good Samaritan establishes a pattern for providing relief to strangers in desperate need. When by God's providence, we cross paths with a stranger in similar hardship, we have a duty to intervene. Instead of referring such poor folk to some "Department of Accosted Strangers," Jesus recommends personal attendance to the man's needs. Moreover, a compassionate family will also provide hospitality and personal gifts to local widows and orphans by means of the "third year tithe," which, for the Israelites, amounted to about 3.3% of their annual income (Deut. 26:12ff). Thus, biblical charity requires personal connection and moral accountability between giver and receiver. God's idea of charity requires both sincere gratitude on the part of the recipient and love on the part of the giver - and that is precisely what is missing in the federal and state machines that crunch out millions of welfare checks each month. We should also note that biblical charity avoids the problem of welfare dependence by providing only occasional gifts.

The second line of offense in the biblical struggle with poverty is the church. If a widow is destitute without family and over sixty years old, the church is then responsible before God to take care of her (1 Tim. 5:9-15; Acts 6:1-7). Throughout most of its history, the church typically assigned a full 1/3 of its income to the care of widows and orphans.[7] Regrettably, this is far from the case today and that is one of the reasons why the church is now almost entirely irrelevant to modern social life. One conservative evangelical church in Colorado with a budget of $700,000 would not assign a single dollar to the *diaconate* fund! As long as this is the case, we will never see an iota of change to the social problems that afflict this nation in the cities and across the countryside. Ten thousand more conservative and Christian leaders in politics will be unable to make any appreciable difference in the illegitimacy rates, the burgeoning of government, the abortion rates, or any other problem that afflicts this nation, as long as churches are unwilling to establish a meaningful *diaconate*. When I speak of a "*diaconate*," I refer to a body of men who are assigned the task of attending to the needs of the widows and orphans in the local church (Acts 6:1-7). The billions of dollars that pour through government systems, United Way, and other non-local charities where there are no long-term accountable relationships, will only perpetuate the problems. Those who play a part in the Second Mayflower must begin to rebuild a *diaconate* in thousands of churches that will support tens of thousands of widows in an honest, caring, biblical, church-based charitable system. And the world will wait until the local church assumes its biblical responsibilities outlined in 1 Timothy 5.

All of this assumes that the hearts of the poor will repudiate the anonymous, bureaucratic approach to charity and seek out long-term, local, and accountable relationships in families, churches, and

---

7 John Calvin, *Institutes of the Christian Religion.*

communities across America. Most of the poor will not do this as long as it is easier to take the free handout in a sanitized, relationship-free, anonymous context. If this vision is to be realized in our lifetimes, the Spirit of God must work in the hearts of both giver and receiver to reject a system that perpetuates government larceny, the breakdown of the family, and the moral degradation of the poor.

What makes such an undertaking seemingly impossible is that we are already taxed 40-50% of our income to support a corrupted government system. Under such oppressive conditions, one would think it an impossible imposition on the family to assume responsibility for medical care, shelter, and food for widow and orphan. But consider this: since 1980, millions of families of faith have already reassumed the funding and control of their children's education, while rejecting all government aid in the form of vouchers and tax credits. They did it in spite of the oppressive tax system levied by the modern socialist state that continued to prop up an expensive, failing public school system. God blessed the faith of these home educators. Why would the care of our widows and aging parents be any different? If we were to wait for the tax credits and the defunding of the welfare system before beginning the implementation of a godly system, it may never happen. Herein lies a true test of faith.

The transfer of education back to the family also reordered the economics of education, as it is far less costly and far more effective overall, when families take ownership over that which properly belongs to them. While the average public school student in Colorado costs the state $7200 to educate, homeschoolers like our family can do it for less than $200 per year. (Our family saves the state almost $36,000 per year by home educating our own children.)

The solidarity of the family, economic freedom, and political freedom from big government cannot be realized without family and church returning to biblical norms. For example, political freedom cannot be achieved and maintained without the privatization of charity. Human beings will seek security somewhere - either they will find it with family, church, and local community, or they will turn to government for it.

The Jurisdictional Free-for-all

The purpose of this chapter is to set forth an alternate social context to the humanist power state. Effectively, these two systems mark the difference between the city of God and the city of man realized in social relationship. What Christians work to build and what the humanists work to build are two different things, with a different emphases and different goals in mind.

In a biblical framework, the family and the church are the key social units. The humanist, on the other hand, sees both as irrelevant and works for their minimization or total elimination. Karl Marx was intimately involved in this agenda. Included in his *Manifesto* is this sardonic remark concerning the ideological irrelevance of the church (as of 1848), and the critical importance of eliminating the family as a viable social and economic institution:

> "When Christian ideas succumbed in the eighteenth century to rationalist ideas, feudal society fought its death battle with the then revolutionary bourgeoisie ... But communism abolishes eternal truths, it abolishes all religion, and all morality ... Abolition of the family. The bourgeois family will vanish as a matter of course when its complement vanishes ... The communist revolution is the most radical rupture with traditional relations."[8]

Three spheres represent the three jurisdictions that God has instituted for human social relation - the family, church, and state (Gen. 2:18, 24; Matt. 16:18; Rom. 13:1-5). When men refuse to acknowledge God's law as the standard that lays out jurisdictional limits of each sphere,

8 Marx, *The Communist Manifesto.*

and as the Christian church refuses to teach and apply God's law, a "jurisdictional free-for-all" ensues. The fruits of such autonomy are devastating to life and liberty.

Many of these jurisdictional violations can be attributed to the expansion of the state since 1860. But the church has also contributed to the disorder by assuming its attempt to violate family jurisdictions. The Bible clearly lays out responsibilities and obligations of the church by directing its exhortations towards specific spheres, including husbands, wives, families, churches, and civil rulers. To the extent that we neglect the specific addressee to which God's law is directed, we perpetuate the jurisdictional free-for-all that marks the current age in which the state interferes with the family, the family interferes with the church, and the church interferes with the matters of the family.

For example, the clear mandate of Scripture places the responsibility of the training of a child in the hands of the father. Paul considers this normative in 1 Thessalonians 2:11 and Ephesians 6:4, indicating that there is no perceptible change taken from the Old Testament pattern set forth in Deuteronomy 6 and the book of Proverbs. In fact, this is fundamental to a biblical social system. The health of the church is dependent upon the presence of godly men who rule their households well, for it is only those who rule their own households first who are fit to rule in the household of God (1 Tim. 3:5). Thus, rather than circumventing or displacing fathers in their duties, the church is obligated to equip fathers in the congregation for this ministry work which God requires of them (Eph. 4:11-12). Yet family discipleship and father-led devotions have all but disappeared among families in this country, particularly since the advent of Sunday Schools and children's ministries in the church. It appears that in the minds of parents today, these programs make up the essence of "Christian education." Some denominations will even refer to their committees responsible for the Sunday School programs as "Christian Education." This is a far cry from the biblical normative; Christian education for children is primarily a parental responsibility. To the extent that the church's children's ministries have displaced the father's responsibilities and the family's obligations (laid out by the biblical normative in Deut. 6:7, the book of Proverbs, 1 Thess. 2:11, Eph. 6:4, etc.) in the minds and lives of individuals or institutions, those church's activities should be reconsidered and reconfigured.

Those who study the demographics of the church tell us that the fastest growing movements in the church today are the mega church and home church movements. While it is quite appropriate for a church to meet in a home, unfortunately a sizable proportion of the home church movement is a loosely configured association of friends without a biblical eldership and structure that would provide the discipline and order required in 1 Corinthians 5, 1 Timothy 3, and Titus 1. Occasionally, individual families violate the jurisdiction of the church by taking the sacraments into the home without any consideration of church authority, eldership, or discipline. The jurisdictional free-for-all continues and the biblical social order unravels.

"And every man did that which was right in his own eyes."
Judges 17:6, 21:25

The Recovery of the Church as a Relevant Social Institution

Even as the church fails to maintain the biblically mandated jurisdictions, it also fails to impact a dying culture and has surrendered its own relevance. If we are to engage another Mayflower, we must somehow recover that social unit the Bible calls "the church." I say "recover," because much of what God instituted for the "church" has been lost over the last centuries. From the perspective of this father and pastor, the recovery of the church will be even more of a challenge than rebuilding the solidarity and integrity of the family.

A church is a local expression of the body of Christ that loves one another, preaches the Word of God, exercises the sacraments of baptism and the Lord's Supper (1 Cor. 11:21ff), installs qualified elders and deacons (1 Tim. 3:1-12), and exercises church discipline in accordance with 1 Corinthians 5 and Matthew 18.

Perhaps the most obvious reason why the church is irrelevant in our day is because the tithe is hardly practiced anymore. The average American churchgoer gives 2% of his income to the church, a ratio which is even lower than what was contributed during the Great Depression! With such a low rate of giving, it is impossible for a church to function with any less than 300-400 people attending. This is one reason why churches are increasingly pressed to cross the "200 barrier" and then the "500 barrier" into the mega church. These are real trends. Over the last decade, church attendance has fallen in this country, while the mega churches have grown. I look at it as a last-ditch effort to salvage a church in our generation.

What is the real problem facing the church in America? As the church grows in number without sufficient biblically qualified elders, it becomes almost impossible for two or three pastors to carefully shepherd so many people. Recently, one mega church pastor in Colorado Springs, commented to the secular press on why the divorce rate was higher in the "Christian Mecca" of El Paso County than anywhere else in Colorado. "I feel like I'm re-arranging deck chairs on the Titanic," he said. What has happened is the elder/pastor to congregant ratio is unmanageable. *Often, these pastors do not even know the names of their people!* This inability to create depth in relationship will inevitably force the pastors to water down the message, which will only perpetuate the 2% commitment. It is an impossible catch-22 from which we cannot escape unless we radically reconstruct an all-pervasive biblical social system from the bottom up.

There are two root issue problems here. Preeminent is the devastating lack of godly fathers who rule their own families well, and consequently the lack of godly elders who can rule in the household of God (1 Tim. 3:5). There is a severe dearth of biblically qualified elders in this country, and it is killing the church as an institution. Secondly, the mega church is not growing by the strength of its relationships. Employing the "crowd attracts a crowd" philosophy, it will rely on its employees, its buildings, size, and sheer institutional force to retain its momentum. But the shallow relationships that result only perpetuate the anonymity of postmodern city life. Church discipline becomes a virtual impossibility, and the church must water the message down to the least common denominator in order that it might continue to process the masses through the system. Even its small groups will speak to narrowly defined, common, and therefore, short term interests. Inevitably, these short term relationships will fade quickly once the shallow common denominator that first brought the small group together becomes obsolete.

Are people really getting saved? How much of what we are doing is a lot of wood, hay, and stubble that will burn up when the fires of tribulation burn? If the church is called to make disciples by teaching them to observe everything Jesus has commanded, are we really accomplishing this task? These are the sorts of questions that Christian leaders must answer. If the elders are called to shepherd the sheep, and if they must one day give account to Christ Himself for that oversight (Heb. 13:17), shouldn't they know the names of the sheep? Shouldn't they know when these people are struggling with anger issues or pornography addictions? Even if they knew of these issues, I wonder if they would be able to do what it takes to protect, admonish, warn, comfort, encourage, and strengthen their sheep. Much of this work must be direct, personal, and individualized (Acts 20:20; Luke 22:31; Phil. 4:2, etc.). But what has happened to postmodern shepherding? It is not uncommon for churches to shuffle their members off to Christian counseling centers that offer short-term help at $200 an hour - at least when they reach a Galatians 6:1 spiritual crisis. What a contrast between the non-relational, strictly economic, anticovenantal model of the modern church and that which Christ and the Apostles exemplified for us! Where is the biblical shepherding where real pastors have real relationships with real people over a really long time?

While there are some instances of faithful shepherding, godly fatherhood, family discipleship and relational churches in this country today, this is far from the norm. Instead, shallow relationships, a transient society, and the inherent anonymity in the large church have all served to render the church irrelevant in modern times. As one fellow told me once, "I'm glad we're attending a large church. I don't need to know these people's problems and they sure don't need to know mine." This is what makes in depth, long term discipleship and meaningful moral accountability a pipedream.

After at least 100 years of disintegration, relationships are tenuous things today. Modern man set out to construct all of his social systems *such that they would disallow anything but shallow, short term relationships.* This is why small churches are dying, and the younger generation abandon the smaller towns for the large cities. Anonymity in the city, the university, the corporation, the church, and in the family is the preferred lifestyle today, because that sort of environment conveniently removes the obligation and opportunity to love.

The Problem with the Small Church

It is true that the small churches provide greater opportunity for people to get to know each other, but this is why so few survive. Many will die if they cannot "break the 500 barrier" within a decade or so. Most small churches have learned to whisk their people into a few narrowly defined, age or interest-appropriate small groups or Sunday School classes. Some churches become a narrowly defined group with little integration of ages, maturity levels, interests, and backgrounds. Once the worship service is over, congregants quickly vacate the building limiting human contact in the foyer to a polite greeting or two, "Oh, hello there Mrs. Jones. You look lovely today! See you next week."

Some small churches find that they can stay together for some period of time only if they can define themselves as narrowly as possible and distinguish themselves sharply from every other church. In other words, if they can establish themselves as the paradigm of orthodoxy and subtly imply that all other churches lack in orthodoxy, spiritual maturity, zeal, etc., this forms a temporary solidarity among the members. The members begin to think, "I am part of this group, because I am not a part of all of these other groups." This sort of unity provides some longevity, but eventually these churches split into increasingly smaller groups unless they can be kept together by a charismatic, authoritarian leader.

Many great reformers today preach a strong message of truth, but they have missed the critical component of relationship. I am not saying that truth is unimportant in the unity of the church. But truth may never be alone. It must be joined with humility that prefers others above ourselves and love to the point of sacrificing our lives for our brothers (Eph. 4:1-6).

The Real Test of Relationships

Most leaders in the church are critically aware of the tenuous nature of relationships, and are genuinely concerned about the survival of the church. If people really come to know each other, the depth of relationship will begin to identify their doctrinal and practical differences. This can only mean conflict, and in the experience of most pastors, conflict ruins churches.

Many pastors and elders avoid relationships in their church like the plague and rely on transience to avoid long term, irresolvable conflicts. Too often the pastor becomes a scapegoat for church conflicts, and he relieves the congregation of resolving conflicts and dealing with heart issues by simply transferring to a new church. Today, the average pastor stays just five years with a congregation before he moves on to the next church.[9] As one seminary professor told his practical theology class, "These people are not your friends. If you want a friend, get a dog." But what does such advice have to do with the church of Jesus Christ, who called His disciples "friends?" Of course, they denied Him and abandoned Him on the day of His humiliation and torment. But after that, He died for them because they were His friends. A few days later, He returned with peace on His lips and restoration of His friendships (John 20:19, 21, 26). How have we come to this place where church relationships are as shallow as the world's? The church in America hardly lives out the power of the Gospel of Jesus Christ anymore! The salt has lost its savor.

However, the problem with the church extends far beyond pastors. The hearts of many a parishioner in the modern city bear thick layers of scar tissue from a long history of dishonorable departures and "bad goodbyes." Broken relationships in the family and church community strew the paths of the wanderers. When brothers do not part ways with a clear declaration of peace, they leave with the impression that they are holding something against the other. This usually results in another relationship broken beyond repair, or, at the least, in a pseudo-civil, hyper-superficial relationship. Moreover, when brothers part with unresolved differences, they have to live that way for the rest of their lives, unless they engage in biblical peacemaking. Bad goodbyes signal the beginnings of apostasy and the undoing of the foundational concept of church relationships. Like stretching a rubber band too many times, the very notions of loyalty, brotherhood, and love become meaningless. Often those who have been casualties of too many bad goodbyes will find themselves reluctant to risk new relationships. Each successive relationship becomes even more superficial. Thus, they migrate away from relationships to the more shallow, anonymous system offered in the city of man. And the church as a whole gives up on relationships, peace-making, loving the brethren, and all of "that sort of rot." This is

9 http://www.barna.org/FlexPage.aspx?Page=BarnaUpdate&BarnaUpdateID=98

how the problem of "bad goodbyes" gradually erodes love and unravels the gospel.

Consequently, the very reference to the church as a "body" is void of meaning for many today. The unity of the covenant body of the church is in even worse shape than the family, and I include conservative Presbyterian, Baptist, and Lutheran churches in this assessment. Referring to older men as "fathers," older women as "mothers," and the others as "brothers and sisters" is strange and awkward in those churches where parishioners remain strangers to one another. If we would live the life of Christ in the biblical social covenantal units of family and church, we will find relationships preeminent, and terms connoting *phileo* love predominating in both family and church. As one more obvious example, men who understood *phileo* love would certainly not consider the "holy kiss" as odd (Rom. 16:16; 1 Cor. 16:20; 2 Cor. 13:12; 1 Thess. 5:26).

The Return of Relationships

The ones who are closest to us are the hardest to love. While humanist institutions are carefully constructed in ways which insulate us from this challenge, Christians find great blessing in relationships. These things provide opportunity for the exercise of the fundamentals of the Christian life - forgiveness, confession of sin, and love. As you get closer to somebody, the more you will see of their warts. Such graces as humility, longsuffering, and love can only grow in the seedbed of relationships. There is tremendous spiritual growth that takes place in these relationships, and that can be painful. But the confession of sin, self-sacrifice, and godly sorrow that come in relationship produce repentance unto life.

There are more churches than ever that are serious about renewing long-term, committed, accountable relationships. They are serious about building biblical community. And they have seized upon a single practice to displace the shallow, program-based system - the practice of *hospitality*. This concept derives from the biblical Greek word *phileoxenia*, or "love of strangers." Christians today are rediscovering what it takes to cross boundaries and establish new relationships by means of the biblical practice of hospitality. Again Jesus is our example here, for did not the Son of God Himself cross a *universe* to sit down for dinner with a publican and a sinner? If Jesus can cross boundaries in this way, then certainly we can do the same thing. We can sit down for dinner with a divorcee or a prostitute, instead of placing her in yet another program for "twice divorced children of alcoholics," or a focus group for "recovering prostitutes."

Beginning with those "strangers" within their own congregations, many of these brothers will engage in hospitality for as many as five, ten, or twenty hours per week. While this may cut into their leisure time in front of the television or the computer, a new lifestyle does begin to emerge in this new social construct. Some will open their homes for long term hospitality to accommodate mentorship and discipleship, or to provide closer accountability for singles.

There is no doubt that churches such as these are taking great risks in crossing over into relational living. The message they bring produces a sharp contrast with the dominant man-centered, self-consumed worldview in which most people have been raised. But they bring that message in the context of renewed relationship. They bring a hard message in the hand of love.

Radical things begin to happen in these churches. Instead of loving the world and hating their brother, they actually begin to hate the world and love their brother. By God's grace, there are more sanctified hearts that can actually tell the difference. As the relationship enables depth in conversation, in doctrine and application, the risks of fracture in the relationship only multiply. But wisdom from above is first humble, and it is able to carefully discern between majors and minors in the differences. These doctrinal differences are seen as *opportunities* to exercise love, joy, peace, and longsuffering in the struggle to keep the unity of the spirit in the bond of peace (Eph. 4:1). This is considered a worthy struggle among this people of faith who are building covenant community.[10]

I hope my reader is beginning to see the difference in the two social constructs. The world builds its cities on power bases. We build our communities on God's truth, love, peace, godly penitence, and forgiveness.

Political Freedom

I have already made the point that politics is only a derivative of what happens in the family and church. Nevertheless, as we form another movement towards liberty under God's law, we should not underestimate the power and the commitment of the other worldview especially in this area of politics. The state is the core of the faith for humanists. Make no mistake about it, they are in hot pursuit of increasingly centralized power, even world government under powerful dictatorial rule. To underestimate the zeal of their commitment would be fatal for they are truly, religiously committed to power and the state as savior. If you doubt this, attend an education committee meeting of your local legislature. Indeed, they are committed to the state with a fervency I wish more Christians had for the true and living God.

While being careful not to fall into the socialist trap of assuming the government is the only way to social reformation, we should not neglect involvement in that sphere. But there is never a more important area in which Christians should pick their battles. As one gentleman put it, "You cannot water every plant with your blood." Yet in a field that is almost entirely controlled by a pragmatic ethic, it is essential that we begin with our principles and let the strategy be driven by those principles. God's laws and God's priorities must set our political agenda. Putting it in simple terms, we should first consider where

---

10 The renewal of the church will not happen without a thorough knowledge and application of the principles of biblical peacemaking. Reference *The Peacemaker,* by Ken Sande (Shepherd Press), for an excellent synopsis of these principles.

government is most grievously involved in the wrong things and curtail those activities. Then, we look at its worst sins of omission, and attempt to correct these. Our first concern must be to protect those who are doing the work to rebuild the Mayflower, protecting them from the Tobias' and Sanballats of the world, who long ago did what they could to thwart the work of Nehemiah as he rebuilt the walls of Jerusalem. This is why government regulation of homeschools and family medical decisions are particularly egregious violations of freedom. Secondly, the use of tax money to fund those organizations which oppose life, liberty, and property rights must be opposed. And third, the right use of government to defend the nation and prosecute criminals with the sword is essential (according to Romans 13).

Even as those who are driven by principle over pragmatism in politics, we still seek success in our agenda; or, put in more biblical language, we seek repentance at an institutional level. Therefore, it is important that we make honest assessment of our actions and progress in politics. We should at least state the questions and face the facts. Did the partial birth abortion ban save a single baby? Did George W. Bush increase the size of the federal government (in non-defense spending) more than any president since Lyndon B. Johnson? When Republicans support pro-homosexual policies, what makes them any different from a Democrat president like Bill Clinton? Without honesty, our political efforts will be nothing but a sham and vision fades. We should also honestly reassess our goals. For example, is it our goal to get the Ten Commandments posted on the inside walls of the Tower of Babel, or is our goal, more fundamentally, to dismantle the tower? Do we want prayer in the public schools or would we rather pull the plug on government controlled education? Above all, our children must learn the principles of godly civil government.[11]

11 For the last seven years, Colorado's Christian homeschool organization has sponsored a Future Statesman program in which they have educated literally thousands of Colorado youth in the principles of godly government. Each year these young people come to a "Day at the Capitol" event, complete a workbook, and attend workshops on the relationship of family, church, and state, and the principles of liberty. Other organizations like Teen Pact, Worldview Academy, and Summit Ministries are doing the same thing with thousands of young teens from across the nation.

A free country will falter quickly if it is not built on principled economics and proper government. And there will never be a free haven without a government based on biblical principles and citizens who will maintain that government by electing godly men who are committed to these principles.

The truth of the matter is that in all political realms it is always those who are uncompromisingly evil or those who are uncompromisingly biblical who yield the most influence. You might think of political and cultural trends as sitting on a balance, with a few stalwarts on the far left side of the scale, and a few stalwarts on the far right side of the scale. These are the ones who are most self-consciously committed to their principles. But the bulk of the politicians, citizens, and churches are crowded into the middle and have very little effect on the cultural and political climates. We must teach our children that it is always the few who stand uncompromisingly for what is right who are most effective in swaying the masses and bringing a country to righteous rule and political freedom. One mistake that Christians make is placing their support behind candidates who will never make much of a difference, although they may be identified with the "better" party. This wastes what little time and resources we have for political elections. It would be much better to support principled candidates who would risk all - life, property, and sacred honor (or re-election) for those principles. Moreover, a little political savvy would be helpful. It should go without saying that political candidates lie. Remember, politicians can woo the conservative Christian votes by convincing rhetoric, while their real voting record betrays a completely different story. The most important rule for the voter is to vote according to the candidate's established record rather than relying on campaign positions and slogans. Choose a candidate by his character according to the principles contained in Exodus 18:21 and 2 Samuel 23:3, knowing that his character is more betrayed by his voting record than by the front of the campaign brochure.

Finally, dollars and hours put into a godly campaign in any state can be even more effective than voting, especially if there are few if any godly candidates running for office in one's home district. A Christian should certainly support a godly candidate with his vote, but it is always far more effective to focus support on those candidates that fear God and keep His commandments even if they run in a different district. Occasionally, a Christian finds himself in a state where righteous candidates who fear God are few and far between. He should remember that five hours or $200 donated to a political campaign of a righteous candidate in any district is far more influential than placing a single vote for men who do not fear God in his own district. Typically, it takes only 200 righteous men who are willing to donate $200 to get the 10,000 votes necessary to elect a state representative in a state like Colorado.

Spiritual Preparation

As we purchase the ticket to ride on the next Mayflower, let us remember ultimate freedom is freedom from sin. That is because sin is living in opposition to the purpose for which we were created. The strong hindrances that oppose those of us who have boarded the Second Mayflower are not only the enemies without, but also the enemy within. Isn't it the weakness of the flesh within us that makes us vulnerable to other enemies?

What can stop the Second Mayflower is that which crushes the human spirit. Among other vices, we strive against discouragement, faithlessness, ignorance, slothfulness, lust, pride, and strife. So the question that meets the very heart of our topic is: how can we strengthen ourselves against these vices that would tear us down? To affect any meaningful cultural change, we must achieve spiritual change. In fact, I would venture to say that history is not changed with large numbers of people. Great movements achieving positive good must be spearheaded by those who have achieved some significant spiritual maturity.

America was founded 75 years after the spiritual revival of the great reformation of the 16th century. Then the colonies formed a nation twenty years following the Great Awakening, paved by the preaching of Jonathan Edwards and George Whitfield. The Second Mayflower will be no different in this regard. Without reformation of heart and life, there will be no Christian community; there will be no "city on a hill."

Spiritual maturity will come by way of the powerful, convicting preaching of God's Word in the church (2 Tim. 4:2), the daily study of God's Word in the home (as individuals and families), and, of course, in the application of it in our lives. It comes by faith in Christ's salvation and passionate love for Christ and His kingdom. Where there are no works there is no faith, and where there is no faith there will be no works. These are distinct but not separate in the life of the Pilgrim and the Puritan.

If God is going to bless us in our endeavors, if it is to go well with us in the land that the Lord our God gives us, *we must revive honor for parents.* This has wide-ranging implications for education, courtship, dress, music, and entertainment. Our cultural expressions, music, and art must develop out of an honor for God and an honor for past generations. Honoring parents is a lost concept to a world which has steadily degraded art from Bach to the "rape rap" that takes the Top 40 charts in popular music today. But then again, wasn't the abolishment of the family the humanist, statist agenda? When a teenage son honors his parents, he takes his father's culture, which is his father's applications to God's laws and ties them around his hands and around his neck (Prov. 3:3, 7:3). Of course, he should honor God first, but to the extent that his father's culture does reflect an honor for God and His law, that is where he starts. Then, he builds upon his father's legacy. He stands on his father's shoulders; and this is how cultures advance and righteousness prevails from generation to generation.[12]

12 The San Antonio Independent Christian Film Festival has provided a strong reforming element to culture and art that self-consciously endeavors to honor God and to honor our fathers. Over 1200 producers, directors, photographers, artists, musicians, and culture changers attended the 2007 festival. Reference www.saicff.org.

Finally, as we board the Second Mayflower, we dedicate every area of life to the Kingly rights of Jesus Christ, acknowledging His law as supreme. Then, we continue to search the Bible for purpose, direction, and concrete principles in order that we might apply them in every area of our lives. God's law-word must be applied to our family life, work, government, education, art and entertainment. This has been the vision for the daily radio program called *Generations*, which is now heard in all fifty states and in least sixty countries around the world. On this program, we take the issues of the day, from politics to church relationships, from teenage rebellion to paintball wars and look at them through the eyes of a biblical worldview, with the goal of returning truth and relationships to modern family life.[13]

The Second Mayflower is already afloat and thousands of families are in various stages of preparation for the voyage. Of course, God has placed people in different positions in life and they enter the boat from various vantage points. Some are more focused on biblical economics, some on biblical family life and education, and some on rebuilding the local church. But all of them are bringing truth and relationships back to a lost and lonely world. They build the ship by applying the Word of God to every area of life, self-consciously, with consistency and courage. Being careful not to despise others if their contribution is meager or of different focus than ours, let us encourage one another to this new life of faith. In truth, it is nothing more than living life the way God designed to be lived in family and church. It is simply returning to the sufficiency and life relevance of God's Word, and incarnating it into real life and real relationships. Our goal is a different world than the one we know today where 37% of children are born without fathers, half of marriages end in divorce - and where half of our income is taxed.

It is a life of victorious Christian living! It is the life of blessing.

---

13 Listen to Generations everyday, anywhere in the world at www.kevinswanson.com

7

CHARTING THE COURSE

At what point will you rise to defend what you believe? Is there anything worth putting your reputation or your life in jeopardy? Will you object if your children are routinely indoctrinated in homosexual ideology in the government schools? Will you object if imperfect babies are killed in our hospitals? Will you object if involuntary euthanasia becomes widespread in nursing homes? Will you object if the state tells your pastor or priest what he can say from the pulpit? (In Sweden, an evangelical pastor who preached a sermon on Sodom and Gomorrah was convicted of "verbal violence" against homosexuals and sentenced to a four-week prison term.) Will you object if the church loses its non-profit status and is heavily taxed? Will you object if the state assumes "ownership" of children and tells parents how they must raise them - under penalty of losing custody? Will you object if every teenager in America is given immoral advice and a supply of condoms to implement it? Will you object if each family is permitted only one baby, as is the official policy today in China?

"Will you object if Christian business people are required to satisfy a quota of homosexual and lesbian employees? Will you object if churches are not exempt from that quota obligation? Will you object if universities refuse to grant degrees to outspoken Christian students? Will you object if daughters or sisters or wives are drafted into the military and required to fight in combat? Will you object if obscenity laws are repealed and child pornography is ignored by the government? Will you object if the schools teach 'death education' to students beginning in elementary schools? Will you rise to speak if every tenet of your faith is legislated against in Congress and in your home state? ... Is there any freedom or principle you would defend with your life?"[1]

* * *

Such stirring language like this from a strong advocate for the Christian family in our day attempts to encourage Christians on to some kind of action. But then we must ask: "What action? What do we do next?" Once you have captured a vision for something different, something better than what you have, you still must develop a strategy to make it a reality.

Would, for example, six phone calls to a senator's office and an election of a Republican president solve the problems facing us, restore the family, and build back a moral and a free nation? What about more radio talk programs on the family, a million-man march on Washington DC sponsored by another Christian men's organization, a "Why Wait?" campaign to curb teen promiscuity, and hundreds of rallies, crusades, and conferences? To those of us who have lived through a hundred years of programs, rallies, crusades, and conferences of one sort or another, we wonder how much of these efforts consisted of wood, hay, and stubble.

Let me repeat the challenge I leveled earlier. The principle revived must be fundamental enough to sustain a reformation that would last for hundreds of years, and the applications must be robust enough

---

1 Listen to Generations everyday, anywhere in the world at www.kevinswanson.com.

to incarnate the principles into the way that we live. Having laid out the fundamental principles, we must now find a way to incarnate the principle into real-life applications. So what do we do next?

It should be abundantly obvious from the extensive analysis of present trends contained in the previous chapters, that the family is breaking down, while morality degrades and freedoms wane everywhere in the Western world (and wherever the Western humanist worldview has infiltrated the education systems).

After taking in such a dismal view one cannot help but ask, "When the foundations are destroyed, what will the righteous do?" This could be the most defining biblical passage of our times. Times like these do not call for some mere carpet cleaning, for the foundations of our systems are split clean through to the bottom. Our task, therefore, must be to chip out the old foundation and lay down a new foundation (Jer. 1:10).

The False Premise

Unfortunately, both conservatives and liberals instinctively look towards politics to solve the problems that plague the nation, although they will define the problem differently. This instinct stems from the basically socialist worldview that sees the civil government as the solution to society's problems. Actually, it is this viewpoint itself that is the problem. It is this idea that has undermined the family and destroyed the fabric of our nation.

Considered in a proper framework, the state is only a derivative of the individuals, families, educational institutions, and churches of a nation. Thus, if there is a problem with state policy, it is because there is a problem with the individual hearts, families, schools and churches that make up the nation. While the state should not be ignored as a necessary component of a reformation agenda, it is much more of an effect than a cause; it is more of a derivative than an initiator. Contrary to popular belief, the state has no redemptive element within. It is quite the opposite. Government can further aggravate the problems, well demonstrated since 1865 by the salvific efforts of Western governments with their social and education programs. But as far as improving social conditions by bringing a change about in the hearts and lives of people and families, government is at a loss to accomplish any of this.

This is where the goal of humanists today conflicts sharply with a biblical teleology.

In a humanist world, societies are built upon power centers, structured by government programs. The state imposes itself into every area of human life, and no government institution is more important than its education programs. Set against the humanist concept of society is the Christian concept. The biblical conception of social relationships relies far less on state-enforced coercion. There is no need to impose our ideology by means of government funded schools, art museums, welfare programs, regulatory agencies, and the like. This is not how we change the world. A civil government arranged according to the jurisdictional limits of God's law limits government's purview to defense and justice. When humanists say they "want to make an impact," they always assume a *political impact*. When Christians say they "want to make an impact," they refer primarily to making an impact directly upon the hearts and lives of individuals, families, and churches. We are not building empires. We build faithful families with hearts changed by the Spirit of God. From there we build faithful churches on faithful families. Eventually, communities and civic commonwealths emerge from people whose lives are firmly rooted in healthy, biblical families and churches.

The Limits of Religious Freedom

But how does this happen when there is very little agreement on what constitutes a standard for morality, and when God's law is not seen as the standard to govern society? This is not an easy question, for the limits of pluralism are always a challenge. If multiple communities of Christians covenant together to walk in God's ways, do we prefer Christians for our leaders as the first Supreme Court Chief Justice of the United States recommended? What are the limits of pluralism? Everybody draws the line somewhere. I have yet to meet a pluralist who would invite some religionist that practices human sacrifice into his community and allow him to practice his religion without restraint. The limits of pluralism are set by the proximity of relationships and the depth of convictions concerning certain truths. For example, a local body of 200 believers in a church or a homeschool support group would have a much tighter set of requirements for membership than 2,000,000 citizens of some body politic in an entire state. The limits of pluralism are always spelled out in the founding documents whether that be the Constitution of the United States or the Statement of Faith of the support group.

Nevertheless, every community group and every state will acknowledge a faith of some sort. Humanist states put man at the center and create governments that are humanist, and over time they will build their towers so high they fall down. Christian states set God at the center, create limited governments with limited powers, and maintain bottom-up power structures. They recognize the God-ordained institutions of family and church and their proper biblical jurisdictional powers. And they would allot even less power for county and state governments. When the states federate, they provide an even smaller degree of power to the centralized entity that is hardly an entity but only a covenanted conglomerate of individual states. The limits of the power provided to these governmental entities are severely limited by written contracts called constitutions. These governments are bound in their jurisdictions by the laws of God contained in the Bible. This defines a Christian country. It is, in fact, that unique vision held by the founding fathers of this nation.

What we are setting out to build is a Christian country, but here is the challenge: because it is a bottom-up government structure, it *simply cannot be built from the top down.* It cannot be structured by gaining control of the civil magistrate and manipulating the body politic into a bottom-up framework such as that which I just described. *A Christian country is defined as a Christian social system. If we expect to have a Christian country we must begin by building families and churches that function according to their biblical jurisdictions. It can only be built from the bottom up!*

All of this brings us back to us to the original question. What shall we do now? As long as there is liberty to do so, the godly Puritans and Pilgrims of our day must set themselves to rebuild biblical families and church communities. But we are still left with the question: is it possible to establish a Christian nation when the foundations are destroyed and where almost all of the institutions are anti-Christian? It should be pointed out that those who came to America were motivated by political and moral forces that threatened to hamper the church and seriously hamper the reformation vision held by these fine people. Certainly, such is the case for us today as well. Therefore, if there will be a Second Mayflower, how will it materialize? Either the Puritans will change this place or the Separatists must take it elsewhere. In this chapter, I will review the biblical basis for political resistance and flight.

Political Resistance

"Resistance to tyranny is obedience to God!" That was the war cry of the fathers of this country who fought our War for Independence, and it was the premise of many a sermon preached from Presbyterian and Congregationalist pulpits during those formative years.

As people begin to sense a rising tyranny wrapping its tentacles around them, they immediately begin to wonder about the question of resistance. How does one resist, or should he resist, a tyranny? This concern is evident in Francis Schaeffer's work - an early pioneer in the modern effort to produce a distinctively Christian way of thinking. In his final published work, he considered the use of civil disobedience and force in opposition to tyranny.[2]   "We ought to obey God rather than men," was the policy of the early Apostles who quickly discovered that the message of the Lordship of Christ was an offense to Jew and Gentile alike.

When government policy and other social institutions oppose our world and life view, what does the Christian do? Of course he resists. He pushes back. He insists on change and may even disobey government mandate; but all of this must be constrained by God's laws.

There are, effectively, four kinds of political resistance to which good men have resorted in the history of the world: verbal resistance, civil disobedience, flight, and civil conflict. To the extent that political forces prevent him from living a righteous life in family, church, and business, he is called to resist that force. This resistance takes on different forms for different persons depending on a number of factors including God's unique calling on each person and the political climate.   However, resistance is inevitable when there is a clash of values between the world and the Christian.

The term "persecution" for most of us connotes the torture chamber and the stake, but the biblical term is much broader and includes subjection to any form of opposition, resistance, mockery, criticism, and ostracism. For the Christian, persecution taken rightly is a blessing, one of God's means of purifying, strengthening, and establishing his kingdom in the hearts and lives of men.

There are at least three escalating levels of resistance to tyranny prescribed biblically.

Verbal Resistance

Our primary channels for verbal resistance include lobbying, supporting political action committees, casting a vote for a godly leader, and the use of the pulpit and media to raise a standard for righteousness. Lawful attempts to bring about change in policies, social mores, and

2 Francis A. Schaeffer, *A Christian Manifesto*, Crossway, Westchester, IL.

practices that clearly violate God's law might include communication, media, money, and political involvement. The strategies we use in our efforts to bring about social change should always be framed in terms of God's law. Moreover, one's talents, abilities, and calling are critical in the determination of the strategy. Some strategies have proven to be more successful than others and this ought to be a consideration as well. For example, some argue that sidewalk counseling in front of abortion clinics has been more successful at saving human lives than forcibly blocking abortion clinics at the risk of arrest. Regardless of the outcome of the debate on strategy, suffice it to say that, "the only way for evil to prevail is for good men to do nothing." From the very beginning of the long, sad, historical record of the permeation of evil throughout social and political institutions, good men have always faithfully corrected ungodly policies and actions of tyrants. For example, I think of Elijah, John the Baptist, and Jesus. (1 Kings 19:20-22; Mark 6:14-22; Luke 13:32)

Flight

As man pursues his endless quest for absolute power in every era of world history, he always conceives new tyrannies, violent revolutions and wars. Typically, these horrific circumstances will bring about migrations made up of those families who desire "a quiet and peaceable life in all godliness and honesty" (1 Tim. 2:2). Flight is an unfortunate, but often necessary, form of resistance to which good men and women must sometimes avail themselves. There are a number of examples of flight recorded in the Bible, including Mary and Joseph who took the baby Jesus to Egypt in order to escape the evil hand of the megalomaniac king, Herod (Matt. 2:13, 14, see also Matt. 10:23; 23:34; Heb. 11:37, 38; Jer. 26:20-23; 1 Kings 19; Acts 9:23-25).

Civil Defense

Occasionally, tyrants are not satisfied with tyrannizing their own people and they seek greater power over increasingly large geographical areas. Resistance to these imperialistic forces may be conducted by a small state which has its own organized government and militia (Neh. 4:7-17; Luke 22:36). Such was the perspective taken by this country in its War for Independence in 1776.

Nevertheless, a Christian does not participate in armed insurrections, revolutions, coups, and mobs organized to overthrow governments. Fundamental to a Marxist worldview is the concept of violent revolution, something that tyrants have found useful to foment anarchy, which always gives birth to tyranny. Such revolutions are common in South America, Africa, France, and Eastern Europe since the 18th and 19th centuries when Karl Marx and Jean Jacques Rousseau promulgated their revolutionary ideology for the modern world. Since then, many modern nations have lived the doctrine of perpetual revolution and suffered the mass murder of hundreds of millions as they threw off one tyranny only to invite even worse tyrannies into their civil state (Matt. 12:44, 45).

The Bible contains principles for warfare that should be carefully observed by any who should ever engage in violent resistance. Much of modern warfare does not respect these principles. Those nations that are drawn to a continual state of warfare do not understand the priority of peace. And those anarchists who think the battle for freedom comes primarily by the sword rather than by the preaching of the Word and the building of godly families, churches, and communities still have a humanist perspective. That is because they have abandoned God's law which is the only law system that can effectively balance the one and many, the anarchy of the many and the tyranny of the one.

Perhaps the best example in all of history of one who had the right perspective was Nehemiah who led the effort to rebuild Jerusalem in

457 BC.[3] The men were prepared to fight, but the real project at hand was to rebuild the church and homes for the people. In one hand the men held a sword - but in the other was a trowel. The goal was to build the wall, not to cut human flesh. Therefore, our task at hand is to structure a community on the principles of God's Word first. Then we will have something to defend.

Civil Disobedience

Civil disobedience is arguably a fourth area of resistance. Sometimes it is a favorite discussion topic among liberals, conservatives, anarchists, or anybody who dislikes certain government policies and laws. Unfortunately, civil disobedience tends to appeal to the baser instincts of a man, especially attractive to those who resist authority. Some of the most outstanding Christian theologians and pastors have recognized a role for civil disobedience, including Francis Schaeffer, Samuel Rutherford, and John Calvin,[4] not to mention the Apostles themselves (Acts 5:29).

Nevertheless, civil disobedience should never be seen as anything more than a temporary measure. Some have seen civil disobedience as an excellent means by which to gain media attention and move public opinion in favor of some policy change. But this strategy is far more effective for those who call themselves "liberals" than for those who call themselves "conservatives." As individuals persist in civil disobedience over decades and generations, the possibility of arrest, imprisonment, and execution at the hands of the state increases.

When all legitimate efforts to resist tyranny have proven useless and as the risks of imprisonment and execution rise, serious consideration must be given to flight. For example, the German home educators who have of late refused to check their children into the public schools for state indoctrination with its purely naturalistic and materialistic

3 Reference the book of Nehemiah in the Bible.
4 Reference Francis Schaeffer's *Christian Manifesto,* Samuel Rutherford's *Lex Rex,* and John Calvin's *Institutes of the Christian Religion,* Book 4, Chapter 20, Sections 31 and 32.

worldview are left with little recourse but to flee. This is nothing new. The *diaspora* of the early church in the first century came on the heels of severe persecution in Jerusalem and Judea, but that was the means by which the Gospel reached nations to the "uttermost parts of the earth." While the early movements to New England were motivated by the tyrannical policies of kings and queens, this was also the beginning of the missionary movement of the 1700s and 1800s. The first protestant missionaries in history were ministering with the native Americans as early as 1663.[5] We can rest assured that God has his purposes even for persecutions and *diasporas*.

Reasons to Resist

Indeed, spiritual life seems to be flourishing in nations where the biblical faith is persecuted. When communists took over China in 1949, there were an estimated 700,000 Christians. Mao Tse Tung proceeded to mercilessly persecute these poor people for decades, which turned out to be a less than a brilliant strategy to bring about an end to the Christian faith. As the faithful emerged from what was probably the most severe persecution ever experienced by the Christian church, the number of professing Christians topped 60,000,000. Again, it would be hard to miss the message. Hell's worst rain of fire against the church would do nothing but fortify it for further assaults on hell's gates (Matt. 16:18).

But do you know why these good folks were persecuted? They were persecuted because they refused to register their church with the official "Three-Self State Church," and they still insisted on congregating on Sundays to worship the living God. If they had only registered with the "Three Self Church" or cancelled their Sunday services, they might very well have avoided imprisonment. Yet, while the pastors were imprisoned for twenty years, their children attended the communist schools, receiving a worldview indoctrination that many Christians

5 As a missionary to the Indians in Massachusetts, John Elliot first translated the Bible into a native American language in 1663. It became the first Bible printed in America.

here would find repulsive. Should we condemn these families when they do not fight the battle for parental control of education or the one-child-per-family policy or the egalitarian economic system? Yet they are fighting. They fight their battles against state control over the church, and they suffer for it.

These pastors in communist countries have often commented that, "We are not a threat to the state. All we are doing is preaching the Gospel of Jesus as Saviour." To which I must answer, "Oh but you are, kind sir. You are a threat to the state. If you will not have the state control the church because you hold that Jesus alone is Lord of the church, then you have set yourself against the basic ideology of the modern statists." They have drawn the battle line, and they resist.

Therefore the question for those of us in the West is this: Where is our battle? Where will we draw the lines? We may not be fighting the same battle that our Chinese brothers fight, but where will we fight? Some have said, "Maybe some day we will be persecuted in this land just as our brothers are persecuted in Vietnam or China." Again I must answer, "You can meet resistance with resistance here and now if you so desire."

If we define persecution as resistance, trials, difficulty, and pain or if we define it as taking up the cross and obeying Christ against all resistance, one could do any of a number of things to receive the blessing of persecution, depending on his place in life. Here are several ideas which come to mind. Any parent could engage the struggle for the freedom of the family from government control by pulling his children out of government funded and certified schools. He could stand up in a university ethics class and tell them all, "Homosexuality is clearly an abomination against God and homosexuals must repent of their wicked behavior, as we all need to repent of our sins." Surely that would do more than raise a few eyebrows; expulsion would not be outside of the realm of possibility. It won't be long before such language will constitute a "hate crime." I can think of 1,000 things to do, each one legitimate by the laws of God and illegitimate by the laws and social mores of a relativist age. But I do not intend to specify precisely where each person needs to address the war. Nevertheless, those who refuse to fight at any point are those who contribute to the decline of the faith. We aren't fighting the Chinese battles or the German battles that Christians out there have to fight. *The reason we live in a post-Christian age is because somebody stopped fighting.* In the words of Luther, that great instigator of the first reformation:

> "If I profess with the loudest voice and clearest exposition every portion of the truth of God except precisely that little point which the world and the devil are at that moment attacking, I am not confessing Christ, however boldly I may be professing him. Where the battle rages, there the loyalty of the soldier is proved, and to be steady on all the battlefield besides is mere flight and disgrace if he flinches at that point."[6]

Certainly, we need to be careful not to judge our Chinese brother who isn't fighting the same battles on the same fronts that we are fighting. He is fighting for the right to assemble with brothers in the same house, and he may not be able to address the problem of socialist, secular education. Moreover, it should be obvious that the single man can hardly pull his children out of public schools and refuse to register his children with the state (even as our Chinese brothers refuse to register their churches), and thereby stave off the socialist control of the family. Similarly, not everyone can oppose the self-centered existentialist worldview that doubled the square footage of homes and halved the number of children in the homes since 1900. God doesn't give children to every family equally. Nevertheless, unless and until Christians oppose the gods of materialism, existentialism, and socialism, and draw a battle line *somewhere,* they have given up the battle. We would then

6 Martin Luther, Weimar Ausgabe Briefwechsel 3, 81f.

be pressed to conclude that they have no real faith through which they would overcome the world (1 John 5:4). There must be real, concrete battles and real resistance if we will salvage faith, family, and freedom in the 21st century.

> "Blessed are those who are persecuted for righteousness sake for theirs is the kingdom of heaven." Matthew 5:9

A Time to Flee

The First Mayflower brought pilgrims to the new land who were fleeing persecution in the mother land. Indeed England lost many a devout Christian pastor and their pious congregations between the years of 1620 and 1690. In many cases, the families and churches most committed to the Word of God abandoned England and Scotland because of harsh reprisals at the hands of a tyrannical state. This nation was formed out of an exodus. Therefore it would not be unrealistic to expect to see more flight as migrations and consolidations of godly people form decentralized states covenanted to the one true and living God.

> "If they persecute you in this city, flee to another." Matthew 10:23

Given that Jesus Christ Himself recommends fleeing, how does one discern the right timing for such a move? A full study of the context in which this admonition was given is in order to rightly understand the concept of fleeing. Obviously, the Lord did not intend this to mean a total avoidance of risk. In the same passage Jesus commends putting one's life on the line for the cause of Christ (v. 39). Furthermore, He predicts that some will be arrested and persecuted for the cause of the kingdom (vv. 21, 22, 25, 28). While Jesus sees fleeing as a viable option, He is careful to warn His disciples not to act out of fear of man (v. 28). Rather, the reason for flight is the hard-heartedness of the residents of the city that utterly rejected the message. "And whosoever shall not receive you, nor hear your words, when ye depart out of that house or city, shake off the dust of your feet. Verily I say unto you, It shall be more tolerable for the land of Sodom and Gomorrah in the day of judgment, than for that city" (vv. 14, 15).

Hence, we must never for a moment see fleeing as primarily motivated by a spirit of fear or even self-protection. The leaving is a proclamation of judgment on a city. This was precisely the sentiment expressed by the Puritans who left New England in 1629. Indeed, John Winthrop knew what he was doing from the outset:

> "It wil be a great wronge to our owne Churche and Countrye to take awaye the good people, and we shall laye it the more open to the Judgment feared."[7]

When godly leaders, pastors, and churches leave a city, they take their salt, yeast, and light with them, and the message is clear, "It shall be more tolerable for Sodom than for you in the day of judgment." But the major point Jesus impresses on His disciples is to be careful not to act of out of a fear of man. "For God hath not given us the spirit of fear; but of power, and of love, and of a sound mind" (2 Tim. 1:7). Whether one is abandoning a business, an investment, a school, or a city, he must never act out of fear of men or the circumstances surrounding the situation. Fear is the wrong motivator, and if the decision to act is based in that fear, it will be a bad decision.

I would conclude, therefore, that any efforts on the part of reactionaries to escape government tyranny that are based in fear are bound for failure. Unfortunately, there is a great deal of paranoia among those who have witnessed abuses of power.

---

7 Morgan, *The Puritan Dilemma: The Story of John Winthrop*, Little, Brown, and Company, Boston, MA, 1958, p. 41.

A Community of Pilgrims

A careful review of the First Mayflower and the things that contributed to its remarkable success would quickly center upon the value of covenant community. While there were the "adventurers" who participated in the movements to the new world, most of the early migrations came as covenant communities already intact. *They fled together.* In fact, the first settlement in Plymouth, Massachusetts was a church community which had already moved as a unit to Holland. Later, a significant portion of the community came aboard the *Mayflower* to America under the leadership of William Bradford. If there had not been strong covenant bodies of believers already established in England, these early ventures would have been an utter failure. These folks came as brothers and sisters who were willing to *live and die together*; and this they did. Their commitment to each other enabled them to establish community and agree to a form of government under incredible hardship in America. Granted, there was not perfect unity. Problems with dissenters like Anne Hutchinson and Roger Williams surfaced within a few decades. However, there was sufficient unity amongst them to create a commonwealth. It was a unity that had already been forged in England before they came, developed under the duress of persecution at the hands of the state.

In recent years, I have witnessed several attempts to create "Christian" communities out of a motley collection of dissenters, curmudgeons, and independents. These efforts seem to inevitably end in embarrassing failure. They lose sight of a common enemy or the common vision. Eventually, every disagreement becomes "a hill to die on" for both parties. Love, joy, peace, and longsuffering often come at a premium in the relationship. If the covenant community has never learned to resolve differences biblically and maintain peaceful coexistence, the project will surely be a total loss from the outset.

In the 17th century, people lived in the same community and attended the same church together for hundreds of years. Today, relationships are shallow because they are transient and because our cities and mega churches have created opportunity for almost total anonymity. Therefore, without the restoration of true community in the hearts and lives of men and women here and now, there will be no hope for a Christian community in the future. The Second Mayflower begins when the hearts of a people begin to seek out relational living in Christian community. In a day where the individual and state (civil government) are the primary entities, the family and the church must be restored before we will see renewal of a Christian community. Remember, our present institutions have been carefully arranged as to ensure shallow, short term relationships and anonymity within the church, which in the end disallows any real shepherding and church discipline. This kind of community simply doesn't exist when solitary men and women meander through four different churches in six years, participating in five or six different small groups in ten years. Is not this merely the perpetuation of the same anonymity and shallow relationships of the modern world? This may explain why the church is powerless to re-structure social relationships. It also explains why biblical social systems seem strange and idiosyncratic to millions of Christians who have grown accustomed to the ways of modern life. Unless we can revive true Christian community where love, joy, peace, and longsuffering have the opportunity to grow and function, we are offering no reasonable alternative to the modern socialist state.

I pose the question to my reader: if the tyranny in America should get any worse would your church, as a body, be willing to move 3,000 miles to a new land? What would it take to make the decision as a body? Of course it would take persecution. But it would also take time to establish those relationships. If a body stays together long enough and is willing to work through difficulty, conflict, trials, and the challenges of life together, that is enough to establish the requisite strong bonds. Generally, it would take a minimum of ten to fifteen years for this to happen. Yet, think about how the average church changes its membership dramatically over that length of time. The transience of the body makes it almost impossible to do what the first Pilgrims did. Only a church community that had stayed together for many years, having grown in honor and love for one another, could have faced such a challenge as they did. The Second Mayflower will begin right now with the restoration of relational living in family and church and true Christian community. Chapter six laid out the necessary preparations for such a journey.

When the Pilgrims Fled

We are amazed to see the faith of the Pilgrims who first left England with their unlicensed pastor, then abandoning Holland as well as their youth were corrupted by other youth in Leyden. One wonders what they would have thought about the American public school today where evolution is taught in the science room and the gay and lesbian club meets every other Friday in the cafeteria, while the amateur thespians make generous use of the "F" word and take the name of Christ in vain in the theater building. I wonder if they would have found this place corrupting.

The Pilgrims fled England because they thought they would have a better shot in the new land at raising godly families, establishing the kingdom of God, and worshiping God free from state control. It turned out to be a good call. America did provide opportunity for the Christian faith and church to flourish, and that heritage continues on, even through a two-hundred year decline into the modern humanist state.

On one hand, the Christian is one who can endure persecution and holds to the hope that one day he will stand in glory with Christ. In the words of the Apostle Paul, "To be absent from the body is to be present with the Lord, which is far better." Yet the man of God still retains a strong sense of responsibility for his tasks on earth. So he is not afraid to die, but neither does he shrink back from the battle on this side of the river. Take for example the father who feels his responsibility for providing his family's physical provision lest he be found "worse than an infidel" (1 Tim. 5:8). He feels a deep obligation to raise his children in the nurture and admonition of the Lord, and he would rather not leave them to the *paideia* of John Dewey, Hollywood, and MTV. We must do all in our power to protect our own lives without disobeying God's laws. The delicate balance to strike between resistance and acceptance, between risks and responsibility, is found only in Wisdom. What do we resist, when do we resist, and how do we resist? I believe that we can combine biblical principles with historical lessons and find a way to navigate the perils that lie before us.

So is there ever a time when a Christian is impelled to escape an impending persecution? When does one make that decision to escape tyranny sweeping over his country? This kind of question is of life-or-death import. It is a question that should certainly have been answered by Christians in pre-revolutionary times like 1770s France, 1890s Russia, 1930s Germany, or even in present day America.

Why Would We Flee?

A variety of factors play into such a decision. Taking in the big picture, a believer is concerned first with the kingdom of God. A life lived for the highest purpose of all is a life lived for that kingdom. To the extent, therefore, that the kingdom would be better served in some other place, one should consider such a move. "Seek ye first the kingdom of God and His righteousness, and all these things will be added unto you" (Matt. 6:32). The driving principle simply cannot be financial prosperity or personal comfort - the factors that appear first on the list of materialists. If persecution and resistance is serving the kingdom of God well where you are, then perhaps it would be good if you stayed where you are.

Some have accused the Scottish reformer, John Knox, of cowardice for his retreat to Geneva or England when his life was threatened at the hands of the Queen. But sometimes there are men who are of better service to the kingdom of God on earth alive than they would be dead.

One's marital status is also a serious consideration when facing a persecuting state. This seems to be Paul's point as he commends singleness for the "present distress" in 1 Corinthians 7. Bearing less responsibility for a family's sustenance, those men in the unmarried state will experience more of a freedom to risk imprisonment and death. Under a persecuting state like today's Germany, it would be harder for a married man to engage his kingdom work which is, *first and foremost*, the right ruling of his household and the bringing up of his children in the nurture and admonition of the Lord. As parents, our primary mission on earth resides in our homes. Even if we were barred from the streets, church buildings, and media, we would need to instruct our children in the ways of God. This is our first and most important responsibility in the kingdom of God. But when the state imposes on family and church, which happen to be the spheres where the core work of God's kingdom is done, good men must seriously consider flight.

The Bible also gives the father responsibility for protecting the lives of his family members (Neh. 4:14; Ex. 20:10). The Westminster Shorter Catechism addresses the Sixth Commandment with the following question and answer:

"What is required by the Sixth Commandment?"
"The Sixth Commandment requires all lawful endeavors
to preserve our own lives and the lives of others."

Again, the interests of the kingdom of God will, at times, trump the value of our own lives. It is never a dishonor to give up our lives for the kingdom of God; indeed, that is what is expected of any follower of Jesus Christ. Nevertheless, a father has an obligation to protect the lives of his precious ones - his little piece of the kingdom - and that may involve removing his family from some city or state if persecution or criminal activity threatens life and limb.

Another City on a Hill?

Perhaps the bigger question that Christians must consider is whether there really is an opportunity to better the kingdom of God elsewhere. Often, people make moves because they assume that anything must be better than their present condition. But, as the common expression goes, they move out of the frying pan into the fire, or even into another frying pan. Before considering a move one must be sure that there is ample opportunity to raise up another city on a hill elsewhere.

The blessings of a Christian country are inestimable. Think of the unprecedented freedoms and prosperity enjoyed in this country. Despite great diversity of cultures, this nation retained its constitutional foundations with its bill of rights for nearly one hundred years before it began to centralize power. By the turn of the 20th century, America had also become the largest missionary-sending nation in the world. When Christian missionaries are backed at home by a strong political force that supports the Christian faith (as this nation once did), they will enjoy some measure of protection while they do their work in pagan or Muslim countries. Another Mayflower will give Christ's advancing kingdom another foothold in the strong man's house (Mark 3:27). Political strength can be, and has been, used effectively to facilitate the free delivery of the Gospel to the darkest strongholds of Satan.

Generally, the combined effect of 50,000 people in one area who have covenanted together can yield more salt and light than 50,000 individually fragmented people could. As the righteous/unrighteous ratio in the populace drops, at some point, the impact of the few righteous men dwindles and their net effect is far less than what could be produced if they covenanted together. When a few good people gather in one area and base their community and government on godly principles, freedom and prosperity will flourish. The diluted effect of the few principled people scattered around America has done nothing to quell the general drift towards tyranny. If there had been ten righteous men in Sodom, God would have preserved that fertile country. But alas, there was but one and the destruction was inevitable. When Jesus speaks of the righteous as salt and light in Matthew 5, the second person, plural is used. "You all are the light of the world." It is the combined effect that is important.

In our world economy today, any nation blessed by God will stand out like a city on a hill. Other countries always benefit from the economic prosperity of a free, God-blessed country. As productivity exploded in the United States as a result of political and economic freedom, other nations (not controlled by Marxist-Leninists and other tin-pot dictators), such as Japan, Taiwan, Philippines, and South Korea benefited greatly. These countries borrowed technology, engaged in trade, and received missionaries who taught the faith and life of the Old and New Testaments of the Bible. With the added blessing of another Mayflower, some nations will receive the blessings that always attend true godly faith and some will also receive the faith that produced the economic blessings as well. Either way, they are blessed.

When the nations come to trade freely with a God-blessed nation, they will ask, "Who is this God who has given this people such freedom and blessing?" Will they miss seeing thousands of inner-city children born into the world both welfare and crack-dependent? Will they miss the unraveling of the family, the 50% divorce rates, and 37% of children born without fathers? Will they miss the retirement institutions filled with elderly people, forgotten by all but some well-paid social worker? Will they miss the abortion mills, the pornography shops, the branding and tattoo parlors, the raw numbers on the top-40 charts extolling the virtues of rape, murder, and suicide? Will they miss the campus mass murders at the hands of students who really believe in "natural selection?" Will they miss the 50% taxation on money exchanging hands? Will they miss government regulation on every movement of innocent citizens while the common peace is daily held hostage by street thugs? Will they miss the prevalence of drive-by, random gang shootings, the convicted murderers and rapists walking the streets, the ubiquitous, sue-crazy litigants, and the arbitrary "justice" of the modern humanist state?

When the poor, the down-trodden, and the oppressed come to our shores escaping the brutal tyranny of socialism and other totalitarian schemes, what will they see? Will there be great opportunity? Will they see our free enterprise, our limited government, our safe streets, and our fair justice that is not afraid to exercise biblical law? Will they take note of our families - solid and strong - children raised with faith and character, and education systems that yield strong, competitive, productive economics? Will they find generous, voluntary charitable systems, millions of fathers who disciple their children for Christ as they sit in their house, families who tenderly care for their own elderly, and churches that preach the Bible? Only then will they ask, "What other nation is so great, and what other nation is so great as to have such righteous laws?" (Deut. 4:6-8). These are the blessings of a Christian nation. This is the City on a Hill of which Winthrop spoke. It is the vision rooted in the biblical principle that non-Christian nations benefit from the light of one Christian community (Is. 60:3-16).

Second Mayflower

8

THE NEW WORLD

The rapid social and political changes of the last 100 years, engulfing most of the civilized world, destroying the family, and increasing the power of the state is enough to stagger all human comprehension. Never in the history of the world has such a radical agenda overtaken so much of the world in such a short time-frame! The changes are both ideological and technological. Of all the technological changes that have taken place, travel and communication are probably the most important. Travel is now relatively easy and communication virtually instantaneous. These things make for a smaller world and a more homogenous socio-political situation among developed (or developing) nations. The worldview that guides most political states in Africa, Asia, Europe and the Americas is that which was formulated by Karl Marx and Jean Jacques Rousseau. With the incorporation of a basically humanist and socialist construct in most Western countries, at present the world seems to be torn between only two basic worldviews: Islam and Secular Humanism. Although the secular humanist nations are still somewhat affected by a heritage of 1,500 years of Christian thinking, there is little of that heritage remaining in the cultural lif of these nations.

Even countries that have received some semblance of a Christian "gospel" never really received a strong Christian worldview, or a biblical metaphysic, epistemology, and ethic. While Christians may hear something about a Savior named "Jesus" in a church service, the rest of the week they are educated in secular humanist schools and colleges. Whether they live in Japan, New Zealand, Indonesia, the United States, South Africa, or Russia the teaching is almost exclusively rooted in a metaphysic based upon evolutionary thinking and a purely naturalistic materialism. Thus, the approach most "Christians" take to education, economics, family, gender roles, and politics is far less informed by the Bible than by John Dewey, John Maynard Keynes, Betty Freidan, Karl Marx, or Jean Jacques Rousseau. This contributes to a relatively homogeneous socio-political situation the world over, at least among the developed nations.

Where the Christian faith has penetrated new territories like Africa and South America, it is a mile wide and an inch deep. A gospel stripped of a God-centered worldview will not penetrate very far into culture and life. While I do not want to disparage the missionary work that has been done over the previous two centuries, the trade-off of quality for quantity in the work of the church becomes counter-productive to the kingdom's interests. As the fire burns, it reveals far more wood, hay, and stubble than gold, silver, and precious stones (1 Cor. 3:12, 13). If the faith is so weak that it can no longer influence social and political institutions with a God-honoring law-order and life, then the gospel message has become too thin on truth and it leaves little hope for another Mayflower in any other area around the world.

The previous several centuries have produced a widely dispersed faith which has lost much of its "saltiness." And, while pockets of individual faith exist here and there, little depth of faith is evident in human relationships, Christian communities, economic relationships, and political covenants. Our task for upcoming generations is clear. From the remnants of Christian faith found dispersed throughout the world, we must begin to form concentrated centers of faith - building godly families, churches, and communities that reflect the principles of God's Word.

The Destination for the First Mayflower

Should any fledgling group of faithful men and women envision another haven of freedom or that city on a hill, where would they begin the construction of the ship? It would be good to first consider the example set by the Pilgrims aboard the first Mayflower. Remember that it was the Protestant Reformation which laid the groundwork for the venture; it provided a highly concentrated form of Christianity, individual piety, family worship, and strong church covenants. Our Christian forefathers chose a barbarian land which was relatively unpopulated, rich with mineral resources and untouched by Christian civilization. They moved off the map to a land where few cared to go. They came with very little technology and built a civilization from the ground upwards. They came with a vision to build a country on the principles of the Bible. They came with a resolute, immovable faith in God, confident that their venture was indeed part of the will of God. They came with a long-term vision, fully aware that they may not be raptured within ten years following their arrival. They dug in for the long haul and built Christian educational institutions, Christian government, and a Christian culture, the echoes of which can still be heard faintly across our country to this day. They built a godly culture with great commitment to God, at great risk to their own lives and fortunes. This was their commitment.

It was only a small minority that led the movement for the first several decades. Four hundred settlers made Virginia by 1609. Nine years later, the population stood at 1,000, and by 1640 the population of the American colonies had reached 40,000. Still, this constituted less than one percent of the six million that populated the English isles at that time.

Some Nations are More Free Than Others

Here at the beginning of the 3rd millennium AD, it is helpful to review the present state of the nations of the world in terms of the biblical values of freedom and morality. There is much homogeneity across the developed nations, but there are also remarkable differences. By contrasting several different world surveys on economics, faith, values, and church attendance, the impact of worldviews made on the socio-economic situation of the nations becomes obvious. Five hundred years after the Protestant Reformation, it is still truly amazing to witness the long-lasting and deep-seated effects produced on world economies.

First, consider the Heritage Foundation's Freedom Survey. This annual study of economic freedom bases an overall index value on specific indices such as freedom from regulation, free trade policies, government taxation, monetary freedom, investment freedom, financial freedom, property rights, freedom from corruption, and labor freedom. What follows is a summary of the results for 2007:

The Ten Most Free Nations	Index	The Ten Least Free Nations	Index
Hong Kong	89	North Korea	3
Singapore	86	Cuba	30
Australia	83	Libya	35
United States	82	Zimbabwe	36
New Zealand	82	Burma	40
United Kingdom	81	Turkmenistan	43
Ireland	81	Congo	43
Luxemburg	79	Angola	43
Switzerland	79	Guinea-Bissau	45
Canada	79	Chad	46

According to this particular study, of the ten most free nations in the world only Luxemburg has a heritage of Roman Catholicism. The other nine countries are predominantly Protestant nations, or in the case of Hong Kong and Singapore, impacted by the Protestant worldview by virtue of their long term colonial relationship with

Great Britain. On the other hand, the most economically oppressive nations in the world hold their strongest religious commitments to Islam, Animism, Communism, and Theravada Buddhism (in the case of Burma). The authors of this study recognize a connection between economic blessing and economic freedom noting that "the world's freest countries have twice the average per capita income of the second quintile of countries and over five times the average income of the fifth quintile of countries."[1]

Of course, economic freedom is not the only measure of freedom, especially if many, if not all, of the nations studied have consciously rejected God's laws as a standard for their institutions. However, to the extent that there is less stealing and political dishonesty in one nation over other nations, we have to acknowledge that there must be some remnant of a subscription to the eighth commandment still extant there. But this does not necessarily mean that these nations are subscribing to the other commandments of God. Economics does not give the whole story. For example, Mexico still protects the right to life for the unborn, something our nation has neglected since 1973. Portugal retained its pro-life commitment until 2007. It would seem that the right to life should be at least as fundamental as the right to property.

Another organization (the World Values Survey) produced a helpful study which contrasts nations that retain a strong commitment to "religious" or "traditional values" with those that claim "secular-rational values." (The study defines traditional values as strong parent-child ties, deference to authority, and a rejection of divorce, abortion, and euthanasia.) The nations most committed to traditional values in this survey include El Salvador, Puerto Rico, Venezuela, Nigeria, and Columbia. Finally, the nations which have almost entirely rejected traditional values include Japan, Sweden, Norway, Finland, Estonia, Bulgaria, Russia, East Germany, West Germany, Czechoslovakia, China, Netherlands, and Denmark. As might be suspected, America,

1 Ibid.

Portugal, Poland, and Ireland are the swing on this survey[2] which means they are already experiencing a value transition. Also of significant note, these are countries where church attendance remains relatively high. The following table provides church attendance by nation, and some correlation with the above values survey should be immediately apparent:[3]

Nations with Best Church Attendance		Nations with Worst Church Attendance	
Nigeria	89%	Russia	2%
Ireland	84%	Japan	3%
Philippines	68%	Sweden	4%
South Africa	56%	Iceland	4%
Poland	55%	Estonia	4%
Puerto Rico	52%	Finland	4%
Portugal	47%	Denmark	5%
Slovakia	47%	Norway	5%
Mexico	46%	Latvia	5%
Italy	45%	Azerbaijan	6%
United States	44%	Belarus	6%

The United States lags several decades behind nations like Sweden, Russia, or Holland when considering "progressive" social trends. For at least one hundred years the battle for secular humanism has waged hot in this country, yet its biblical foundations were much stronger than anything Russia, Japan, or Holland had ever known. Even the pilgrims who left Holland in 1619 did so while noting the nation's distinct lack of Christian piety and unsavory influence on their youth. Meanwhile, Russia's access to a Christian world and life view was severely curtailed for the lack of any substantial reformation influence during its 1,000-year Christian history.

2 http://www.worldvaluessurvey.org/
3 http://www.nationmaster.com/graph/rel_chu_att-religion-church-attendance

One should note from the above data that almost every nation which has embraced secular humanist "values" has a history of significant Christian influence and has received the concomitant blessing of material prosperity. It is only the poverty-stricken nations like Columbia, Nigeria, and El Salvador which hold on to any semblance of family solidarity, strong parent-child ties, and an aversion to abortion. The rest of the West has willingly sacrificed the values of family relationships on the altar of materialism. Even in this country, while the birth rate dropped from 4.0 to 2.1 between 1900 and 2000, the average square footage of homes doubled in size. Such statistics betray the real values that have settled into the hearts of men in the modern age who, evidently, have come to love dry wall and mortar more than children.

The pattern is unmistakable and repeats itself again and again in history. First, a nation enjoys the blessing of a Christian heritage in the form of a biblical world and life view, with the attendant blessing of maximum possible freedom in the marketplace. Peace and prosperity inevitably come with this freedom. But what follows almost immediately on the heels of prosperity is rebellion as the nation turns to money and materials as its chief value and purpose in life. Instead of trusting God and being grateful to Him who gave them these blessings, their trust shifts to themselves, their money, and their institutions.

"God resists the proud, but gives grace to the humble." 1 Peter 5:5

The lesson from both history and scripture is clear. God works with the humble and, in the words of Jesus, how difficult it is for a rich man to enter the kingdom of God! He is far too self-secure in his riches. This does not mean that it is impossible for a wealthy nation to fear God and walk humbly before Him, because nothing is impossible with God. But it does mean that God draws near to the humble and rejects the proud. Multiple warnings in scripture make it plain that rich people and rich nations are easily taken in by the traps of wealth and materials (1 Tim. 6:9-11, 17-19; James 5:1-5).

We must conclude therefore that the blessing of another Mayflower - another nation that might receive a blessing from our bountiful and faithful God - is not possible with a proud people. However, may be possible if a people is humbled by economic distress, disease, war or persecution, and it must be a people humbled under the mighty hand of God. So, you ask, where will the next Mayflower take place if it is to be? It will probably come where least expected, in an obscure corner of the world with a humble people who will face hardship, pain, and loss with courage and faith in God.

A Brief Analysis of Several Nations

The age of colonial rule is over. Much of the impetus behind colonialization came from man-centered empire builders seeking power and wealth by mercantilism, and the fruits of it have been less than stellar. In some countries, such as Hong Kong, the Philippines, Singapore, and America, the transition to self-rule was successful. But across the continents of Africa and South America, the transition was rough; to this day hardly a nation on those continents has been capable of self rule without giving way to civil wars, communist dictatorships, or criminal anarchy. Colonial states like South Africa and Zimbabwe were beneficiaries of Western Christianity by way of the Dutch, but the worldview heritage was shallow, the impact upon the native populations minimal, and these nations have been torn apart by virulent criminal elements, Marxism, and dictatorships.

Australia and New Zealand provide interesting possibilities. Though they have imbibed deeply of the secular humanist worldview and their Christian foundations lack the depth of the United States, their overall "freedom index" is still as high as that of the United States. Nevertheless, a self-conscious commitment to a biblical worldview among the populace, or even among a remnant, is still barely in evidence.

The United States

Truly, no other country can claim a righteous heritage as rich and as deeply ingrained as America. At the beginning, it was a vision for a "city on a hill," a vision that yet lives in the hearts of those who still remember and cherish it. Thus, in the opinion of this author, it is inevitable that the first Mayflower will give birth to a second. If there will be another Mayflower it will begin in the hearts of those who are heirs of the first. One nation today produces most of the Christian curriculum for Christian schools and homeschools. One nation has produced a massive homeschooling movement with a legal support system that influences governments all over the world. One nation has produced the vast majority of Christian worldview academies, creation ministries, and radio programs that call for an application of God's Word to all of life. Though it may be but a remnant holding out against the force of humanist domination in virtually every institution in the West, this remnant still constitutes the heart and soul of a self-consciously consistent Christian worldview in a world dominated by humanists and Muslims.

This slowly building Christian undercurrent is contributing to a definite polarization in the United States. The socialists and humanists are increasingly committed to their ideologies while those interested in freedom based on biblical law are becoming even more committed to their position.

Over the centuries, this Christian nation was able to retain a strong unity despite its widely varying cultures. But now a dangerous mixture forms as a widening diversity in languages and cultures combines with the breakdown of the Christian faith and a rejection of biblical law which would have enabled a healthy form of cultural diversity. Only the law of God, Who is the One and Many, will provide for maximum unity and diversity in human society.

As the polarization widens between those who embrace abortion, homosexuality, and socialism and those who reject such lifestyles, the nation will have its hands full with other sources of disunity, not to exclude the cultural, economic, and political elements. Either this nation must return to its original covenants, including the decentralized federalism embodied in the original intent of the U.S. Constitution, or it must face the consequences of its own demise. So, if the next Mayflower comes out of the first, either the nation will return to its original commission or we will be forced to start over again with a similar vision.

This is why it is critical to understand the debates that surrounded the issuing of the founding documents of this nation, whether it be Patrick Henry's cautionary notes made on the floor of the Virginia convention, James Madison's Federalist Papers, or the debate over the first three words of the Constitution. Should the Constitution have begun with "We the people," or "We the states?" A seemingly minor issue spelled out the real difference between two philosophies of government. Our children, especially, should carefully study the writings and speeches of the men who were torn between covenant and empire in the century following the adoption of the Constitution. What they will learn is that the difference between freedom and tyranny or between empire and covenant always comes down to a heart commitment to either God or man. It is the difference between pride and humility. All nations will rise and fall on the very same things on which individuals rise and fall: pride, lust, and idolatry.

If the Second Mayflower grows out of the first, it is critical that both we and our children thoroughly understand the first founding of the nation. Of course the founding fathers made mistakes, but we must teach our children that as long as sinful men initiate new projects, they will always plant the seeds of their own demise at the beginning. This teaches us that our confidence must always be in God, not in mere men. But God still gave us these men as examples, and we stand upon their shoulders.

Should the United States disintegrate for its abandonment of the unifying principles that could hold a diverse nation together, Christians will be pressed to decide whether to continue to support a form of union or rebuild another federal republic.

Federal control over the states has increased dramatically since the early days of the Republic, far more than even the reluctant Patrick Henry could have predicted. First came the 14th amendment. Then a Federal Reserve Bank centralized control of the monetary system and direct taxation by means of the Internal Revenue Service. As the federal government continued to fund and legislate beyond the strictures of the U.S. Constitution and enforced a host of funded and unfunded mandates, the lines that once distinguished the states on the map began to blur and then they disappeared altogether. We have come a long way since the Virginia and Kentucky resolutions of 1798:

> "Resolved that the several states composing the United States of America are not united on the principle of unlimited submission to their general government but that by compact under the style and title of a constitution for the United States and of Amendments thereto, they constituted a general government for special purposes, delegated to that government certain definite powers reserving each state to itself the residuary mass of right to their own self-government; that whensoever the general government assumes undelegated powers, its acts are unauthoritative, void, and of no force."

Combine the expansion of federal powers with the states' present level of dependence on the federal government, and it is hard to imagine that the states will ever regain any more sovereignty, short of some crisis point. But this problem is inextricably tied to Benjamin Franklin's statement, "Either you'll be governed by God, or by God you'll be governed." Tyranny becomes inevitable when the people refuse to govern themselves by the laws of God. Without a core foundation of self-government, family government, and church government, there will be no bottom-up government in the civil sphere. Power will continue to flow uphill.

Secession

Secession is still a favorite item of discussion among some conservatives and patriot groups in this country. But what these activists forget is that the nation is made up of states, and the states are made up of people who have consistently voted for centralized government and candidates that increase taxes and state spending. In fact, it would hard to find a state government anywhere that has not increased state funding as a percentage of the people's income over the last one hundred years. Unless and until we build institutions on biblical principles within the state, secession is another worthless pipe-dream. As long as education is conducted in a socialist context paid for by the state, as long as the government taxes property and inheritance, and as long as the family and the church remain dysfunctional, we might as well continue to live with centralized government.

Charting the Course

Restructuring a civil government to a worldview like ours does not come about by revolution, but by slow and steady rebuilding. This does not preclude a providential opportunity brought on by a crisis sometime in the future, but the opportunity will only present itself to a people who have already regained a vision, and who have the foresight to act upon this vision. For now, God has given us the opportunity to build family and church communities and to educate our children on the principles of a biblical world and life view. And we are building.

As I pointed out in chapter five, the Second Mayflower was born in 1960. The ideas revived in those early decades now take shape in the way we raise our children and in the way we live our lives. Compare this with the First Mayflower. God opened a door of opportunity for our Pilgrim and Puritan forefathers about 75 years after the spiritual revival and reformation that formed these people groups. These were the men and women whose faith laid the foundation for the movement that turned into America. If the first Mayflower provides any pattern for the second, the opportunity for another Mayflower could present itself in the lifetime of our children or our grandchildren.

Western Civilization has entered the dark ages of humanism. Disguising itself in terms like "progressive" and "liberal," humanism has institutionalized both existentialism and gender egalitarianism in lieu of the biblical family and church. Humanist ideologies are now firmly entrenched in lifestyles, in education, the university, economics, politics, church and family. What are the fruits of such a world and life view, self-consciously realized and lived out? Within just a few generations, the existentialist, self-oriented humanism will rot the cultures that it infects. Birth rates are already plummeting in most Western nations. The family is dying in most "developed" nations. Economies stagger. Terrorism and weapons of mass destruction threaten our cities. The city of man is about to implode.

Yet for those who are at work constructing the city of God, prospects could never be brighter. This has to be the perspective of any man of faith who reads the Psalms. Those empires built by men who refuse to fear God and keep His commandments will always be short-lived. Among other passages of Scripture, Psalm 37 presents a universal principle that we have seen enacted again and again in the history of our world:

> *"For yet a little while and the wicked shall not be: yea, thou shalt diligently consider his place and it shall not be. But the meek shall inherit the earth; and shall delight themselves in the abundance of peace ... The wicked plotteth against the just, and gnasheth upon him with his teeth. The Lord shall laugh at him; for He sees that is*

day is coming ... Wait on the Lord and keep His way, and He shall exalt thee to inherit the land; when the wicked are cut off, thou shalt see it. I have seen the wicked in great power, and spreading himself like a green bay tree. Yet he passed away, and lo, he was not: yea, I sought him, but he could not be found." Psalm 37

The First Mayflower has already birthed a second. It began with a new- found respect for the Bible and its ethical and epistemological authority for all of life, which is precisely where the First Mayflower began 75 years before it set sail for America. We begin by molding our lives around the law of God. Initially, the Second Mayflower will have little to do with the civil government, but in the long run it will bear deep socio-political effects on a nation - and many other nations at that. To a world which has lost any concept of true freedom from tyranny, it will return the notion of blessed freedom and the truly good life. It will return to many an understanding of and an experience with that which is of true value, something besides the cold materialism and the "tranquility of servitude" embraced by the modern man.

If we prepare now, we will be ready in seventy-five years when God opens a door of opportunity for us. That is the subject of the next chapter, for not everyone who registers interest in the struggle for freedom fully perceives what is involved in this struggle, and thus their success is often short-lived. However, should the end of the world be delayed and Christ tarry, the world will wait for another city on a hill. Somewhere a movement will achieve critical mass in quality and quantity, in both strength of principle and in numbers. By God's grace, and by great faith, persistence, and obedience to the holy law of God, we will have our Second Mayflower.

*   *   *

"It cannot be emphasized too strongly or too often that this great nation was founded not by religionists, but by Christians, not on religion, but on the gospel of Jesus Christ."

-Patrick Henry

Second Mayflower

9

SETTING SAIL

"We have staked the whole future of American civilization not on the power of government, far from it. We have staked the future of all of our political institutions upon the capacity of each and all of us to govern ourselves according to the Ten Commandments of God."

    -James Madison, fourth President of the United States

"The highest glory of the American Revolution was this: that it tied together in one indissoluble bond, the principles of civil government with the principles of Christianity."

    -John Quincy Adams, sixth President of the United States

"God has given to our people the choice of their rulers, and it is the duty, as well as the privilege and interest of our Christian nation, to select and prefer Christians for their rulers."

    -John Jay, first Chief Justice of the Supreme Court

The destination of the Second Mayflower is not so much a matter of geography as it is ideology. As we pull away from the shore we are certain of our course. We navigate the craft towards a social order that conforms its institutions, laws, and practices towards the ethical standard of God's law. Already the journey is well under way for thousands of families and hundreds of churches across this land!

Beginning in 1960, the movement began with a return to a distinctively biblical epistemology and ethics. Throughout the 1980s, it took a hard turn towards civil government as the primary incarnation of the vision. But now, the vision deepens. Those who gain the vision usually get it because they have studied the history of the First Mayflower and the age-old battle for liberty, and they feel that they must carry on this legacy. Some awake to the tightening force of government tyranny. But without exception, they must catch a vision for God's order set against the antithesis of the humanist system.

The Motivating Factor

Although there were many things that motivated our forefathers to take the supreme risks of life and property, there was a chief motivating factor which tipped the balance in their minds. Edmund S. Morgan in his excellent biography of John Winthrop, sums up the Puritan vision in these words:

> "The advantages of such a move [to the New World] to the Puritans who composed the majority of the membership were obvious. If the company moved to New England, it could become in effect a self-governing commonwealth, with the charter a blank check justifying everything it did. It would thus be able to enforce the laws of God and win divine favor. It could create in New England the kind of society that God demanded of all His servants but that none had yet given Him. The colony would not be a mere commercial enterprise, nor would it be simply a hiding place from the wrath of God. It would be instead the citadel of God's chosen people, a spearhead of world Protestantism."[1]

1 Morgan, p. 46.

Above all, these godly men had a vision for the kingdom of God. Their vision was not the typical vision found driving humanist nations who build their empires around power centers. The motivating force for these men was not a passion for money and materials as the chief end of human effort and progress. What they were after was God's blessing, obedience to His law, and investments in a kingdom which would certainly produce long term, even eternal, returns. This is a far cry from what drove the empire-building of Babylon, Rome, Spain, France, and England.

If the kingdom of God is not foremost in our minds, it is doubtful we will ever summon the motivation and courage necessary to establish a movement that will raise another "city on a hill." Sometimes severe persecution will awaken this motivation, as it did for many in the 17th century. Still, clarity of vision is the key - the vision to see the struggle between good and evil, liberty and slavery, God's law and man's law. If men could only see the scope of the battle, the crux of the battle, and its cosmic importance, they would engage it. But this sight comes only by faith, and it is faith that overcomes the world.

Formation and Maturation

The Second Mayflower will develop over the generations as we pass the vision on to our children. When it finally comes to fruition, its impact could well be greater than any other movement, eclipsing even the work of the Bradfords, the Winthrops, the Adams, and the Henrys of our Christian heritage. As long as it is a movement that self-consciously conforms itself to the law-order of the Creator of the universe, the work will be blessed.

We do not seek a utopia because we know that human nature is depraved and given to sin. That is why we seek distribution of powers, balance of powers, and decentralized government in our social construct. Perfect unity is not possible and perfect justice is unobtainable. For this reason we resist efforts to create a tyranny of a police state even if it were to promise a righteous agenda. Contrary to what the socialists have taught us for over a century now, we assert that *government is not our savior, and it plays only a minor part in our social construct.*

From the outset, we should recognize that this movement will end, as all good things will come to an end; even in the very best of reformations, the men who lead will unwittingly plant the seeds of their own destruction. Nevertheless we will pray to God that the good seeds we plant will fall again and again to the ground, and new plants will spring up anew in the hearts and lives of our posterity (Ex. 20:6). While we are on earth, we are about the business of building the kingdom of God. The Puritans called it "the kingdom militant." Later we will find a city whose "builder and maker is God" in the consummation at the end of the world (Heb. 11:10). But for now we build a kingdom that reaches into every sphere of life: evangelism, family, church, art, music, economics, and civil government. We occupy until He returns.

We are long term strategists. We build for long term relationships, long term investments, long term discipleship, and long term returns. Thankfully, men of faith and foresight built a long term investment 350 years ago that still bears fruit in our nation today. In like manner, we want to plant trees that will yield fruit generations hence. We work with an eye for permanence and endurance. Hopefully, the Second Mayflower will not be a ten-year-blip on the historical time line, soon forgotten and largely unimportant in the progress of civilization.

The Basic Strategy

Every era fights its own battles. Our Pilgrim and Puritan forefathers fought their war against forces that would stymie their reformation: state control of the church, the dissolution of morals, and centralized power in the monarchy. Now we fight our own battle. In this book, I have, to the best of my ability, laid out the battle lines which mark the war of our times. To summarize the content of the previous chapter, the following is a list of the five foundational elements which make up our new "city on a hill."

1. The reunification of the family and the decentralization of business.
2. The reempowerment of the family in discipleship (education), care for elderly parents, and inheritance.
3. The reviving of church relationships, God-centered worship, and a healthy *diaconate*.
4. The decentralization of civil government.
5. The application of God's law to family, civil government, economics, education, and culture.

It is always hard to picture a social context much different than the one in which you live. So if I were to describe the destination of the Mayflower, it would be a distorted picture at best. At the very least, I can simply say without risk of mischaracterization that life in this new world must capture a better balance of liberty and law. To describe the destination in rough form, I would expect to see civil government make up far less of life and family and church make up far more. Government-controlled education will be a thing of the past. Churches and families will care for their own widows. Churches will provide medical care with hearts of true charity. Families will engage in daily worship together, reading the Word, singing psalms, and praying. Families will spend much more time engaged in hospitality than watching television. Culture, business, and government will be decentralized and localized. What I describe here is effectively a "covenant" perspective of life; where power is never centralized with men, and love and peace make the bond for human relationships. This is the city of God.

Technology and the Second Mayflower

Some have blamed technology for the disintegration of family, faith, and freedom in the 21st century, for it was technology that enabled the proliferation of pornography. It was technology that enabled the rise of the mega corporation, the mega school, the mega church, and the mega government that can monitor and control every aspect of our lives. It was technology that gave us non-interactive forms of entertainment that further corrupted family relationships. But why blame technology when it is the hearts of men that misuse technology to corrupt themselves and the nuclear family? While it is true that technology has enabled a homogeneity of the "MTV culture," it was the hearts of men who refused to honor God and honor their progenitors, that corrupted their art forms.

The same technology that created the division of labor which removed father and mother from the home and fragmented the family can bring them back to a reintegrated home. Telecommuting is on the rise today thanks to computer and communication technologies that enable more flexibility in work location. As our worldview shapes the way we think, it will shape the way we live and the way we use technology. However, the principle we are working for is still the empowerment of the family and the decentralization of business. This great decentralization of corporate and government bureaucracies will inevitably create a much better economy than ever before. Wealth, productivity, and growth are best cultivated in our own fields, with our own investments, and on our own time. However, the success of this facet of the Second Mayflower relies upon principled, limited civil government that will not impose graduated taxation, regulation, price-fixing, or subsidization on the free market. It is also dependent on the character of a people who will favor slower growth over investing with debt, who choose honesty over quick gain, and who would rather work hard and trust God than covet security.

The food market will favor local growers again, placing some limited restraints on global competition. Obviously, automation and innovation will continue to be key elements in business success of any kind. Product and process design in manufacturing as well as the service industries must also take into account the above mentioned principles. Also, education will begin to recognize dual tracks in preparing young people for this decentralized business world: the corporate college track and the entrepreneurial track. Preparation for the entrepreneurial track will require a broader skill base, a closer focus on character, mentorship from a true master of the craft, and more rigorous life application.

Unity and Diversity

"Either we will hang together or we shall hang separately."
- Benjamin Franklin

Humanist governments strive for absolute unity under a tyrannical state and absolute diversity of religions, laws, cultures, and languages at the same time. The modern world is soon to discover that this is an impossible combination. The only way to maximize liberty while maintaining order is by the law of God.

In the struggle for religious liberty prior to the 18th century, monarchical governments overcompensated in their control of religious practices by confusing the roles of church and state and ignoring the laws of God carefully laid out in the Scriptures of the Old and New Testaments. Nevertheless, the right to rule eventually fell to those who denied the laws of God, and absolute religious liberty became the byword in the latter half of the 18th century. Madison questioned any restrictions on religious liberty when he wrote, "If religion be not within the cognizance of Civil Government, how can its legal establishment be necessary to Civil Government. During almost fifteen centuries has the legal establishment of Christianity been on trial. What has been its fruits?"[2] After two centuries of abandoning God's law as the ethical standard for family, church, and state one must conclude that secularism, evolution, and atheism in the public schools, 50 million dead babies, and the most tyrannical governments in the history of the world have not yielded a good record either. Within the last two centuries, in the name of religious pluralism, humanism has displaced the recognition of the Christian God, the Christian faith, and the Word of God in every major institution - and the consequences to human life, the family, medicine, private property, and economics have been devastating. All legal systems including political law systems, are religious, for law is only a derivative of the God or god acknowledged as the source of that law.

Of course, religious liberty cannot be absolute in any sphere of human life. For example, if a Muslim seeks citizenship in a Christian country with a copy of the Koran in one hand and the words, "Kill the Infidel" tattooed on the other, would it not be appropriate for an immigration official to take exception to the man's religious leanings? This will become increasingly obvious even to the more liberal polytheists in years to come. When the early absolutists insisted on total religious freedom for "heretics, Turks, or whatsoever,"[3] they did not realize that a man's religious faith would always exhibit itself in religious actions and that those actions must be governed by laws and those laws would be a derivative of a basic worldview or belief system.

Clearly, the only reason why a Christian would insist that the civil magistrate prosecute some cult engaging in human sacrifice in downtown Los Angeles is because he happens to believe that the true and living God does not require human sacrifice for sins, beyond the sacrifice of his Son. When a cult insists upon rendering a human sacrifice to satisfy the demands of his god, a Christian government will be forced to curtail the activity based upon the civil requirement of

2 *Madison Papers*, "From George Nicholas," April 22, 1785, 8:264.
3 Thomas Helwys, *A Short Declaration of the Mystery of Iniquity*, 1612.

Deuteronomy 13. It is only the law of God which places limits on the civil magistrates that maximizes liberty, while preventing the abuses of anarchy and tyranny. It was only when the church refused to preach the law of God and limit the civil magistrate to the powers enumerated in the Word of God, that civil governments in all Western, post-Christian countries assembled their modern tyrannies.

This does not solve all of our problems. We are still left with a question concerning the limits of religious freedom. Samuel Davies, a more balanced voice in the battle for religious liberty in the founding of the nation, would write: "I readily concede, That Principles subversive of Civil Society & of the Foundations of Natural and revealed Religion, then propagated, may justly be checked by Civil Authority & the Propagators of them punished with condign Punishment."[4] But how *does* one determine the "Foundations of Natural and revealed Religion?" Does the promotion of jihad, or the denial of the Trinity, or the denial of the existence of any god undermine the civil society and the foundations of revealed religion? Such questions are not easily answered.

Each family, each church, and each political state must choose the god that they will serve. Joshua and his family insisted on serving Yahweh (Josh. 24:15). When a nation refuses to acknowledge the Creator of heaven and earth, the God of the Old and New Testaments, in favor of polytheism, atheism, or Islam, it will fail to receive the blessing promised the nation whose God is Yahweh (Ps. 33:12). On the other hand, when a civil ruler enforces church attendance or church membership, he has created tyranny and reached beyond legitimate jurisdictional boundaries laid down in Scripture. There is no law of God that forces one to be a member of the church. Even in the Old Testament the stranger could live among the people without participating in the sacrifices and the sacred meals.

---

4 *Letters of Patrick Henry, Sr., Samuel Davies, James Maury, Edwin Conway, and George Trask*, "Rev. Samuel Davies to Rev. Patrick Henry, 21 April 1747," *William and Mary College Quarterly Historical Magazine*, Vol. 2, No. 1, October, 1921, p. 269.

No nation should ever enforce absolute unity of thought and belief. Nevertheless, there should be basic unity on some basic propositions before a community of people can covenant together for a common government. Somehow, each colony that formed this nation at the beginning made covenant on basic issues and formed their governments. Then the United States formed around a Constitution, another covenant document. The foundation of a nation is vitally important; when its foundations are strong, it can bear the weight of many generations and give much life to a nation.

All of the early covenantal documents acknowledged God the Creator, and sometimes even God the Lawgiver. Read the following preamble of the "Fundamental Orders of Connecticut" from 1638 and you will understand the foundations of this nation.

"Forasmuch as it pleased the almighty God by the wise disposition of His divine providence so to Order and dispose of things that we the Inhabitants and Residents of Windsor, Harteford, and Wethersfield are now cohabiting and dwelling in and upon the River of Conecticotte and the Lands thereunto adjoining; And well knowing where a people gathered together the word of God requires that to maintain the peace and union of such a people there should be an orderly and decent Government according to God, to order and dispose of the affayres of the people at all seasons as occasion shall require; do therefore associate and conjoin our selves to be as one Public State or Commonwealth; and do, for our selves and our Successors and such as shall be adjoined to use at any time hereafter, enter into Combination and Confederation together, to maintain and preserve the liberty and purity of the gospel according to the truth of the said gospel is now practised amongst us; As also in our Civil Affairs to be guided and governed according to such laws, Rules, Orders and decrees as shall be made, ordered & decreed, as followeth;"[5]

The state constitution of Delaware instituted this oath of office for the House of Burgess State Assembly:

"I, A.B., do profess Faith in God the Father, and in Jesus Christ His own Son, and in the Holy Ghost, one God blessed for evermore; and I do acknowledge the Holy Scriptures of the Old and New Testament to be given by divine Inspiration."

Even the more "liberal" colonies as Pennsylvania and Rhode Island included references to the Trinity or to the Christian Bible. Note the Rhode Island charter of 1683:

"We submit our persons, lives, and estates unto our Lord Jesus Christ, the King of kings and Lord of lords and to all those perfect and most absolute laws of His given us in His Holy Word."

Charters like these represent the very essence of what made America the recipient of the blessings of God - blessings that would extend into many centuries of our history. These public covenants were critical to the strength of the community, the perpetuity of the blessings, and to the success of their ventures. This is precisely where we ourselves must begin as the First Mayflower gives birth to the second. Our compacts must be based on the acknowledgement of God as both Creator and Lawgiver, and the Bible as the source of law. Freedom cannot exist without morality, and morality can only be defined by the God who, by definition, is the source of law. In our compacts we must promise to apply the law of God to the law of the land. Arbitrary law and natural

5 Henry S. Commager, ed., *Documents of American History*, pp. 22, 23.

law are utterly inadequate - for it was the abandonment of God's law that led to the foundering of the First Mayflower and the demise of the Republic.

Understandably, such monotheistic formulations as those which founded this nation would frighten the polytheists and "pluralists" who mistakenly believe that a nation can be atheistic, monotheistic, and polytheistic at the same time. Every social unit will choose its god and its law system. Socialists choose the state as the source of law and power. Muslims submit to Allah and his law. But Christians will form a "nation whose God is Yahweh" (Ps. 33:12).

Of course God allows a measure of religious freedom within a Christian nation, but that freedom must always be in accordance with His law. For example, God's law restricts religious freedom in the area of human sacrifice, a practice that has been legitimized by pluralist (or polytheist) nations in history.

"And because of all this we make a sure covenant, and write it; and our princes, Levites, and priests, seal unto it ... They clave to their brethren, their nobles, and entered into a curse, and into an oath, to walk in God's law, which was given by Moses the servant of God, and to observe and do all the commandments of the LORD our Lord, and his judgments and his statutes."
Nehemiah 9:38 - 10:29

Leadership - The Catalyst

There should be no question in our minds that this country would not exist had it not been for fathers, pastors, and leaders like Richard Mather, John Winthrop, John Cotton, William Bradford, Patrick Henry, Samuel Adams, John Adams, and George Washington. These were the men God determined to use in the forming of this country. Leadership is the catalyst of any great movement. Without godly leaders with vision in homes, churches, and communities, this world would be nothing but tyrants, bloody pogroms, anarchy, bloodshed, slavery, and misery. Godly leaders have always made the difference throughout history. There would have been no kingdom of Israel without a David and a Solomon. Some movements of righteous men are short-lived, and some last for a few hundred years. Certainly our present situation is no different.

What we lack today are godly fathers like Richard, Increase, and Cotton Mather. Tyrannies and top-down hierarchical structures in civil or ecclesiastical realms simply will not survive where godly fatherhood is cultivated, where fathers daily disciple their children in God's Word as they sit in their houses (Deut. 6:7; Heb. 3:13). Moreover, godly fathers who carefully shepherd their families in accordance with Ephesians 6:4 and 1 Corinthians 14:35, will grow into men who shepherd the wider church community. Without godly shepherding in the family and without godly shepherding in the churches there is no hope whatsoever for a community that is self-governed and able to be free. Yet shepherds are what we lack, that is, men who rule their own families well, so they can rule well in the church of God (1 Tim. 3:5).

The Second Mayflower must grow from the bottom up. We cannot begin with politics and expect a "really good" president to change our world. For us it begins with godly fathers and capable elders. There should be at least one elder for every ten families in a church, and these men should be mature and capable to lead these families spiritually and hold the fathers morally accountable to their obligations.

It is of great significance that the cry of our own hearts is identical to that of John Knox, the great Scottish reformer, the grandfather of the First Mayflower. His dying words were, "Lord, grant true pastors to thy kirk."[6] Such was the last prayer of a great man, without whom there would have no America - no America as we know it today. There would have been no Puritans, no Pilgrims, no Scottish covenanters, no Presbyterians (and therefore no War for Independence against Great

6 Douglas Wilson, *For Kirk and Covenant - The Stalwart Courage of John Knox*, Cumberland House, Nashville, TN, 2000, p. 223.

Britain), no Patrick Henry, no Samuel Adams, no George Washington, and no pastors and elders in the "kirk."

Could it have been so simple? John Knox's agenda was far from political. All he wanted was more pastors and elders. This is our agenda.

Lord, grant true pastors to thy church!

Training the Pastors

The cultivation of elders for the church must focus primarily on the character requirements laid out in passages like 1 Timothy 3 and Titus 1. This is just as important as a man's knowledge of the Word, church history, homiletics, hermeneutics, apologetics, theology, biblical languages, and so forth. Therefore, preparation for the office will happen only in heart-deep discipleship under the direct tutelage of a man who is willing to disciple another man. To separate theology from the classroom is tantamount to separating faith and works (James 2:26). The heart of the church was removed when seminary professors became less interested in the discipleship of the character of the man than in the content of their lectures.[7] But for us, training in the ministry will take on more of the form of mentorship and discipleship within the context of the local church, where the man has opportunity to apply what he has learned each day as he shepherds his own family and as he begins shepherding in the local body, under the direction of an experienced pastor. In short, the man will learn his Greek while mucking out the sheep stalls.

What follows is a short summary of the 1 Timothy 3 requirements for those who will fill the critical role of elder or pastor in the church:

Ability - One who has the self-discipline, experience, and confidence to lead.

7 This is the legacy of secular university education that gave birth the Renaissance. Tragically, the church borrowed the secular university model with the seminary training of Oxford, Cambridge, Harvard, Yale, and Princeton. The separation of church and education, character and academics, discipleship and intellectual training, and faith and works (in theology) devastated the church.

Blameless - One who lives his life without gross sins that would bring reproach on himself, his family, or his church.

Temperate - One who is clear-headed and vigilant; reserves decisions until he has enough information.

Sober-minded - One who is self-controlled, is not ruled by emotion and lust.

Hospitable - One who is generous with his accommodations, caring for the needs of others. He is exemplary in building relationships in the church by regular hospitality in his home.

Able to Teach - One who has gained both the wisdom and the respect to counsel others; and he knows the Word of God well enough to teach it.

Not Violent - One who does not resort to physical violence except as a last possible resort to protect the lives and property of others.

Not Coveteous - One who is either in the financial position not to be overly concerned about wealth, or it is plain by his generosity and his talk of money that God's Kingdom is more important than "filthy lucre."

Not Given to Wine - One who is not dependent on alcohol, food, or entertainment for his only or primary comfort and enjoyment.

Gentle - One who is not quick to judgment out of an over-interest in his own position.

Not Quarrelsome - One who has achieved the maturity to speak the truth plainly and firmly but without anger and pride. He understands the difference between majors and minors and will resist the temptation to debate every issue.

Of Truth - One who roots himself in the truth of God's Word.

Righteous - One who judges by the law of God, not by human tradition or personal opinions.

Ruling His House - One who has proven that he can motivate by discipline and love; his children are obedient and faithful and his family functions as his team.

If a Second Mayflower happens in our generation, we will focus on working these virtues into our own lives and into the lives of our sons. This is our manifesto. Karl Marx and Jean Jacques Rousseau proposed their deliberately crafted agenda and millions subscribed to it. They built a system of top-down government built upon bureaucracies in just about every developed nation. In contrast, ours is a system of bottom-up government built upon fathers and pastors. I know that our vision is different from anything we have ever seen before, but it is our project. If we set out today to equip fathers and elders to be the leaders that God wants them to be, we will find a better world forty years from now. If we begin now, we will see the fruit in the lives of our children. And if they catch the vision they will take it even further and a Second Mayflower may arrive at its first destination by the year 2040.

Civil Leaders

We cannot find enough godly leaders for our communities, because there are so few godly men who lead their families well. Good leaders are cultivated through years of purposeful training, discipline, and development. Much of leadership ability is learned through early experience and by observing good leaders in homes, in churches, or in business. If we want our children to become leaders, we must demonstrate good leadership in the home. The only reason that men of stalwart integrity, courage, and righteousness surfaced at the founding of this nation was because they were products of generations of godly fathers.

The Bible provides a clear set of requirements for both civil and ecclesiastical leaders. Before supporting a man for political office, we must be sure he conforms to the Exodus 18:21 pre-requisites.

> *"Moreover thou shalt provide out of all the people able men, such as fear God, men of truth, hating covetousness; and place such over them, to be rulers ..."*

Besides being competent for the job, these men must fear God, speak truthfully, and hate covetousness. That is, they should neither be ambitious for power nor greedy for money.

Working on All Four Sides of the Boat

Another helpful way some have summarized the Christian worldview in the area of sociology is by breaking it down into four spheres. There are, effectively, four God-ordained spheres of life: self-government, family government, church government, and civil government. These four spheres act as the four legs of a stool. If one leg was missing, the stool would fall. Likewise, if we expect any real social reformation in our culture, we must call for total reformation over each area of life. Just as four keys are turned in unison to open the bank vault, we must reform all areas of life in unison if we are to expect any meaningful, long-lasting cultural change. We cannot attend to family and church while neglecting civil government; and neither can the leaders attend to issues of civil government while neglecting family and church.

a. **Self-government** - Self-government promotes community. If you have a man who is gentle, generous, hard-working, considerate of others, and righteous in his dealings with others, you have a man who builds community and removes all justification for the existence of any sort of big government. One must conclude that many South American, African, and Asian countries are open season for communist and other revolutionary dictatorships because they lack sufficient self-government which enables political freedom. This is why the Gospel of Jesus Christ which cleanses a man from sin and fills his heart with a new principle is basic to changing our world. No exportation of "democratic ideals" or "secular ideals" will quench the bloody revolutions, civil wars, and cruel dictatorships that have plagued the world since Cain built his city, and Nimrod, the mighty hunter built his big tower. The problems run too deep in the hearts of men. Indeed, both communist and socialist governments predominate when there are few neighbors helping neighbors and families who refuse to take care of their own. Not surprisingly, undisciplined, rude, dishonest, and careless relations predominate among the citizenry. We can see this everyday in our own country. Excessive petty regulatory laws come about when people are too eager to take their selfish irritations to court instead of seeking personal and direct resolution of their problems with their neighbors.

b. Family government - As defined by God Himself, the head of the family is the father, with his wife serving as vice-regent and home ruler (or *"oikos-desposteo"* in the Greek). The family has the rights and responsibilities of educating and disciplining the children, family health and diet provisions, saving an inheritance, and all other prerogatives as spelled out in the Bible. If children are not properly raised by parents and subsequently launched into their own families by careful oversight in courtship and betrothal, everything else will unravel. The family is God's intended means of building society, but when parents do not raise their own children according to the biblical norm (Ex. 12:26; Deut. 6:7ff; 1 Thess. 2:11; Book of Proverbs; Eph. 6:4) and delegate it to church or state, inevitably the biblical social construct will unravel. Therefore, it will only be those who recognize the vital importance of renewing family relationships and engaging family discipleship who will make up the vanguard of our movement.

c. Church government - Perhaps the sphere which has been most neglected is the church. Robust preaching of the Word, God-centered worship, and careful church discipline have been replaced with feminized sentimentality, emotional highs, narcissistic experientialism, and shallow self-help messages. Every culture is defined by sentiment and emotion, but if that emotion is self-oriented and unbiblical, there will be no Christian culture. A right view of worship will capture the proper sentiments towards human life including fear, love, grief, and joy, in proper direction and proportion. Sanctified emotions do not come naturally for the Christian without careful nurture of these things in worship. To recover a right understanding of worship, I recommend that every family conduct a thorough study of the Psalms, the most emotional book of the Bible, as part of family worship.[8] Psalms is God's book on worship.

Genuine shepherding, meaningful accountability, long-term relationships, hospitality, and care for widow and orphan on the part of the *diaconate* will reinstate the institution of the church as a relevant social unit in our world. Indeed, the rebuilding of the church is essential to the rebuilding of a Christian society.

It is essential that families wholeheartedly support the work of building the church, an institution precious enough to Christ that he gave His life for it (Eph. 5:25). Though many do scoff at it, church government is spiritual and bears power in people's lives which is far more influential than one might think upon first consideration (Matt. 18:17, 18; 1 Cor. 5:5). While not all churches are equipped with elders, it is normative that multiple elders rule faithfully in each church (Titus 1:5).

d. Civil government - Finally, the civil magistrate is a power ordained by God Himself. Even as God distributes certain powers to his rulers in the church and the family, He has laid out responsibilities for the civil magistrate according to his laws in Old and New Testaments (Rom. 13:1; Matt. 15:4). It is our duty to support the civil magistrate by obeying lawful laws (Rom. 13:4-7; Acts 5:29). Just as Paul exercised his rights as a Roman citizen to protect his life, we ought to also exercise our rights to protect our lives and the lives of others (as well as to promote other laws of God).

How would you know that a godly vision had blessed a nation but that men would start living their lives in accordance with God's righteous laws? Of course, the blessings of Deuteronomy 28 will descend on that nation. Instead of spousal abuse, divorce, disunity, and imploding birth rates, we will find families living in harmony because wives are fulfilling their God-given calling as fit helps and home managers; and husbands

---

8 For family devotionals on the Psalms compiled into a Family Bible Study Guide, reference www.generationswithvision.com.

are loving their wives as Christ loved the church. In place of the curse of irresponsible fathers will be men who disciple their children in God's Word each day and carefully oversee the courtship of their daughters to good men who will build their own godly households. Our nation is no different than any pagan nation living outside of God's law order. Those pagan, humanist countries have always seen infanticide, abortion, euthanasia, and state-funded programs as the only solutions for their problems, Christians find the solutions in God's social order of families and churches that function according to his law. As the pagans abort their children and euthanize their elderly, Christians will adopt the orphan and show compassion for the widow. As pagans worship themselves and the gods they have formed out of plastic, metal and wood, Christian nations will worship the true and living God who is the source of all good gifts made from plastic, metal, and wood.

Counting the Cost

I do not assume that my reader would be immediately inclined to take on such a venture as this one. It may be that our venture can be undertaken without great danger, severe hardship, and loss of life. But then again, has anything significant ever been accomplished without great hardship, danger, and threat to life and limb? Over the first eight years of colonizing Virginia, thousands lost their lives from disease and tragedy at sea or on land. It is doubtful we will escape without some difficulty in this exploit.

Might a little opposition come from those who despise our Pilgrim-like separatism as we build our families and churches? Or might it come from those who resent our Puritan inclinations to impact institutions that touch their lives? Either way, I think you can count on the world's opposition to the faith at some level (John 15:18, 19; 2 Tim. 3:12).

However, do we have any other alternative? The faith is dying in Europe where Muslims are poised to take on a dominant position in what used to be Western culture, now burned out by raw humanism and existentialism. With its undying penchant for socialist governments, birth implosions, and any system that might further disintegrate the family, humanism continues its death march across our country as well. The family in America is reported to be the weakest of all Western countries and the church has become insignificant as a cultural force. We are on the brink of losing faith, family, and freedom. If there is anything we have learned from the last centuries, it is that these three foundational imperatives are interdependent. Without freedom, the family and faith cannot survive. Without faith, we will see freedom and family languish. And without family, man will give up on a generational commitment to faith and freedom. Again, I ask, *do we have any other option but to pursue the Second Mayflower?*

This venture begins today as my reader will make a pact with himself and his family. Only those who have assumed the faith and commitment to live righteously according to the law of God will attempt a brave and challenging course of action for the future.

The First Voyage

The Second Mayflower launches either one of two great voyages that must inevitably change the course of Western civilization. We can change this place by obeying God in all spheres of life. Whatever efforts we expend raising our children for God, reforming the church, and changing our government will never be wasted. Though we may fail to save the nation, our efforts will not be in vain. If we plant the seeds of freedom here, they may be transplanted to another place in the future. Nothing done for the kingdom of God is ever wasted. Like yeast spreading through a bread, social change will spread gradually and geographically. Many committed Christian families worked hard for social change in the church and the state in England for several generations prior to the founding of this country; and it was that strong philosophical, political, and cultural capital which was later invested into the development of a Christian culture in the American colonies.

This, then, is our project. We must develop our own capital in ourselves, our children, and our churches. We must learn what it is to live as free men. Then we must prepare ourselves and our children for leadership by active involvement within our families, churches, and communities. Leadership is dependent on clarity of vision, strength of convictions, and the ability to motivate others to follow.

The Second Voyage

If we fail in our attempt to build something here, if opportunities for active involvement disappear, *then we will go somewhere else and build it there.* However, there is no reason to consider this second course of action for several reasons. First, there is yet much we can do here and now. We can still build our families here without imminent threat of imprisonment. We can still leave our children with a vision that will surely impact both culture and politics in their generations. Secondly, this vision for a Second Mayflower is relatively new, having developed out of the 1960s among those who began to see the differences between a biblical worldview (a God-centered epistemology, metaphysics, and ethics), and the secular humanist, man-centered worldview. Many of us have never really understood and realized a vision for family, church, and commonwealth like that which formed this God-blessed nation so many years ago. So for the first time that vision is forming in our hearts and taking shape in our lives. We find ourselves in our present condition because there was precious little biblical vision for many generations before us. May I encourage my readers to patiently work with this vision and see what it will bring in 75 years?

Thirdly, if we were to launch forth to build a community elsewhere, where would we go? It is only in this country that there is to be found much of a biblical vision for family, church, and state. New Zealand has just approved a law prohibiting biblical corporal punishment. Most South American and African nations are torn apart by anarchical and dictatorial forces that portend a total lack of any Trinitarian, biblical worldview.

We have nothing to do but to rise and build our families and church communities now.

"Then answered I them, and said unto them, The God of heaven, He will prosper us; therefore we His servants will arise and build." *Nehemiah 2:20*

Wherever Christians live they are obligated to build a culture that will be counter-cultural to the world around them. Regardless of where they live, the mandate is the same. Christians are bound to build culture according to the principles of God's law or they must go somewhere else where it can be done. Neither conforming to the world's system or attempting to escape the world entirely are acceptable options for the believer.

In Hebrews 11 the biblical author encourages us to mark the men of faith who went before us. If we were to do so, we would still conclude, "We have not resisted to blood, striving against sin." But that is what they did.

"Through faith, they subdued kingdoms, wrought righteousness, obtained promises, stopped the mouth of lions, quenched the violence of fire, escaped the edge of the sword, out of weakness were made strong, waxed valiant in fight ... They were stoned, they were sawn asunder, were tempted, were slain with the sword ... Of whom the world was not worthy." Hebrews 11:33-38

So what about us? Is there any principle of righteousness for which we would give our lives? Is there a kingdom of evil that we would not subdue for Christ our King? Is there any imagination we would not bring into conformance to the rule of Christ (2 Cor. 10:4, 5)? Far too many Christians are afraid to be counter-cultural, yet that is how the salt has lost its savor. They may be afraid of losing property, political capital, or even their lives. But as Jesus put it, "He who loses his life for My sake will save it." Therefore, Christians must be committed to standing firm in their convictions despite the possibility of loss of influence or even their own lives.

FAQ's

Before boarding the ship, some prospective passengers have raised several important questions concerning the voyage of the Second Mayflower which will be addressed in turn.

Question #1 - *Shouldn't we accept the libertine philosophy that government should endorse homosexuality, abortion, and adultery, because government's purpose is to prevent coercion?*

First, coercion is hard to define because some practices which libertarians refer to as "victimless crimes" do bear a coercive effect on others. Individualism tries to deny the corporate nature of life, but God made man such that there would be connections among them that would create a "oneness" in human experience. What we are all trying to prevent is an unjust coercive force of the one body politic upon the many individuals and an unjust coercive force of the many individuals upon the one. But the immorality of the individuals who commit adultery and abort children harmfully effects individual families and the institution of the family in a body politic. These arguments hinge upon what we know about the interactions of the one with the many and vice versa. But alas, our knowledge is not comprehensive. We might point to history and discover that empires and nations that tolerated sins like abortion and adultery eventually saw their civilizations die. Ultimately, we must turn to the God who is both the One and the Many for the standard of His law. He created us to live both as individuals and as corporate units; and His law perfectly balances the liberties of the many with the power of the one political unit.

Moreover, how can we expect the blessings of freedom or the blessings of God if we refuse from the outset to keep His laws? Free states are constantly pressed on every side by both external and internal forces. Our peace and prosperity do not hinge upon a thousand delicate relationships with rogue states, anarchical terrorists, or competing empires, any of whom could torch our cities in a heart beat. Rather, our peace and prosperity hinges upon the God in whose hands lie the hearts of the kings of the earth (Prov. 21:1). A nation whose ways please the Lord would make even its enemies to be at peace with it (Prov. 16:7).

Libertarians who deny the importance of defining liberty by God's law are largely irrelevant to history. If anything, they only contribute to the moral decay of the age which must inevitably lead to greater governmental tyranny. "Either you'll be governed by God, or by God you'll be governed."

Question #2 - *But have you ever found two Christians who agree on anything? Could Christians ever covenant together in a social compact?*

While it is doubtful that a Christian covenant could possibly materialize anytime soon, anywhere in the world today, my hope lies not in the present, but in the past and the future. If in 1620, God could bring a godly group of people into a small ship on the high seas to make covenant, He can do it again in the future.

Indeed, there is little maturity or unity in a church that cannot distinguish between majors and minors, and cannot apply the humility and longsuffering to hold some issues in abeyance while working for unity. It is true that there is precious little consistent truth or character in a church with ten thousand denominations; but with a little mercy from God in heaven, two or three generations could make a difference.

Perhaps it will take a bloody persecution to force a righteous people to acknowledge the fundamentals instead of quarreling over how much water to use in a baptism or concerning the year Christ returns. But if freedom is ever going to surface, it will be on a ship built by a virtuous, self-governed people who are willing to unite together in a covenant and live with it. If they haven't learned to do this in a church, they will never come close to making a civil covenant.

To be a part of the Second Mayflower does not mean that everyone must agree to every particular of doctrine. But they must agree that the source of truth, indeed, the source of moral and civil law, is the Bible. Even the particular applications of such a principle are not always clear and may be debated with patience, integrity, and grace in our churches, our courts and legislatures.

Question #3 - *If Christians were to vacate one area and assemble in another, what salt and yeast would remain in the land left behind?*

Such a question assumes that the Second Mayflower is going somewhere else, which may or may not be the case. But it is interesting that this is precisely the argument that was raised against the Puritans who left England to build a Christian nation here. John Winthrop's biographer, Edmund S. Morgan, writes,

> "But one other thought kept recurring to Winthrop, a gnawing doubt not easily downed: would it not be deserting the world and one's fellow sinners to flee into a brave new land? Though one professed affection for all the saints and all the true churches of England, was it not in fact an act of separation to put three thousand miles of water between oneself and them? Though there might be opportunities to serve the Lord in New England, was it not a duty ... to stay in England and keep on striving to bring righteousness there?"[9]

In the end, Winthrop would pull away from the mother country for the prospects of seeking the kingdom's interests elsewhere and to protect his family from corrupting influences. If Jesus would encourage His disciples to abandon a hardened, apostate town in Israel that rejected the Gospel, then one should not be surprised to find such towns in

9 Morgan, p. 46.

the apostate Christian nations of Europe and America. Persecuted and suppressed Christians who hide in their homes from governmental intrusion have limited influence on their culture for good. And when they have given up their children, their freedom of speech, and their freedom to worship, they have nothing left. Christians must resist, and that resistance necessarily takes different forms in different places.

Generally speaking, we would do little good for ourselves or others in prison camps or in a place where the freedom of speech is severely curtailed. Consider, also, that free countries, once established, have provided the flourishing economies sufficient to fund massive missionary movements. I only thank God that John Winthrop fled to a "brave new land" and deserted the mother country as he led the first Puritan movement to America. We still enjoy the blessings of these first faithful endeavors.

Question #4 - *But would this world's empires or world government permit a free country to exist?*

Fear is always a natural reaction when you finally enter the age-old battle between good and evil, tyranny and liberty. Certainly, the enemy promotes fear because of the paralysis that comes with it. What we fear may be the strength of the opposition, the great centralization of power in the hands of tyrants, and the possibility of failure. But think of the great men of faith mentioned in Hebrews 11. If we are to receive the reward of heaven, why should we fear mere men, especially if our intent is to obey the God of heaven? Jesus warned His disciples not to fear men, but "fear rather Him who has power to destroy both body and soul in hell."

The question, therefore, is put wrongly. More to the point, "Would the God of heaven, the King of all kings, grant the grace to this world to allow one free country to exist?" God is still with us and He is still sovereign. Concerning the great empires of previous millennia who oppressed Israel, the Old Testament prophets testify:

"And all the inhabitants of the earth are reputed as nothing: and He doeth according to His will in the army of heaven, and among the inhabitants of the earth: and none can stay His hand, or say unto Him, What doest Thou?" Daniel 4:35

"Remember the former things of old: for I am God, and there is none else; I am God, and there is none like Me, declaring the end from the beginning, and from ancient times the things that are not yet done, saying, My counsel shall stand, and I will do all my pleasure: Calling a ravenous bird from the east, the man that executeth My counsel from a far country: yea, I have spoken it, I will also bring it to pass; I have purposed it, I will also do it." Isaiah 46:9-11

If we were to live in obedience to the King of kings and Lord of lords in covenant together to obey His laws, why would He curse us? There is no question that any social covenant takes a measure of faith. Of course we must believe in God, but we must further believe that He is absolutely sovereign over all of the affairs of this world. And we must believe that He blesses nations who subscribe to His laws - a principle that is repeated throughout the Old and New Testaments (Ps. 33:12; Deut. 28:1-10; Gal. 3:8). Has he not already demonstrated this pattern in our own nation? Study the history of the United States from 1610 to 1776 as written by contemporaries of the time (not the revisionists of today). Study the direct quotations, the autobiographies, the sermons, the speeches, and the writings of those righteous men who founded this nation and you will understand why God blessed the nation from 1776 to the present day.

Moreover, empires that refuse to acknowledge Christ as King always break down and fade away. That was the legacy of Spain, France, and England; and promises to be the destiny for this nation also. As the chief financial and political supporter of the United Nations, the

United States itself is facing increasing cultural and ideological disunity. Whereas, at one time, a biblical model of morality, Christian freedoms, and Christian laws held this nation together despite cultural differences, today there is little left to bind us together. National morality is all but gone and our freedoms are quickly unraveling. A nation divided is a nation without strength and peace within. Its national character will not last and it will weaken, causing militarily, politically, and finally geographically.

> *"And I looked, and rose up, and said unto the nobles, and to the rulers, and to the rest of the people, Be not ye afraid of them: remember the Lord, which is great and terrible, and fight for your brethren, your sons, and your daughters, your wives, and your houses ... our God shall fight for us." Nehemiah 4:14, 20*

Consider also how difficult it must be to rule the world. How successful is the United Nations or the United States at bringing peace and "democracy" to revolutionary and dictatorial states? I began this book with the proposition that anarchy plays off of tyranny. Man's attempts to the rule the world without Christ will always end in frustration. The more that governments attempt to centralize power, the more they will be consumed with quelling anarchical squabbles, civil wars, and religious conflicts in every corner of the globe. World government will bankrupt the economies that fund it. As many of the psalms attest, the wicked are destined to fall into the traps they prepare for the righteous. Some may attempt to centralize power with the United Nations in order to tyrannize the righteous, but in the end they will fail. God often defuses their wicked intentions by pitting them against themselves, while the righteous prosper in peace (Prov. 11:5; Ps. 141:10). Could Islam consume its energies fighting against Humanism while Christians prosper in peace? God is sovereign and we need not worry about the plight of the wicked and the sum result of their deeds,

"The wrath of men shall praise Thee, and the remainder of wrath shalt Thou restrain" (Ps. 76:10).

A biblically-based free economy will flourish because it inspires innovation, hard work, and healthy competition. Taxation will be minimal to enable capital to continue to flow into productivity, equipment, and technological development. Moreover, God may bless us with great technological developments in energy resources (cold fusion), defensive capabilities against nuclear missiles, breakthroughs in medical science, and privatized methods of environmental control that produce greater health and wealth for the nation. Socialism and communism destroy economies and environments so ably proven by the government bureaucracies in the United States, Romania, and the Soviet Union. Who knows, but that God may bless us at least if we are obedient to Him. Psalm 107:33-42 reminds us that God can bless the righteous even if they are forced into a barren wilderness!

> *"He turneth rivers into a wilderness, and the watersprings into dry ground; A fruitful land into barrenness, for the wickedness of them that dwell therein. He turneth the wilderness into a standing water, and dry ground into watersprings. And there He maketh the hungry to dwell, that they may prepare a city for habitation; And sow the fields, and plant vineyards, which may yield fruits of increase. He blesseth them also, so that they are multiplied greatly; and suffereth not their cattle to decrease. Again, they are minished and brought low through oppression, affliction, and sorrow. He poureth contempt upon princes, and causeth them to wander in the wilderness, where there is no way. Yet setteth He the poor on high from affliction, and maketh Him families like a flock. The righteous shall see it, and rejoice: and all iniquity shall stop her mouth. Whoso is wise, and will observe these things, even they shall understand the lovingkindness of the LORD."*

Question #5 - *How can you expect to ever accomplish anything when there are so few people who would agree to so basic a vision as looking to the Word of God as the source of law? How can a few thousand people impact millions?*

This was precisely the argument facing the colonials at the point that Patrick Henry gave his famous speech.

"They tell us, sir, that we are weak; unable to cope with so formidable an adversary. But when shall we be stronger? Will it be the next week, or the next year? Will it be when we are totally disarmed, and when a British guard shall be stationed in every house? Shall we gather strength by irresolution and inaction? Shall we acquire the means of effectual resistance by lying supinely on our backs and hugging the delusive phantom of hope, until our enemies shall have bound us hand and foot? Sir, we are not weak if we make a proper use of those means which the God of nature hath placed in our power. The millions of people, armed in the holy cause of liberty, and in such a country as that which we possess, are invincible by any force which our enemy can send against us. Besides, sir, we shall not fight our battles alone. There is a just God who presides over the destinies of nations, and who will raise up friends to fight our battles for us. The battle, sir, is not to the strong alone; it is to the vigilant, the active, the brave. Besides, sir, we have no election. If we were base enough to desire it, it is now too late to retire from the contest. There is no retreat but in submission and slavery! Our chains are forged! Their clanking may be heard on the plains of Boston! The war is inevitable - and let it come! I repeat it, sir, let it come. It is in vain, sir, to extenuate the matter ... Why stand we here idle? What is it that gentlemen wish? What would they have? Is life so dear, or peace so sweet, as to be purchased at the price of chains and slavery? Forbid it,

Almighty God! I know not what course others may take; but as for me, give me liberty or give me death!"

None of us should be even slightly disturbed by our small numbers. History has always been changed by small minorities of men and women who were committed to a set of basic convictions. The Bible is replete with examples of men who accomplished great things with very little: Gideon, Samson, David, Jesus Christ and His 12 disciples. God would have spared Sodom from judgment if there had been even ten righteous men in that city. Our own countrymen fought against overwhelming odds in the War for Independence against the greatest of all world powers - and won. Only a small minority of Americans actually supported the War for Independence.

Conclusion

In conclusion, those that will be a part of the great historical venture called *The Second Mayflower*, must commit to this navigation plan. They will commit to changing this place by taking an active role in building family, church, and state according to the Law of God. Fathers will capture a vision for their families and begin to re-integrate family relationships. They will give their children an education rooted in the fear of God, and raise sons and daughters to be godly fathers and mothers with kingdom vision. Then, they will covenant together in a true church with believers who are committed to the Word of God. Finally, they will support godly candidates for office who will rule in the fear of God.

But if the culture continues to decline and we fail to see repentance on a national scale, and if we find this place intolerable, we will go somewhere else that can be made acceptable to a freedom-loving and moral people. We commit to these two goals. I, for one, refuse to accept slavery to a government and a culture that has utterly rejected the laws of God. For me and for my family, a culture with 37% of children born without fathers, 95% of married persons admitting to pre-marital sex, and half of marriage ending in divorce is unacceptable. I fully intend to leave my children a better place to live than the place in which I was born. I will either change this place or leave it and build a God-fearing nation elsewhere.

I challenge my reader to commit to an uncompromising position of godly living, godly government, and a godly culture. Accept no less. Either change this place, or go somewhere else where it can be done.

"So built we the wall; and all the wall was joined together unto the half thereof: for the people had a mind to work." Nehemiah 4:6

Second Mayflower

POSTSCRIPT

"'Men who have assurance that they are to inherit heaven, have a way of presently taking possession of the earth.' This courage and confidence enabled them to fight, with economic, political, or military weapons, to create a new world worthy of the God who had so signally blessed them ... Previous theologians had explained the world: for the Puritans the point was to change it."[1]

A s the kingdom of God stretches from "shore to shore," and as the frontiers of Christ's rule move from one culture to another and from one area of cultural expression to another, we do not see immediate and complete victory in all realms of man's experience. Rather, we see the rise and fall of Christian influence in various cultures around the world. We may see an end to polygamy, human sacrifice, and chattel slavery, quickly followed by the rise of statism (slavery to big government), pornography ("polygamy lite"), and abortion ("infanticide lite"). Men are accustomed to being slaves to sin, to lusts, to cruel masters, governments, and large corporations. Some are more explicit about their sin and others paper it over with a thin veneer of hypocrisy.

But we cannot deny the inevitable ruin of communism and any culture that insists on defying God and His holy law. Neither can

1 Douglas Kelly, *Emergence of Liberty in the Modern World - The Influence of Calvin on Five Governments from the 16th Through the 18th Centuries,* P&R Pubishing: Phillipsburg, NJ, 1992, p. 125.

we ignore the constant thrust of God's kingdom into Moslem and communist countries, nor can we deny the unprecedented political and economic freedom that broke into this sin-darkened, people-enslaving world for the first 200 years of this nation's history.

Christian culture produces capital; the capital is then spent by those who are more concerned with building the empires of men than building the kingdom of God; so the towers come down when the capital is spent. But those who are focused on the kingdom of God and His righteousness (Matt. 6:32) continue to build godly families, godly churches, and godly culture through it all.

Today we have the benefit of many great theologians, Christian philosophers, and writers who have over the previous centuries gone to great lengths to advance a biblical worldview of man, salvation, life, civil government, law, art, family, church, and personal devotion to God. If we have studied the Bible with the preconception that the Bible speaks with authority to all areas of life, then we know what to do. We know our duty to our families, our churches, our culture, and our government. Now we must doggedly pursue those duties and commitments.

We will not succeed in this venture either with the timid conservative or the flash-in-the-pan activist. We look for those who understand the fundamental nature of the change that needs to occur and who are willing to build homes, churches, and communities out of a wilderness over the span of many generations. Not unlike those who laid the first foundations of this land, they may have to work against the opposition of savages and pagans - risking life and limb. This project must involve more than a face lift and a "carpet cleaning" for each of the political, economic, social, educational, and cultural institutions that form the modern world. We must renew relational living and biblical ethics in the reconstruction of each of these institutions at their very foundations. It will take time, great patience, and care to lay these foundations. Therefore, each member of this venture must be willing to take on a long-term project that will span generations.

POSTSCRIPT

Today we have the example of our forefathers who planted freedom on this continent, freedom not seen for thousands of years. We are inspired by this single success, keenly aware of the possibilities. We can aspire to these heights once more by looking to these fathers' examples of courage, hard work, endurance, commitment, and faith. We must press into the future of His story, endeavoring to apply the Bible, our great blueprint, to every area of life. Now let us prepare for the Second Mayflower.

> "Arise, shine; for thy light is come, and the glory of the LORD is risen upon thee. For, behold, the darkness shall cover the earth, and gross darkness the people: but the LORD shall arise upon thee, and His glory shall be seen upon thee. And the Gentiles shall come to thy light, and kings to the brightness of thy rising. Lift up thine eyes round about, and see: all they gather themselves together, they come to thee: thy sons shall come from far, and thy daughters shall be nursed at thy side. Then thou shalt see, and flow together, and thine heart shall fear, and be enlarged; because the abundance of the sea shall be converted unto thee, the forces of the Gentiles shall come unto thee. The multitude of camels shall cover thee, the dromedaries of Midian and Ephah; all they from Sheba shall come: they shall bring gold and incense; and they shall show forth the praises of the LORD ... Surely the isles shall wait for me, and the ships of Tarshish first, to bring thy sons from far, their silver and their gold with them, unto the name of the LORD thy God, and to the Holy One of Israel, because he hath glorified thee. Therefore thy gates shall be open continually; they shall not be shut day nor night; that men may bring unto thee the forces of the Gentiles, and that their kings may be brought. For the nation and kingdom that will not serve thee shall perish; yea, those nations shall be utterly wasted." Isaiah 60:1-11

Second Mayflower